To Sr. M. Alberta
from
Fr. Pastorek
Dec. 25, 1964

Saint John Eudes

A Spiritual Portrait

St. John Eudes

Saint John Eudes

A Spiritual Portrait

by Peter Herambourg, C.J.M.

Translated by Ruth Hauser, M.A.
Edited and Annotated by Wilfrid E. Myatt, C.J.M.
Introduction by Edward A. Ryan, S.J.

The Newman Press · *1960* · *Westminster, Maryland*

Imprimi potest:
A. F. Le Bourgeois, C.J.M.
Moderator Generalis
Congregationis Jesu et Mariae
Romae, die 6a Januarii, 1959

Nihil obstat:
Edwardus A. Cerny, S.S., S.T.D.
Censor Librorum

Imprimatur:
Franciscus P. Keough, D.D.
Archiepiscopus Baltimorensis
May 16, 1960

The *nihil obstat* and *imprimatur* are official declarations that a book or pamphlet is free of doctrinal and moral error. No implication is contained therein that those who have granted the *nihil obstat* and *imprimatur* agree with the opinions expressed.

Library of Congress Catalog Card Number: 60–14810
Printed in the United States of America

Foreword

SAINT JOHN EUDES *A Spiritual Portrait* is a biographer's analysis of the profound interior life of a great saint as manifested exteriorly by his characteristic devotions and his day-to-day practice of virtue.

St. John Eudes, contemporary of St. Vincent de Paul, was an outstanding personality of the Catholic Church in seventeenth-century France. This analysis dates from the early eighteenth century.

Its author is Father Peter Herambourg. Although he entered the Eudist Congregation in 1682, two years after the death of its remarkable founder, Herambourg based his work entirely on eye-witness accounts, records and documents contemporary with St. John Eudes.

Father Herambourg's indefatigable research stemmed from his deep personal devotion to St. John Eudes, but it was carried out with exact and thorough scholarship. The result was an invaluable two-volume biography, which reflected the taste of the eighteenth century both in presentation of subject-matter and style. Father Herambourg's work contained a minimum of biographical data confined to the first volume, and a maximum of edification, skillfully worked out in the second, a systematic presentation of virtues and devotions defined and illustrated from the Saint's spiritual writings and correspondence.

The second volume, here entitled *Saint John Eudes: A Spiritual Portrait* was first given to the public over a century after its composition by Very Reverend Ange Ledoré, Superior General of the Eudist Fathers, in response to the general interest in the cause of beatification of John Eudes. The first edition published in 1868 was followed the next year by a second in which Father Ledoré elaborated and illustrated the original Herambourg work with the introduction of biographical matter taken largely from the first volume. Some years later a third edition was brought out by Lethielleux of Paris. The Ledoré editions enjoyed widespread popularity. Italian, German and Spanish translations were subsequently published.

In 1926 Father Denis Boulay, C.J.M. edited the original work of Father Herambourg without the Ledoré additions. This definitive edition is here presented for the first time in English dress. It is an accurate readable translation endeavoring to preserve the authentic eighteenth-century flavor.

It is the hope of the present editor that the reader will find in this book much practical help in developing his own interior life and in furthering the work of divine grace in his soul.

To follow the leadership of St. John Eudes with the guidance of Father Herambourg, it is not necessary to do as the Saint did, that is, found religious congregations, effect social reforms and reclaim prodigious numbers of souls by feats of eloquence and extraordinary personal ministry. Unflagging perseverance in the practice of Christian virtue in daily life is what builds up a life of sanctity. Each one can become heroic by fidelity to virtue and the interior life.

Explanatory notes have been compiled to make the reader

at home with the text. The editor wishes to express his indebtedness to Reverend Charles Berthelot du Chesnay, archivist of the Congregation of Jesus and Mary, and associate editor of its Paris review, *Notre Vie,* for invaluable assistance in tracing patristic and historical references. His thanks are also due to Very Reverend Louis Arand, S.S. of the Catholic University of America for a critical and scholarly reading of the manuscript.

The editor shares with his predecessors the aim of Father Herambourg to widen knowledge of St. John Eudes, whose one desire was to bring each individual soul close to the Sacred Heart of Jesus and the Immaculate Heart of His Blessed Mother through the daily practice of virtue.

WILFRID E. MYATT, C.J.M.

Willowbrook Seminary
Hyattsville, Maryland
February 8, 1959

Contents

Contents

Introduction

THE SIXTEENTH CENTURY saw France, the eldest daughter of the Church, fall into civil strife which threatened to destroy the country. And yet the seventeenth century was *le grand siècle,* the great century of French history. It witnessed one of the most beautiful flowerings of Catholic life in the whole history of the Church. It was the century of St. Francis de Sales, St. Vincent de Paul and St. Margaret Mary, of St. Isaac Jogues and St. John de Bréboeuf, of Bossuet and Bourdaloue. To understand the career and teaching of St. John Eudes, one of the great saints of the great century, we have to know something of the situation in sixteenth as well as in seventeenth-century France. Although the span of his years, from 1601 to 1680, fell entirely in the seventeenth century, his life was conditioned by the events of the preceding century.

The France of St. Louis and St. Joan of Arc stood, during the last half of the sixteenth century, in danger of losing its Catholic heritage. Militant Huguenots abolished the Catholic cult in many regions. Altars were profaned, statues broken, relics burned, churches and monasteries pillaged, priests and religious martyred. But the majority of the French people were determined to remain true to the religious traditions of the nation. The Catholics, therefore, opposed violence violently. And the result was civil war. France tottered on the brink of the abyss. To stop the rising tide of Huguenotism seemed impossible. Catherine de' Medici, mother of three French kings and the real ruler of the country, had recourse to massacre to meet the political threat of the Huguenots. For a time the peril seemed averted. But the danger was more acute than ever when Henry IV became the lawful king of France. For four years Henry, who was a Huguenot, tried to win his kingdom from the Catholics by force of arms. Finally, to save the country, he himself became a Catholic. Catholicism triumphed. It was now possible to introduce into France the Catholic reform which had already been established in Italy, Spain and other Catholic countries.

France was much in need of reform. The Catholic clergy was poorly trained. During the more than three decades of civil strife, priests had lived too close to the people and had become too deeply involved in politics. More at home in the tavern than in the pulpit, they were popular but their spiritual lives left much to be desired. Ecclesiastical discipline had all but collapsed. As a consequence, the French people were poorly instructed in the religion that they had fought so valiantly to save, and their pastors did not have the training required to meet the needs of the day. The religious orders had also suffered in the general disarray. Many monasteries of men and women were far below the level of observance that would have allowed them to leaven the mass of the Catholic people.

But brighter days lay ahead. Henry IV (1589–1610), his son, Louis XIII (1610–1643), and his grandson, Louis XIV (1643–1715) saw to it that France had an episcopate which, taken as a whole, was able to cope successfully with the problems. In 1615 the French bishops introduced the decrees of the Council of Trent into France. Soon the older orders revived while new ones increased their activities. By mid-seventeenth century France had replaced Spain as the leading political force in Europe, and French was replacing Latin as the international language. Moreover, Frenchmen had won leadership in most sectors of Catholic life. French spirituality, in particular, reached a pre-eminent level in the Church which it has, by and large, retained to the present day.

St. John Eudes, whose virtues and devotions are studied in the present work, played a role in the reform of the Church and in the flowering of the spirit which was equalled only by St. Francis de Sales and St. Vincent de Paul. Born at Ri, an obscure hamlet of Normandy, he had as parents an educated farmer, Isaac Eudes, and a local country girl, Martha Corbin. Their marriage had been for some years childless. John in his memoirs attributes his birth to a pilgrimage which his father and mother made to the shrine of Our Lady of Recovery, some eighteen miles from Ri.

John Eudes joined the Oratory of Jesus in 1623, and there enjoyed the advantage of being formed spiritually by two masters, Peter de Bérulle and Charles de Condren. Ordained to the priesthood in 1625, Eudes fell sick, and during a long period of convalescence, his insight into spiritual reality was much strengthened. As an Oratorian, St. John Eudes first distinguished himself by his zeal in taking care of the plague-stricken. In 1632 he began to preach parish missions and was an immediate success. Work in the home missions always remained one of his cherished fields of endeavor. He preached 112 six-week missions in the course of his life. A born orator with a voice of thunder, John Eudes did for Normandy what St. John Francis Regis did for Cévennes, what Blessed Julian Maunoir did for Brittany, what the followers of St. Vincent de Paul and the Capuchins did for all France. God filled these apostolic men with consuming zeal in preaching the Word of God and in turning men's minds from the vain satisfactions of the world to thoughts of eternity and to lives guided by the Gospel precepts. John Eudes yielded to none of them in the fervor and success of this popular apostolate.

St. John Eudes was happy in his membership in the Oratory of Jesus, but in 1643 he became convinced that God was calling him to leave his associates in order to found a congregation of priests who would conduct seminaries as well as promote the home missions. Normandy was badly in need of seminaries where future curés could receive some training in their apostolic careers. Encouraged by Cardinal de Richelieu, St. John Eudes left the Oratory and immediately founded the Congregation of Jesus and Mary, which had as its center the seminary of Caen in Normandy. This was not a seminary in the full modern meaning of the word but rather a kind of retreat house where intensive training, often of not more than a few months' duration, was imparted to recruits for the priesthood. But even this brief formation accomplished much when it was directed by men like St. John Eudes and St. Vincent de Paul. These men and their peers gave France a clergy second to none, a clergy which even the French Revolution was unable to turn from its purpose. The French curé of the nineteenth century, to whom the Church universal owes so much, may be looked upon as the legitimate descendant of the priests formed by the Sulpicians, the Vincentians and the Eudists. In addition to the Seminary of Caen, St. John Eudes founded like institutions at Coutances, Lisieux, Rouen, Evreux and Rennes.

Another foundation of this man of many projects was the

Refuge of Our Lady of Charity at Caen where young women who had been led into disordered lives were sheltered and taught to walk in the paths of virtue. This foundation and others like it accomplished a signal work of charity in pre-revolutionary France. Organized anew in the nineteenth century, the Refuges of Our Lady of Charity have performed outstanding service and continue to do so, not least for the Church in the United States. One branch of this nineteenth-century revival of a part of the apostolate of St. John Eudes, that which owes its beginning and development to St. Mary Euphrasia Pelletier, has spread throughout practically the whole of the Catholic world under the title of the Good Shepherd.

The soul of these activities, which by no means exhaust St. John Eudes' happy initiatives, was the Saint's intense devotion to the Immaculate Heart of Mary and the Sacred Heart of Jesus. The beginnings of these devotions, which are now among the favorites in the Church, owe more to St. John Eudes than to anyone else. Of the devotion to the Immaculate Heart, he was at once the missionary, the poet and the theologian. Before him the devotion can scarcely be said to have existed although it was privately practiced. St. John Eudes from his earliest years had been distinguished by a tender devotion to our Lady. His Oratorian training led him into the interior of Mary and caused him to express his devotion to the person of God's Mother in the form of devotion to her Admirable Heart. As early as 1643, St. John Eudes inaugurated with episcopal approbation the liturgical cultus of the Immaculate Heart of Mary in the Congregation of Jesus and Mary. By 1648 he had composed and received episcopal sanction for a Mass and an Office of the same most Holy Heart.

Our Protestant friends sometimes object that devotion to our Lady interferes with devotion to her Divine Son. The truth seems to be that the Blessed Virgin Mary always fills the hearts of those devoted to her with a still greater devotion to her Son. At any rate, in the case of St. John Eudes, devotion to the person of Mary led to devotion to the person of Jesus. Familiarity with our Lady's interior life led to familiarity with that of our Saviour. Devotion to the Immaculate Heart led to devotion to the most Sacred Heart. Indeed, St. John Eudes disliked separating the Sacred Heart and the Immaculate Heart. He was accustomed to speak of *the Sacred Heart of Jesus and Mary.* In 1668, however, he wrote an Office and a Mass of the Sacred Heart. In 1670 he had the approbation of the Bishop of Rennes for these liturgical masterpieces, and in 1672, where the bishops permitted it, the houses of the Congregation of Jesus and Mary and of the Order of Our Lady of Charity celebrated the Feast of the Sacred Heart. With reason, then, have recent Popes styled St. John Eudes the author of the liturgical cultus of the Sacred Heart. The modern devotion to the Sacred Heart of Jesus stems not only from St. Margaret Mary but also from St. John Eudes.

St. John Eudes, who wrote voluminously to propagate his favorite devotions, and in so doing developed a spirituality which ranks among the most appealing, went into an eclipse during the nineteenth century. But the twentieth century which saw the triumph of the cults of the Sacred Heart and the Immaculate Heart in the Church has also witnessed the canonization of St. John Eudes. Moreover, an excellent critical edition of those of his works which survived the French Revolution has been published. Accurate readable translations of his principal works are also available in English through the good offices of Father Wilfrid Myatt, C.J.M.

and Father Patrick Skinner, C.J.M., now Archbishop Skinner of St. John's, Newfoundland.

The present work, *Saint John Eudes: A Spiritual Portrait,* will find a place in the hearts of all who love the Saint. It was written by Father Peter Herambourg, a true disciple, one who thoroughly assimilated the spiritual doctrine which St. John Eudes lived by and wished to see assimilated by all Christians. The foundation of Eudist spirituality is, it is true, a recognition of the divine majesty which requires from God's rational creatures humble reverence, complete surrender and self-forgotten adoration. Man must ever take in the presence of his Creator the posture that is really his: that of a slave who has no rights save those his Master gives him. In the case of St. John Eudes, however—and this is perhaps the point that separates him from the masters of the so-called French School, while it indicates how far he surpasses them—love of God in Jesus Christ penetrates and transforms the adoration, the service and even the reverence. The slave becomes aware that his Master has elevated him to the rank of friend. He perceives that the life of the Christian, when his actions are performed in and for Jesus, continues the life of Jesus. "It is no longer I that live, but Christ lives in me" (Gal. 2:20).

There is little or nothing of the aristocrat or the abstract in the spirituality of St. John Eudes. It is profound but at the same time concrete and patently based on the Gospel. Sedulously avoiding the subtle and the abstruse, St. John Eudes has a simplicity which springs from a sound and well-digested theology. He has a sweetness of expression that will surprise only those who do not understand how intimately the saints relived the mysteries of the Word Incarnate. He has an abundance and a plenitude which may displease stylists but which is really the result of the stress that human thought and language always undergo in trying to express the ineffable condescension of God in His dealings with men.

In Father Herambourg's work, the doctrine which flowed from the heart, tongue and pen of St. John Eudes has been systematized under headings which are not unusual in treating of the holiness of saints. Just as a lover of jewelry studies the play of light in a beautiful diamond, so the author of this work, having penetrated into the sanctuary of radiant beauty which is the soul of a saint, endeavors to reveal the splendors he beholds. Those who are familiar with St. John Eudes' own works will find here most of his insights and much of the holy fire that consumed him. Those who have yet to go to the originals, have here a competent introduction to one of the masters of Christian spirituality.

EDWARD A. RYAN, S.J.

Woodstock College
Woodstock, Maryland
March 25, 1959

Saint John Eudes

A Spiritual Portrait

Chapter 1. Esteem and Love for Virtue

CICERO, THE PRINCE of orators, in the treatise on the moral duties that he wrote for his son, Marcus, to be the rule and guide of his life, says that if virtue were to become perceptible and were seen as it really is, it would engender a wonderful esteem in the minds and an ardent love in the hearts of men.[1] Wisdom, descending from the throne of God, revealed itself to Solomon, who pursued it with special affection, looking upon it as a sister and calling it his beloved.[2] The diligence and earnestness with which St. John Eudes[3] sought after virtue, even from his tenderest years,[4] would indicate that it had revealed to him some vision of its beauties and that, whereas the hearts of children are ordinarily filled with trifles, as Scripture says,[5] piety had taken possession of his.

St. John Eudes did not seek virtue in the fashion of the pagan philosophers or the politically-minded, who look at it through the eyes of reason alone and value it as a thing most excellent in itself, most necessary for the perfection of man, to distinguish him from animals guided by sense alone. Rather he looked upon virtue in its source, namely in Jesus Christ, the Incarnate Word, in whom it attains infinite excellence.[6] The Saint was convinced that his was the obligation, shared alike by all Christians, to strive seriously after perfection, since our Blessed Lord in the Gospel desires us to be perfect even as His heavenly Father is perfect.[7] He was persuaded, furthermore, that all priests and religious, as well as those aspiring to these states in life, should be living models of the holiness of Jesus Christ, the Sovereign Priest and Perfect Religious, and he overlooked no means to achieve his goal.

This esteem and love for virtue prompted St. John Eudes to strive to avoid the smallest sins. If he had believed that it was sufficient to abstain only from serious transgressions, he might have had reason to fear that infidelity to little things would soon have made him guilty of grave sins. He had learned through the reading of Sacred Scripture that downfall becomes inevitable to one who disregards small sins.[8] Following the counsel of St. Paul,[9] he refrained from all appearance of evil: indecorous language, unrestrained mannerisms, a sophisticated behavior, over-familiarity with degenerate worldings; in short, everything that might lead to the slightest suspicion of irregularity in his conduct came strictly under his ban.

This same love for virtue impelled St. John Eudes to do all the good in his power. He profited by every occasion afforded him by divine providence to perform good works. Never did anyone budget his time with more economy. He used every day of his life to the best possible advantage. He was scrupulously exact in performing all the devotional exercises that he had assigned to himself. He was the image of that faithful servant whom our divine Saviour has depicted in the Gospel, the one whom God rewarded with an abundance of grace in this world and a throne of glory in the next.[10]

The Saint labored untiringly to acquire all the virtues in

their perfection, imitating in particular those which the saints had practiced most conspicuously. As he had had the privilege of being the disciple of Cardinal Peter de Bérulle[11] and of Father Charles de Condren,[12] two priests of outstanding piety, he patterned his life so closely after theirs that he became the best living copy of these two great servants of God. He also delved into their minds and hearts, and through his intimate association with them, he discovered the treasures of grace hidden in those two sanctuaries of holiness, which he always approached with awe and reverence. It was through imitation of his two spiritual guides that he conceived high aspirations of perfection, profound adoration of God, close union with the Word Incarnate, ardent charity toward his neighbor and constant self-mortification. Thus he progressed steadily from one virtue to another, growing unceasingly in holiness, instead of limiting himself to certain devotional exercises with no wish to advance beyond them.

St. John Eudes regarded virtues as gifts of the mercy and goodness of God. Although he was convinced that he should make every effort to acquire them, he relied solely on the help of God, to whom he continually addressed fervent prayers for that intention. If he loved and sought after virtue, it was not in the spirit of those worldly sanctimonious persons who wish to be virtuous only for their own merit and satisfaction and who, filled with pride, have a strange passion for everything that can make them more esteemed by their fellow men. The Saint's incentive was the interest and glory of God, the desire to be like our Blessed Lord, who wishes, for the honor of His heavenly Father, to continue in all Christians the practice of the same virtues that He Himself once practiced here on earth.[13]

This forceful and persevering ambition of St. John Eudes

to practice to perfection all the Christian virtues will be brought out in the chapters that follow. In them the reader will see how greatly this apostolic man contributed "unto the measure of the age of the fulness of Christ."[14]

NOTES

1 Father Herambourg refers here to *De officiis*, a philosophical treatise on the moral duties of man by M. Tullius Cicero. The names, Cicero and Marcus, which are not in the original Herambourg text, have been added to complete the opening sentence. The reference is to the following passage in Book I, chapter 5, of *De officiis:* "My son, Marcus, you here perceive at least a sketch, and, as it were, an outline of virtue; which could we perceive her with our eyes would, as Plato says, kindle a wonderful love of wisdom." Plato in *Phaedrus*, chapter 65, remarks: "Our eyesight is the most exquisite of our senses. Yet it does not serve us to discern wisdom; if it did, what a glow of love would she also kindle within us." It will be observed that Cicero applies to virtue what Plato says of wisdom. See Cicero, *Three Books of Offices, or Moral Duties*, translated by Cyril P. Edmonds, London, 1850, p. 11.

2 Wisd. 8:2.

3 Father Herambourg, who wrote this book between 1687 and 1712, refers to the Saint as "Father Eudes," as he was then called. John Eudes was beatified on April 25, 1909, and canonized on May 31, 1925. In this edition we have used "St. John Eudes," the name by which he is now known.

4 See Daniel Sargent, *Their Hearts Be Praised* (New York, P. J. Kenedy, 1949), p. 10 ff. Also Henri Joly, *A Life of Saint John Eudes* (New York, Benziger Brothers, 1932), pp. 1–7.

5 Prov. 22:15.

6 See St. John Eudes, *The Life and Kingdom of Jesus in Christian Souls* (New York, P. J. Kenedy, 1945), p. 33 ff. In other references to this work we shall use the short popular title, *The Kingdom of Jesus.*

7 Mt. 5:48.

8 Ecclus. 19:1.

9 1 Thess. 5:22.

10 Mt. 25:23.

11 Cardinal Peter de Bérulle (1575–1629) was one of the most prominent churchmen of seventeenth-century France. In 1611 de Bérulle founded the Oratory of Jesus, a society of priests without religious vows, whose main purpose was the renewal of the priestly spirit among secular priests. Father de Bérulle received John Eudes into the Oratory at Paris on March 25, 1623. Eudes made his first retreat there under de Bérulle, who continued to be the Saint's spiritual adviser until September, 1625. See Sargent, *op. cit.*, p. 23 ff.

[12] Father Charles de Condren (1588–1641) was de Bérulle's successor as superior general of the Oratory of Jesus. St. John Eudes made his final preparation for the priesthood under this remarkable man, who, as Father John James Olier says, "was as enlightened as an angel." All through his life Eudes showed traces of the influence of both de Bérulle and de Condren. See M. V. Woodgate, *Charles de Condren* (Westminster, Md., The Newman Press, 1949), p. 90; also Sargent, *op. cit.*, p. 30.

[13] Jn. 13:15; Phil. 2:5.

[14] Eph. 4:13.

Chapter 2. Faith

FAITH IS THE foundation of the Christian religion. It is the door through which we enter the Catholic Church, since baptism is conferred on us only after we have given evidence of faith, either by ourselves or through our godparents. "Without faith," says St. Paul, "it is impossible to please God."[1] Through faith we give sincere testimony of our obedience to His divine majesty, for God is the absolute master of everything in man. Consequently, even as He desires the homage of our will in all things, despite its inclinations, so also does He require the homage of our understanding, its readiness to believe whatever He proposes, notwithstanding its own reasoning and the opposition of the senses. This submission is not the effect of an abject captivity. On the contrary, just as it is the mark of a noble heart to love difficult and trying things, so, too, according to the opinion of William of Paris,[2] it is the proof of a strong mind to believe them.

If this be true, as it undoubtedly is, it would be hard to find a man more filled with faith than St. John Eudes, or one who rendered more glory to God through the submission of his understanding. He made his mind a captive under the yoke of faith, which he used to call the cornerstone of the kingdom of Jesus Christ, in accordance with these words of St. Paul to the Hebrews: "Faith is the substance of things to be hoped for."[3] The faith of St. John Eudes revealed God as He really is, infinite in His Being and in all His divine perfections, true to His words, faithful to His promises, all love towards those who seek Him, all justice to those who neglect Him, all wisdom in guiding and ruling the universe. These views of the attributes of God aroused various dispositions in the Saint's heart: self-effacement through homage to God's grandeur, trust through the realization of His mercy, love through the recognition of His goodness, fear through dread of His justice, self-abandonment through submission to His divine providence. Each day, indeed, provided St. John Eudes with fresh reasons for meditating on these divine perfections.[4]

One of the special objects of the Saint's faith, that he cherished most highly, was the incomprehensible mystery of the most holy and august Trinity. To think about the Blessed Trinity was one of his greatest delights; to speak of it was his most pleasant conversation; to love, bless and praise it was the holiest of his occupations. He contemplated and adored the three divine Persons as the origin and center of all things, the principle and end of the dignity and holiness of the priesthood, the model and ideal of religious communities. To the glory of the Blessed Trinity he directed his whole being and his life. In its honor he used to recite a rosary[5] composed of three decades with three additional beads at the beginning. On each of the first three beads he would say: "Come, Holy Trinity," thus recalling to his memory and understanding the Father, the Son and the Holy Ghost. On the ten small beads he recited the "Glory be to the Father and to the Son and to the Holy Ghost," while uniting himself with all the praise they receive in heaven and on earth, and on the large beads he said with the same intention: "Praise, glory and love to Thee, O Blessed Trinity." All his devotional exercises centered around the glorification of one God in three divine Persons. Whenever he uttered the august name of the most holy Trinity or heard it uttered, he would bow his head reverently in homage to that great mystery of the Catholic faith.

Faith also revealed to St. John Eudes all the grandeur of Jesus Christ, the God-Man, and his obligation to depend on the Incarnate Word through love; the infallibility of the Catholic Church of which Jesus Christ is the head, and the Holy Spirit the guide; and the respect required for the ceremonies, functions, customs, orders, prohibitions and teachings of the Church.[6] Faith taught him that of himself he was only an nonentity, only sin and abomination, and that all the things of this world are but vapor, illusion and vanity. These truths were ever present in his mind. He frequently declared before heaven and earth his firm and entire belief in all that Jesus Christ taught us Himself as well as what He teaches through His Church, and repeatedly expressed the desire to shed his blood and forfeit his life rather than hesitate over a single point of doctrine or endorse any error contrary to it. He would also offer himself to God to make this profession of faith before all the enemies of our holy religion, in union with the faith of the Blessed Virgin Mary, of the holy apostles and of all the saints.

This inviolable attachment to our holy faith gave St. John Eudes a marked aversion toward all novel forms of religious thought, as well as toward all who advocated or taught them. He always courageously resisted their urgent importunities that he support their ideas. He stated boldly and fearlessly that he and the members of his Congregation[7] were as far removed from Jansenism as heaven is from hell, that they were more opposed to it than fire is to water, and that the greatest evil that could befall a city or a diocese would be to entrust the direction of its seminary to priests corrupted by that pernicious doctrine.[8] He most eloquently exhorted all his colleagues to avoid argument with those who were tainted by Jansenism, and to state their attitude frankly when the subject came up, "for we must do so," he said, "without fear of possible consequences. Indifference is strictly forbidden in a matter so clearly pronounced upon by the Holy See, whose decision is accepted by the entire Church."[9] He even drew up a constitution forbidding the introduction of any new religious opinions in his Congregation, particularly of those not in strict conformity with the sentiments held in common by the Fathers of the Church.[10] His love of truth brought down on his head the wrath of many prominent persons who, not satisfied with persecuting him, also vented their spleen on those who were associated with him.[11] Though he did not have the privilege of shedding his blood in the defense of his faith, he certainly suffered extraordinary persecutions during his lifetime in order to defend the articles of the Catholic faith.

His desire to establish and augment our holy faith impelled St. John Eudes to labor for the conversion of heretics. He had the consolation of converting a considerable number of them during his missions through public discussion groups conducted two or three times a week, through individual interviews, and above all through his untiring recourse to prayer in which, pouring out his heart in the presence of the divine Majesty, he would ask God to grant light and grace to those poor blind individuals whose unfortunate condition grieved him deeply. He himself never ceased to thank God for the favor of making him a Christian and a Catholic by birth[12] and of preserving the purity of his faith in spite of the many dangerous occasions in the sphere in which he moved.

St. John Eudes strove in particular to implant this holy faith in the hearts of young people by means of frequent informal instructions.[13] He valued this practice as one which yielded the greatest fruit and the least vanity. He would treat children with both gentleness and friendliness, frankly and kindly making efforts to win them over in every way possible. He also urged members of his Congregation to train themselves for this work, laying down rules to help them do so.[14]

The faith of St. John Eudes was pure and simple, grounded in the testimony of Sacred Scripture, which he studied continually with special devotion. In lifeless print he beheld the eternal word of God the Father who desires to enlighten mankind. He looked upon Holy Writ as the most precious gift bestowed upon us by the Holy Spirit of God. He was convinced that everyone should revere Scripture as the heart of God which contains His divine secrets and is the source of life for His children. Before reading the written word of God, he used to pay homage to our Lord as the self-subsistent Word of God; then he would adore the Son of God in all His divine intentions toward Holy Church and toward himself in particular, while declaring the truths contained in Scripture, or while inspiring those who had written them. He would thank God for the graces of enlightenment that had come to all Christians through that medium; he would humble himself profoundly, considering that he was unworthy to touch or even to look at those sacred books; he would ask pardon for his inadequate use of them.

Mindful that our divine Saviour had read Sacred Scripture publicly in the synagogues as St. Luke tells us,[15] St. John Eudes used to unite himself to the dispositions of Christ and of the saints who were made holy by the reading and study of Scripture.[16] It was his custom to implore the divine Spirit who inspired these words of eternal life to implant these truths in his heart, to make a gospel of his body and soul. It may be said of him, indeed, that he was a living book, written inside and outside with the interior and exterior life of Jesus Christ as unfolded for us in Sacred Scripture. He never concluded his daily scriptural reading without retaining a special text on which to meditate at various times during the day and to use as food for thought, since it is true that man does not live by bread alone but by every word that comes from the mouth of God.[17]

St. John Eudes frequently advised persons to read each day, on their knees, a chapter of the New Testament, and he wished this daily reading of Scripture to be the practice of all Christians, especially of those who desire to labor for the establishment of God's kingdom within themselves, in order to enable them to learn the life of Christ and base their conduct on His words, actions and virtues as revealed in the Word of God.

If faith in its obscurity renders man capable of knowing all things, as Tertullian tells us,[18] it is equally true that it makes us capable of undertaking and accomplishing all things. That is why St. Paul, in praising the heroes of the Old Testament, lauds them for their faith,[19] as the source of all those admirable deeds that merited eternal happiness and glory for them. This same fact led the Apostle to declare that faith is the life of the just man.[20] St. John Eudes considered everything in the light of faith, that he might not err in his judgments. In times of doubt and difficulty faith always presided over his deliberations since he wished to solve his problems on Christian grounds alone. He never allowed himself to be deluded by false ideas that the world might suggest; rather he considered all things according to the judgment passed on them by almighty God. He renounced purely natural viewpoints. Before any undertaking he would cast himself at the feet of the Son of God, adoring Him as the author and consummation of faith, the true light which enlightens every man born into the world.[21] He would acknowledge in the presence of God's divine majesty that he was darkness and blindness; he would implore God to destroy prudence of the flesh and worldly wisdom within him, and not to permit him to follow the maxims of either the one or the other but to grant him instead the grace and strength to prefer in all things the truths of the Holy Gospel.

Thus did this great Saint honor his faith through his virtue, even as those first Christians described by Clement of Alexandria.[22] So also did this same faith give testimony of his virtue because it constituted the mainspring of his acts, for it is virtuous deeds that sustain the life of the just man. Faith without good works, as St. James teaches,[23] is a dead and unproductive faith that will render us guilty before the tribunal of God in proportion to our failure to profit by its enlightenment.

NOTES

[1] Hebr. 11:6.

[2] William of Paris or Auvergne, Bishop of Paris, philosopher and theologian, was born at Aurillac toward the end of the twelfth century and died at Paris in 1249. His works include several treatises on practical theology: *De virtutibus, De moribus* and *De sacramentis.* The reference here is to "De fide" in *Omnia opera* (Paris, 1674), vol. 1, chapter 1, No. 5.

[3] Hebr. 11:1.

[4] See Eudes, *The Kingdom of Jesus,* p. 9.

[5] *Ibid.,* p. 311.

[6] *Ibid.,* p. 10.

[7] The Congregation of Jesus and Mary, a society of priests without the

three regular vows of the religious state, was founded on March 25, 1643, by St. John Eudes. Its members are dedicated to the training of young men for the priesthood in minor and major seminaries and to the preaching of parish missions. See Sargent, *op. cit.*, p. 73; Joly, *op. cit.*, p. 103.

[8] St. John Eudes and the priests of his Congregation were implacable antagonists of Jansenism. See Eudes, *Letters and Shorter Works* (New York, P. J. Kenedy, 1949), p. 129; Father Peter Costil in *Annales de la Congrégation de Jésus et Marie,* vol. 1, p. 325, refers to the vigorous opposition of the Saint to Jansenism; Sargent, *op. cit.*, p. 169.

[9] *Oeuvres Complètes du Vénérable Jean Eudes* (Paris, Beauchesne, 1909), vol. 9, p. 225.

[10] *Ibid., loc. cit.* See also *Constitutions of the Congregation of Jesus and Mary* (Hyattsville, Willowbrook Seminary, 1949), p. 18.

[11] Sargent, *op. cit.*, p. 177 and 269.

[12] Eudes, *Letters and Shorter Works,* p. 287.

[13] *Constitutions of the Congregation of Jesus and Mary,* p. 21.

[14] *Oeuvres Complètes du Vénérable Jean Eudes,* vol. 9, p. 349 and pp. 388–389.

[15] Lk. 4:16–17.

[16] St. John Eudes, *The Priest: His Dignity and Obligations* (New York, P. J. Kenedy, 1947), p. 33–34.

[17] Mt. 4:4.

[18] Tertullian, *De praescriptionibus,* chapter 7, 21; P.L. 2:27.

[19] Gal. 3:7.

[20] Gal 3:11.

[21] Jn. 1:9.

[22] Clement of Alexandria, *Stromata,* vol. 4, chapters 16–17; P.G. 8: 1309–1312.

[23] James 2:26.

Chapter 3. Hope

JUST AS FAITH, according to St. Augustine, lays the foundation of the house of God,[1] which is the Christian religion and the Catholic Church, so also is it hope that gives this divine structure its growth and solidity. Hope is the virtue that prompts us to seek and find our sovereign good in God alone, since He has promised that we shall possess Him for all eternity if we serve Him faithfully here on earth. It affords great happiness to a soul to be bound to carry his hope so far that it includes even the eternal possession of God. Such an expectation can easily sweeten all the bitterness of life. Convinced that hope is based on divine power and goodness and is sustained by the promises and merits of our Blessed Lord, the Christian knows that he will never lack any of the things necessary to reach heaven, and it may be said of him, as of Abraham, that he hopes against hope[2] in the most serious misfortunes that befall him.

Such were the dispositions of St. John Eudes. He believed that God, sincerely desiring to save all men,[3] would not refuse him the means necessary to salvation. He looked upon Jesus Christ as upon Him who had been sent to us by the eternal Father to be our redemption, justice and virtue, our sanctification and treasure, our strength, our life and our all. He frequently meditated on all that our loving Saviour had done and suffered for us in His incarnation, life, passion and death, and still does for us each day in the Blessed Sacrament of the altar. Then he would exclaim: "Let them trust in thee who know thy name."[4] "O Goodness! O Love! O most great and loving Jesus! . . . O my Saviour, surely we are most worthless if we do not have confidence in Thy goodness, after Thou hast displayed so many proofs of Thy love for us."[5]

In all his trials, temptations and repugnances the Saint never allowed himself to become disheartened, but he trusted instead in the goodness of God and in the strength of His grace, as St. Paul would have us do, certain as we are that God will not allow us to be tempted beyond our strength.[6] At such moments he thought of the words which had come from the sacred lips of our Blessed Lord, inviting us to have recourse to Him in time of adversity: "Come to me, all you that labor and are burdened; and I will refresh you."[7] He used to recall these words, too, from St. John: "Him that cometh to me, I will not cast out."[8] Assailed by fear and distrust but sustained by the promises of the Son of God, he would turn to passages of Sacred Scripture such as the following: "To thee, O Lord, have I lifted up my soul. In thee, O my God, I put my trust; let me not be ashamed."[9] "In thee, O Lord, have I hoped, let me never be confounded."[10] "For though I should walk in the midst of the shadow of death, I will fear no evils, for thou art with me."[11] "The Lord is my helper: I will not fear what man can do unto me."[12] "Behold, God is my saviour: I will deal confidently and will not fear."[13] "Although he should kill me, I will trust in him."[14] "O my sweet love," he prayed, "I place my whole being in Thy hands and sacrifice it to Thee, with my life, my soul and all that belongs to me, that Thou mayest dispose of them in time and in eternity howsoever it pleases Thee, for Thy glory." Such were the weapons that he employed to fight against and destroy thoughts of despair, which of all sins is the most injurious to man.

St. John Eudes therefore abandoned himself wholly to God, without worrying in the least about what might happen or what His divine majesty might command, either in this world or in the next. This was also the advice offered by his intimate friend, M. de Renty,[15] in a letter addressed to him: "Simplicity calls for unconditional surrender in those who have given up their souls for Jesus Christ, and in those who belong to Him, as you do."[16]

This is precisely what the Saint himself used to advise individuals under his guidance. To his niece, Mother Mary of the Nativity,[17] religious of the Order of Our Lady of Charity,[18] he wrote: "Let us take care not to allow our spirits to become narrow and depressed through sadness and discouragement. Let us try, rather, to gladden, sustain and heighten them through trust, and through our love for Him who is all love and goodness toward us."[19] Replying to another of his religious daughters, who was greatly worried about her salvation, he said: "Rid your mind . . . of all these thoughts that disturb you, and put your trust in our benign Saviour and His most holy Mother, who love you far more than you love yourself, for they are all affection and love toward you."[20]

In his conferences to the Sisters of Our Lady of Charity, one of the things he most frequently counseled was never to become discouraged, even though they realized their many imperfections, but to humble themselves instead and to love their own abasement.

St. John Eudes deemed it an outrage to flee from the

presence of God after one has offended Him, as did the wretched Cain in the wake of his crime.[21] On the contrary, he desired souls to return to God as soon as they had failed Him, and to cast themselves at His feet in the sentiments of the Prodigal Son.[22] Hope was for him a firm and steadfast anchor, as St. Paul would have it be.[23] It always made him happy, safeguarding him from his enemies and surrounding him with divine protection. Indeed, Sacred Scripture teaches us that none are happier than those who have perfect hope in God;[24] that they will gather new strength from it; that they will soar like eagles above the attacks, perils and corruption of the world; that they will progress rapidly and without weariness along the way of the Lord; and that they will advance untiringly toward the blessed eternity.[25]

The Saint looked upon trust in God as the loving gaze of a devoted wife who deeply moves her husband's heart. He believed confidence in God to be so essential that he frequently asked for it as a special favor from the divine majesty. He honored trust in everyone who possessed it, admiring that virtue in St. Vincent de Paul,[26] the founder of the Congregation of the Mission, whom he praised for his unbounded confidence in God and recommended to his colleagues as a model whom they ought to imitate.

St. John Eudes used to say that it was to strengthen us in hope that Jesus Christ, our Lord, had characterized Himself in Sacred Scripture as the friend, advocate, doctor, shepherd, brother, father and spouse of our souls; that He called us His sheep, His children, His portion and His heritage, His soul and His heart.[27] He listed all the passages from Scripture that expressed the happiness and the reward of those who rely on God, for use whenever the devil tempted him to think otherwise. He compiled another list of passages which point out the love of God for us and the care that divine providence exercises over us in order to sustain our hope whenever we might meet with opposition in our work. The words of Isaias were frequently in his mind and on his lips: "Hearken unto me, O house of Jacob, all the remnant of the house of Israel, who are carried by my bowels, are borne up by my womb. Even to your old age I am the same, and to your grey hairs I will carry you. I have made you, and I will bear: I will carry and will save."[28] Another passage from Isaias that he often quoted was: "Can a woman forget her infant, so as not to have pity on the son of her womb? And if she should forget, yet will not I forget thee. Behold, I have graven thee in my hands."[29]

If the realization of his own unworthiness obliged the Saint to place no reliance on himself, his experience of the goodness of God impelled him to entrust himself entirely to divine providence. Indeed, he abandoned his body and soul, his health, reputation, earthly goods and affairs, the persons with whom he dealt, his past sins, his progress along the path of grace, his life, death, salvation, eternity and everything in general—all these he abandoned to the paternal care of almighty God, in the certainty that divine providence would dispose of them in the best possible way. He applied to himself the teaching of St. Peter: "[Cast] all your care upon him, for he has care of you."[30] Frequently he repeated these words of our Blessed Lord to St. Catherine of Siena: "My daughter, forget yourself and think of Me, and I will think constantly of you."[31] It was in these sentiments of perfect confidence that St. John Eudes wrote to a friend to whom he owed a small sum of money: "I promise to pay you with the first money that comes my way, for I have none at all now; but we possess an Infinity Bounty, an Infinite Wisdom and an Infinite Power who is all things to us for our sake."[32]

When the houses of his religious societies were reduced to difficult straits, the Saint never lost his confidence nor even allowed it to waver. On the contrary, he always found strength, like Abraham,[33] in faith, in glorifying God and believing with the utmost certainty that He is capable of fulfilling everything that He has promised. This he demonstrated on various occasions when he revived the courage of certain superiors whose communities were in dire need.

Beside the spite campaign directed against the Eudist Seminary of Rouen during the early days of its establishment,[34] great suffering continued at the institution for a considerable length of time from the scarcity of even the necessities of life. When the Superior[35] of this institution complained, he received this reply from the Saint: "We must guard well . . . against losing that confidence which the Holy Spirit recommends so highly to us in Sacred Scripture, for it is very pleasing to His divine majesty. Distrust binds His hands and prevents Him from bestowing the fruits of His holy generosity. In short, God never forsakes the needy, but He wants us to pray to Him with trust and perseverance. Make a novena, then, for that intention."[36]

On still another occasion St. John Eudes wrote to the same superior: "I am constantly mindful of the needs of your house, but I cannot believe that our most bountiful Father and our most admirable Mother will withhold their generosity in this urgent necessity. No, no, my dear brother, they will not abandon their poor children, however unworthy and unfaithful; heaven and earth would sooner come to an end. What would become of those divine words: 'who giveth food to all flesh: for his mercy endureth for ever.'[37] . . . For my part, I am sparing no effort or endeavor to do all that I reasonably can in this matter, but, thank God, without haste and without reliance on what I am doing. Do as much on your part."[38]

The priest who succeeded the first superior of the Rouen Seminary,[39] finding it in the same predicament, informed his spiritual father of the situation and received this answer. "Our Lord makes us poor in order to grant us the grace to be in conformity with Him, and to give us the opportunity to humble ourselves, become submissive to His most holy will and place all our trust in Him. Therefore, let us trust in Him without reservation . . . and also in our most holy Mother."[40]

St. John Eudes wrote practically the same thing to the bursar of this house who was gravely concerned about its urgent needs. "If I considered from a human point of view all that you write me of the needs of the house in Rouen, it would trouble me a great deal, but I look upon them as being in the province of God who manages all things in the best possible manner. It is usually His way to found His works on lowliness, humiliation, poverty and nothingness. . . . Let us take care not to lose confidence or allow ourselves to become distrustful, for thus do we bind the hands of divine bounty. . . . Let us be anxious only to please Him and to accomplish faithfully what He asks of us, and He will take care of all that is necessary and expedient for us."[41]

The Rouen Seminary was not the only foundation of his Congregation of priests that suffered from want. All the others, in their early days, were in the same plight, but whenever St. John Eudes was told about it, he would reply in terms of complete confidence and abandonment to God's holy will. The favor of aristocrats and the support of the wealthy he held as nothing. Whenever he was obliged to have recourse to them, he would regard them simply as instruments of divine providence. He never sought their aid with urgency, nor did he worry when he saw himself deprived of it.

"There has occurred to me a way to find help," he wrote

one day to another superior of one of his seminaries, "and I have communicated it to our friends who approve of it. Nevertheless, I am not counting on it in the least, but if our Lord finds it pleasing, He will avail Himself of it. Otherwise, His holy will be done. In Him alone should we place our dependence and trust. He does want us, however, to do what we can on our part. . . ."[42] In another letter to the same superior he said: "May God deign to keep us from depending on anything but His infinite goodness. Let us expect nothing, hope for nothing and wish for nothing save Him, placing our dependence and trust in Him alone."[43]

On many occasions St. John Eudes found that his best friends had abandoned him. Yet he never allowed their desertion to trouble him. Although he saw many rise up against him, he always remained resolutely at peace. He never refused any undertaking through fear of being deficient in health, strength or talent. His confidence gave him the courage to conceive great plans for God's glory and to carry them out according to the grace that was given him. While he never doubted his own inability, he believed, as did St. Paul, that he could do all things in Him who gave him strength.[44] He never hesitated to found new houses, though he had no assured income to maintain them, because he knew that the necessities of life are never lacking to those who serve God faithfully. In all his undertakings he did not trust at all in his own intellect, knowledge, desires, resolutions and prayers, but only in God's mercy. Nevertheless, he would do everything he could in managing the affairs entrusted to him and in carrying out the duties of his position; he was as conscientious about them as if he were not expecting the help of divine grace.

In short, the supernatural trust of St. John Eudes was such that he never abandoned the enterprises begun for the glory of Jesus Christ, no matter what it cost him in suffering. He was convinced that, because it concerned the interests of our Lord, God would grant them success according to His holy will. Whenever his affairs seemed to be in a particularly bad state, then he entertained even greater hopes that God would be pleased to crown his efforts by granting him success, so true is it that almighty God is well pleased with souls that place their complete trust in Him, and He showers His signal graces upon them. On the contrary, God withdraws His blessings from those who rely upon creatures and material advantages.

NOTES

[1] St Augustine, *Sermo* 27, chapter 1; P.L. vol. 38: 447.
[2] Rom. 4:18; Gen. 15:5–6.
[3] 1 Tim. 2:4.
[4] Ps. 9:11.
[5] St. John Eudes, *The Kingdom of Jesus,* p. 56.
[6] 1 Cor. 10:13.
[7] Mt. 11:28.
[8] Jn. 6:37.
[9] Ps. 24:1–2.
[10] Ps. 30:2.
[11] Ps. 22:4.
[12] Ps. 117:6.
[13] Isa. 12:2.
[14] Job 13:15.
[15] Gaston John Baptist de Renty (1611–1649) was born in 1611 at the Castle of Beny-Bocage, in the diocese of Bayeux, Normandy. After completing his education, he took up a military career. An accomplished and energetic soldier, he distinguished himself by his courage and military talents as well as by his piety and virtue. In 1638 he relinquished his rank in the army in order to devote himself zealously to the sick and the poor. De Renty was a faithful friend of St. John Eudes and often accompanied him on his missions. From the village of Citry where he was lord of the manor, de Renty wrote to Father Olier, the founder of the Sulpicians, on June 10, 1648: "Father Eudes' labors here are blessed beyond belief." De Renty died on April 24, 1649. See Father John Baptist St. Jure, S.J., *An Extract of the Life of Monsieur de Renty, Late Nobleman of France* (Philadelphia, 1795), p. 57. Also Eudes, *Letters and Shorter Works,* p. 59.
[16] The original copy of this letter from de Renty to St. John Eudes was

in the archives of the Caen Seminary before the French Revolution. It was lost along with many other valuable manuscripts in the chaos of the political upheaval when the Eudist Seminary at Caen was confiscated by the revolutionaries. The original text from which Herambourg quotes was extant in his time.

[17] Mother Mary of the Nativity Herson (1629–1709) was the eldest daughter of the Saint's sister, Mary. At the age of eleven she entered the Monastery of Our Lady of Charity at Caen. On September 9, 1651, she took the habit of the Order and received the name Sister Mary of the Nativity. She became superior of the Caen Monastery and did much to expand the Order and to establish regular observance. She died on June 4, 1709. See Sargent, *op. cit.*, pp. 135 and 248.

[18] The Order of Our Lady of Charity was established by St. John Eudes in 1641. The first Monastery was at Caen in Normandy. The purpose of the Order is the rehabilitation and education of delinquent girls and women. In the original establishment each house of the Order was autonomous. In 1835 St. Mary Euphrasia with the approbation of the Holy See united several houses under a mother general residing at Angers. This branch, known as the Congregation of Our Lady of Charity of the Good Shepherd, is now worldwide. See Father Joseph Mary Ory, *The Origin of the Order of Our Lady of Charity* (Buffalo, Leader Press, 1918); also Right Rev. Monsignor H. Pasquier, *Life of Mother Mary of St. Euphrasia* (London, Burns, Oates, 1893), vol. 1, p. 129 and 210; *St. Mary Euphrasia Pelletier* (Angers, 1941) p. 88ff.

[19] Eudes, *Letters and Shorter Works,* p. 252.

[20] Ibid., p. 254.

[21] Gen. 4:13.

[22] Lk. 15:11–32.

[23] Heb. 6:19.

[24] Ps. 30:20.

[25] Isa. 40:31.

[26] In the original text Father Herambourg refers to St. Vincent de Paul as "Monsieur Vincent." Vincent de Paul was not beatified at the time when Herambourg wrote. His beatification took place on September 21, 1729, and his canonization on June 16, 1737. In this passage Father Herambourg is simply narrating what he heard from the Eudist Fathers who had lived with St. John Eudes. From several references in St. Vincent's letters we know that he had a genuine admiration for St. John Eudes. See Pierre Coste, *Correspondance, Entretiens, Documents de S. Vincent de Paul* (Paris, Librairie Lecoffre, 1922), vol. 8, pp. 308–310; vol. 13, p. 347.

[27] Eudes, *The Kingdom of Jesus,* p. 55.

[28] Isa. 46:3–4.

[29] Isa. 49:15–16.

[30] 1 Pet. 5:7.

[31] See A. T. Drane, *The History of St. Catherine of Siena* (London, Long-

mans Green, 1899), vol. 1, p. 43. These words of our Lord to St. Catherine of Siena are quoted by St. John Eudes in *The Kingdom of Jesus,* p. 58.

[32] This short excerpt is from a letter that was lost. It is not found in *Oeuvres Complètes* that were edited by Father Charles Lebrun and Father Joseph Dauphin in 1905. Since there are no quotation marks in the original Herambourg manuscript, this fragment was either discarded or overlooked by the editors of *Oeuvres Complètes.*

[33] Gen. 17:10–11; Rom. 4:11–13.

[34] The Rouen Seminary was opened on February 8, 1659. See Eudes, *Letters and Shorter Works,* p. 125.

[35] The Superior to whom this letter was written was Father Thomas Manchon, one of the first five members of the Congregation of Jesus and Mary. He was appointed superior of the new Seminary of Rouen in 1658 and died there on February 6, 1663. See *Letters and Shorter Works,* p. 31, footnote 2.

[36] *Ibid.,* p. 127.

[37] Ps. 135:25.

[38] *Letters and Shorter Works,* p. 128.

[39] The second superior of the Rouen Seminary was Father Louis Faucon, who succeeded Father Manchon in 1663. *Ibid.,* p. 195, footnote 1.

[40] *Ibid., loc. cit.*

[41] *Ibid.,* p. 133.

[42] *Ibid.,* p. 277.

[43] *Ibid., loc. cit.*

[44] Phil. 4:13.

Chapter 4. Love of God

IN THE OLD LAW

God gave Moses a commandment by which He stipulated that there must at all times be a fire burning upon the altar of the temple.[1] Commentators on Sacred Scripture, seeking to understand the true meaning of this symbol, assert that God intended in this way to teach man, whom He had chosen as His dwelling-place, the obligation of keeping the fire of divine love burning perpetually upon the altar of his heart. It is highly probable that such was God's intention, since in both the Old and New Testaments there is nothing so forcefully emphasized as the precept of love. It was this sacred fire which incessantly consumed St. John Eudes, to whom we may apply the words spoken of King David by the Holy Spirit in the Book of Ecclesiasticus: "With his whole heart he praised the Lord and loved God that made him."[2]

St. John Eudes was convinced that the Christian is given life only that he may use it in the service of God from whom he has received it. He wanted to be entirely transformed into acts of praise, adoration and pure love. He found joy in thinking about the Beloved of his soul and made a practice of frequently elevating his mind and heart toward the Most High. This exercise became so easy for him that he was seldom distracted from it by any outward action. While eating his meals, he would make almost as many acts of love as he would take mouthfuls of food. Whenever he talked to people, his soul was communing with God, and although his conversation was pleasant and easy, it did not disturb his interior colloquy with His divine majesty.

Never was St. John Eudes satisfied with his love for God at any particular moment; he would offer further, as an act of his own free will, all the ways in which he would necessarily love God throughout eternity, in accordance with his hope. Since he would have liked to have a million hearts to satisfy his tremendous eagerness for love, and since his own heart seemed to him to be too small and too limited, he used to exhort all creatures to come to his aid in helping him to discharge such a strict obligation. "Come," he would say to them, "come, love this Saviour most worthy of love. Let us employ and consume all our strength and being in loving Him who created us for that end alone."[3]

The Saint longed to see heaven and earth converted into a pure flame of love, and he was sometimes heard to utter these words or similar ones: "If my power were as great as my desire, God would indeed be greatly loved and glorified."[4] Whoever wished to make him happy had only to manifest his yearning to love God. It was his fondest desire for the souls entrusted to his guidance, or united to him by spiritual ties. This is evident from a letter that he wrote to a religious[5] at Montmartre:[6] "I thank you for your kind letter. I am delighted to see that you are persevering in your desire to love our most lovable Saviour and His dearest Mother more and more. I very humbly supplicate them to cast all of you, that is to say, Mother Abbess[7] and all her daughters, who are my dearest sisters, into the innermost depths of the furnace of divine love. I do this daily for you, insofar as I am able, with the most ardent desire for all of you to be inflamed, devoured and consumed by the sacred flames of that divine furnace. . . . The Hearts of Jesus and Mary are burning furnaces of love whose fires and flames are fed only on hearts. Oh, how happy are the hearts that lose themselves in these divine flames! But the Sacred Hearts require hearts that are humble, pure, detached, charitable, faithful, obedient, inflamed with an ardent desire to please God, and utterly filled with trust in the infinite goodness of the Son of Mary and the incomparable benignity of the Mother of Jesus."[8]

Whenever St. John Eudes did someone a favor, he would ask, as a reward for his trouble, that the recipient give himself to God with the resolution to love Him and to make acts of love to Him.

From St. Paul the Saint had learned that everything in this world has a language of its own.[9] To him all creatures were so many voices which cried out unceasingly: "Love God, who is all love for thee!" He believed that God the Creator had inscribed His love upon all things in the universe, as a passionate lover sometimes carves the name of his beloved on the bark of trees. God's love enkindled fresh fires in him, prompting him to declare that, imagining the impossible, even if the obligation and duty to love God no longer existed, he would still long to love Him with all his heart and in every possible way.

Nothing in the world saddened St. John Eudes so much as his observation of how little love God received. This made him want to cry out everywhere with tears and lamentations, that Love itself was not loved, and much though he did love, he suffered from continually feeling that he did not love his divine Master nearly enough.

"Ah, my dear Lord," he used to say, "would to God that

I might be entirely transformed into desiring, longing, wishing and sighing for a greater love of Thee. O consuming and devouring Fire, where is Thy heavenly warmth? Why dost Thou not completely annihilate in me this evil and sinful life, that Thou mayest replace it with Thine own holy and divine life? Ah, my sweet Love, what will prevent me from loving Thee? Will it be my body? I will reduce it to dust. Will it be my past sins? I will drown them in the sea of Thy precious blood. . . . O Love! O Love! Either to die or to love, but rather both to die and to love! O Love! O Love! No longer ingratitude, offense, sin or infidelity, no longer anything but love!"[10]

It was this overwhelming desire to love God more perfectly that impelled him always to long for eternity and for the many mansions of love, where one sees the flow of God's love toward His creature and the ebb of love from the created being toward the Creator. From time to time the Saint would express his longings in words revealing the flames of the ardor that glowed in his heart. "O heaven," he would exclaim, "how you appeal to my desires! O blessed city where Jesus is perfectly loved and His glorious love fully reigns, where no hearts dwell that are not completely transformed into this divine love! . . . Will not that day soon come, that desirable hour for which I have so often longed, in which I shall begin to love most perfectly my most lovable Lord? . . . O my Lord, to Thee do I cry, Thee do I desire, for Thee do I long. Well Thou knowest that I desire nothing in heaven or on earth, in life or in death, except Thy pure love."[11]

Such was the fervor that consumed this mortal seraph who, after he had exhorted heaven and the God of heaven to satisfy in some measure his longing, would turn toward God's chosen ones in the hope that they might obtain for him the speedy separation of his soul from his body which would make him free to love more purely.

"Mother of God," he would pray, "angels and saints of God and all His creatures, take pity on my sorrow; speak on my behalf to the Beloved of my soul; tell Him that I desire nothing in time and eternity but His pure love; I desire neither heaven, nor the glory of heaven, nor the great joys of paradise, nor the delights of His grace, but only His most pure love. Tell Him that I can no longer live without that pure love. I implore Him to make haste, to fulfill in me the designs and work of His grace and to consume me utterly in His divine love, in order to take me soon into His eternal kingdom."[12]

Writing one day to Sister Mary de Taillepied,[13] a Benedictine nun of great virtue, with whom he maintained close spiritual ties, he said: "Ah, my beloved Sister, if you have the slightest bit of charity toward your poor brother, implore our Lord, when you are in His presence, to take me soon from this abode of sin and imperfection and to place me in the state in which I may love Him purely, perfectly and continually."[14]

The Saint's most fervent desire to love God and his own inability to do so adequately, considering the supreme loveableness of God, prompted him to seek and find countless ways of fulfilling this obligation as best he could. He frequently offered to the divine majesty of God the perfection of the angels, the faith of the ancient patriarchs and prophets, the zeal of the apostles, the sufferings of the martyrs, the holiness of the blessed, and all this, not in order to obtain anything from God, not even heaven, but only to please Him and to render Him more glory. He made it a practice of uniting himself with our Lord who makes good for what is wanting in our worship of His heavenly Father and in our faithfulness to Him. Since our divine Saviour had given Himself to mankind and to each individual, St. John Eudes believed himself capable in consequence of loving God infinitely since he could love Him with all the scope and all the strength of the divine will of the only-begotten Son of God.

The Saint's love was pure and unselfish. If he worked so hard for the salvation of souls, it was always with the intention that God be glorified in them. When he performed acts of virtue, it was not for the satisfaction of doing so, but solely for the honor and glory of the divine majesty and to render himself more like Jesus Christ, in whose spirit he performed whatever he did. Even when he sought eagerly to gain indulgences, his motive was not to be freed from the temporal punishment due for his sins but to achieve the accomplishment of the holy will of God, who desires that we be speedily united with Him. The Saint's aim was that our divine Redeemer might not be defrauded of the fruits of the Cross, that His precious blood might not be shed in vain, and that, his own soul being purified of the evil effects of sin, he might love God more purely and ardently.

Such a love for God became infectious. It was impossible to converse with St. John Eudes without feeling something of the warmth of his love. His words were like so many flames to set hearts on fire. His conversation usually dwelt on the perfections of God, of our Lord or of His Blessed Mother. If he was fairly well acquainted with persons who met him or who came to visit him, he would first ask if they had great love for God, our Lord and His admirable Mother —a title that he often gave to our Lady.

The love of St. John Eudes was an active love impelling him to wish that he could be in all parts of the world to work for the glory of his beloved Master. M. de Renty, who knew the Saint better than anyone else, remarked when writing to him about the missions then being given: "How fortunate you are to be in the midst of such an abundant harvest! Well do I know how you yearn to open the richness of your heart and to spread it on all sides in order to proclaim the kingdom of God in Jesus Christ."[15] His love rendered him admirable and exemplary in all his actions, modest in church, attentive in prayer, recollected in the celebration of the Holy Sacrifice of the Mass, zealous in the preaching of the Gospel, courageous in his reforms and new undertakings. He made a vow to God to do, in all things of importance, whatever was most pleasing to the most holy Trinity.

St. John Eudes knew that there was no better way of showing love for a person than by suffering for his sake. He therefore besought God, the Blessed Virgin Mary and the saints to obtain for him crosses, persecution, calumnies, and everything that could afflict and torment him. He even offered himself with his whole heart to bear all the sufferings which have ever been and will ever be endured in the world, so that anything displeasing in him to divine love might be destroyed and the reign of Christ might be perfectly established within him.

Such were the Saint's admirable dispositions. His heart was all aflame with love for God. Each day he was consumed more and more in those two furnaces of love, the Sacred Heart of Jesus and the Immaculate Heart of Mary, which he chose as the chief objects of his devotion.[16] May it not be said, without fear of offending the truth, that St. John Eudes resembled that seraph mentioned in Sacred Scripture, who, taking a coal from the altar, purified the lips of the Prophet Isaias?[17] How many coals did the Saint take from those two altars of the Sacred Hearts in order to purify not only his own lips and heart, but also the lips and hearts of uncounted numbers who will burn for all eternity with the ardor of divine charity? He was a captive of love, and he would have liked to conquer the whole world with charity. Happy is the soul who sees and knows nothing except divine love, and who, imitating the example of this great saint, scorns the things of earth, that he may devote himself solely to the preservation of that sacred fire of love within himself and others!

NOTES

[1] Lev. 6:12.

[2] Ecclus. 47:10.

[3] Eudes, *The Kingdom of Jesus,* p. 231.

[4] *Ibid.,* p. 235.

[5] The religious to whom this letter was written was a Benedictine nun of the Abbey of Our Lady of Montmartre. The Benedictines of Montmartre were reformed by Mother Marie de Beauvillier, abbess from 1598 to 1657. Later, under the direction of Mother Frances Renée de Lorraine, a union of prayers was concluded between the Benedictine nuns of Montmartre and the Eudist Fathers on March 25, 1661. This fervent community of Montmartre observed the two Feasts of the Sacred Heart of Jesus and of the Most Pure Heart of Mary with the Masses and Offices composed by St. John Eudes. See chapter XXII of this work, p. 193. See also chapter XI of this work, p. 98, and p. 101, note 29.

[6] The Abbey of Our Lady of Montmartre, founded in the 13th century, was located on the very spot where the Basilica of the Sacred Heart now stands. Nothing remains of the monastery today except the Abbey Church of St. Peter, which is on the west side of the present Basilica.

[7] Mother Frances Renée de Lorraine, also called Madame de Guise, was born on January 10, 1621, and died on December 4, 1682. After having been abbess at Rennes from 1637 to 1644, she became coadjutrix-abbess of the Montmartre Abbey under Marie de Beauvillier and succeeded her as abbess in 1657. Her Royal Highness, the Duchess of Guise, to whom St. John Eudes dedicated his book, *The Admirable Heart of Mary,* was not a sister-in-law of the Abbess but her niece. See *Oeuvres Complètes du Vénérable Jean Eudes,* vol. 6, p. 1. Also *The Admirable Heart of Mary,* p. xix.

[8] Eudes, *Letters and Shorter Works,* p. 274.

[9] Rom. 8:22.

[10] These prayers and aspirations are interspersed in various passages of *The Kingdom of Jesus,* pp. 224, 225, 226 and 228.

[11] *Ibid.,* p. 236.

[12] *Ibid., loc. cit.*

[13] Sister Mary de Taillepied belonged to a noble French Norman family. Out of humility she became a lay sister at Holy Trinity Monastery at Caen. See Eudes, *Letters and Shorter Works,* p. 13, footnote 1.

[14] Eudes, *ibid., loc. cit.*

[15] See notes 15 and 16 of Chapter III. This is another excerpt from a letter that has been lost. Herambourg is quoting from the original copy of the letter that he had before him.

[16] St. John Eudes inaugurated in the Church the public devotion to the Sacred Heart of Jesus and to the Immaculate Heart of Mary. See Eudes, *The Sacred Heart of Jesus* (New York, P. J. Kenedy, 1946), "Appendix," p. 179.

[17] Isa. 6:5–7.

Chapter 5. Conformity to the Will of God

THERE IS NO BETTER way of showing God respect and love than by submitting to His holy will. All creatures render their homage to Him by so doing. According to the Prophet Jeremias, God has prescribed an order for all created things,[1] and they must observe it inviolably; He has set certain boundaries for them and they must not go beyond these limits.[2] This is the way in which man, too, recognizes God's sovereignty, since it is true that a submissive people is a crown of glory in the hand of the Lord and a royal diadem in the hand of God.[3] The motto of a true lover toward his beloved is: "Whatever you wish and as you wish it." St. John Eudes may be ranked among the faithful and loving servants described in the Book of Wisdom.[4] He lived in complete dependence upon the divine will, which was the principal object of his fondest thoughts, the center of his most tender affections and the almost perennial topic of his conversations.

St. John Eudes used to speak frequently of the fact that Christ, the Incarnate Word, from the very first instant of His temporal life, obeyed the will of His Father, as St. Paul testifies in his Epistle to the Hebrews: ". . . when [Jesus] cometh into the world, he saith: . . . Behold I come: in the head of the book it is written of me: that I should do thy will, O God."[5] The Saint would contemplate with astonishment how our divine Saviour had, as it were, annihilated His own will, although it was all holy and deified, saying invariably in all things what He said in the Garden of Gethsemani on the eve of His death: "Father . . . not my will but thine be done."[6] Often St. John Eudes would repeat those words as well as the following: ". . . I came down from heaven, not to do my own will but the will of him that sent me."[7] Reflecting on the infinite happiness with which Jesus Christ had undertaken to accomplish so many things, had suffered so many torments and had envisaged the evils that were to befall this world, because such was the will of His Father, he would submit himself without effort to the pleasure and providence of God in all things.

The Saint said repeatedly that, just as the blessed in heaven find all their happiness and their paradise in perfect conformity to God's holy will, even to the extent of rejoicing over the effects of divine justice towards their loved ones who are condemned to hell, so should we, too, find all our happiness in the will of God. He would offer two proofs of this assertion: the first is the end for which we are created, the sole glory of God, which is evident in all the events of life; the second is the union that we should have with Jesus Christ, our Head, who desires us to be one with Himself and His Father, that is to say, to have the same spirit and the same sentiments.

One day, when a friend advanced in virtue told St. John Eudes to be careful lest he swerve ever so little from that royal road which was to follow everywhere and in all things the divine will of God, who desired to live and reign entirely in him, he replied: "Amen, amen, I offer and abandon myself to God's holy will with all my heart for that intention."

From that time onward he regarded his own will as a poisonous monster, a demon full of malice and an antichrist contrary to our Lord and more opposed to his own salvation than all the devils in hell; he sought to mortify and extinguish it in all things. If he felt the slightest inclination toward any particular object, he would cast himself at once at the feet of Jesus Christ, begging Him to destroy this desire if it were not in perfect conformity with the divine plan. No matter how strong the urge was, he never ceased to renounce it until he felt himself prepared to desire the contrary. He offered himself wholly to our Blessed Saviour that he might be both a bloody and an unbloody victim of the divine will, making a complete renunciation of all use of his body and soul. He wanted God and God alone to dispose of him, guide him and employ him for whatever purpose the divine will might desire.

Those were, in substance, the sentiments that St. John Eudes revealed to one of his spiritual children after recovery from a serious illness. "Help me," he wrote, "to thank our Lord and His holy Mother for having delivered me from a serious illness—it was pleurisy—which lasted only a week. Help me to ask them to give me to the divine will so completely that I may never use a single moment of my life except to do everywhere and in all things what is most pleasing to God. I am most edified and comforted by your obedience to that adorable will. Remain firm in this holy disposition. I entreat our Lord to strengthen and increase it in you more and more."[8]

St. John Eudes looked upon the divine will as the supreme purpose of his life as well as its center, as the favorable environment of his existence as well as its sovereign good. He abandoned himself entirely to God's will with respect to his body and soul, life and death, time and eternity. He wanted no other glory, joy, treasure and paradise, either in this world or in the next. He would rather have died than to do anything deliberately against the will of God. At times he would repeat these loving words: "O dearest will of my God, Thou art and shalt henceforth be my heart and soul, my life, strength, wealth and delight, my honor, crown, empire and sovereign good. Live and reign perfectly and eternally in me." On other occasions he was heard to say: "Live Jesus! Live the most holy will of Jesus! May my own will be annihilated and destroyed forever, and may His reign be accomplished eternally on earth as it is in heaven."[9]

Whenever anything happened contrary to his plans, St. John Eudes was happy because it was the will of God. If, on the other hand, he saw his own desires fulfilled, he would rejoice, not because it was a personal satisfaction to him but because it gave glory to the divine majesty. He always tried to perform all his actions out of pure love for our Lord, and he found joy in doing so because it was Christ's will. "My God," he often said when beginning any task, "grant that I may find all my happiness in doing this, because such is Thy will."[10] He used to say that this practice, frequently repeated, diminished and even eliminated the natural repugnances that one might feel, making it possible for the senses to accept as mild and pleasant whatever might otherwise arouse only bitterness and disgust. Whenever he was attacked by temptations to fear or anxiety about the loss of his health, reputation, friends or similar things, he would adore, love and bless the will of our Lord as if the loss had already occurred, or in anticipation of the time when it was to happen.

In the pains of body and spirit that often assailed him, the Saint would prostrate himself in his room before his crucifix, or if possible, he would go before the Blessed Sacrament, there to perform acts of resignation and abandonment to God. Each morning, in addition, he would make an act of acceptance of all the crosses that were to be his during the day. In short, he desired everything ordained by the Adorable Trinity, and desired it joyfully as Almighty God Himself wished it to be desired. Whenever he believed that it was God's will to undertake something, he would obey at once. Neither human respect nor worldly considerations were capable of stopping him even when it seemed that prudence did not require it just then. His devotion to the divine will never allowed him to postpone its accomplishment.

This absolute abandonment to the will of God in all circumstances produced a perennial peace in his soul. It also accounted for the purity of his love for God, since the sovereign degree of love consists in doing, suffering and accepting with joy everything that takes place by divine command.

St. John Eudes declared that this submission to God's holy will was the most universal of all virtues. It should be the most commonly cultivated, since opportunity to practice it is present at all times. He taught that a person who suffered trials or performed actions in a spirit of submission rendered more glory to God and advanced further in the ways of divine grace than he could progress in a lifetime by other practices. That is why he implanted the idea of the divine will so deeply in the minds and hearts of his spiritual children[11] that it has always remained the soul of his institutes. He gave them as a motto the beautiful words from the Second Book of Machabees: ". . . to worship [God] and to do his will with a great heart and a willing mind."[12] He wanted the members of his Congregation of priests, to have this truth imprinted on their souls before all else: that the maintenance and perfection of their religious society depended upon submission to the divine will, which is their foundation, and therefore the superior and mother that should rule and govern them in all things according to its desires; and that the will of the individuals composing the Congregation was the only thing capable of destroying the divine will.

This is what the Saint sought to explain in a letter written to his Congregation of priests: "The most adorable will of God is our most bountiful mother . . . I call it our bountiful mother, since from it we have received our being and life, in the order of nature as well as in the order of grace. God's will must govern us, and we must obey it and abandon ourselves with the utmost confidence to its guidance, for it has a truly maternal love for us! That is why I urge you, my beloved brethren, to regard, honor and love God's will as our most loving mother. Our principal devotion must be to conceive a strong affection of mind and heart for the divine will, conform faithfully to it in all things, and obey all its orders with a great heart and a willing mind. Let us find all our glory and happiness therein and regard all else as pure folly."[13]

On another occasion the Saint wrote to his spiritual sons: "The accomplishment of the divine will is the sole object of our being in this world; it is our sole business and our *unum necessarium*. It is what we ask of God each day through the words: 'Thy will be done on earth as it is in heaven.'[14] It is our proper sphere and our element, in which we shall find repose, true life, perfect happiness and eternal salvation. Outside of God's will there is nothing but trouble, death and perdition for us. But in order that the divine will may reign over us and govern us, it is absolutely necessary to renounce our own wills. We should strive, with the help of divine grace, to trample our own will underfoot, to crush it like a serpent and an antichrist."[15]

St. John Eudes never allowed a day to pass without paying special tribute to the divine will of God. He had Masses offered by his priests and Holy Communions by those who were not priests, in honor of the divine will in itself and in all its commands, past, present and future; in thanksgiving for all it had been pleased and would yet be pleased to command in time and in eternity; in reparation for the sins committed by men and demons against God's divine majesty; to obtain from His bounty the favor of accomplishing all its purposes in us by destroying whatever might prevent this accomplishment, and by annihilating our own wills entirely, that He might establish His reign perfectly in our hearts.

The Saint gave approximately the same instructions to the Sisters of Our Lady of Charity, whose spiritual father and founder he was, exhorting them to do in all things the holy will of God without giving a thought to the satisfaction or distaste that they might experience. He urged them, instead, to derive all their joy from devotional exercises and good works because God intends us to practice faithfully all the things which constitute our duty.

He inspired the same feelings in individuals under his spiritual guidance, and those who confided in him. This is how he offered an explanation of his abandonment in a letter written to a religious of Montmartre: "Tell the good Mother that she should resign herself without reservation to the most adorable will of God, neither desiring nor asking for anything save what is pleasing to Him. That is the secret of obtaining from God everything we wish, for in all things we should have no will other than His, especially since we are well aware that He desires only what is for our greatest good. . . . What wonderful peace the soul enjoys when it has wholly annihilated its own will and all its inclinations, and has sacrificed all its desires, interests and satisfactions to God, neither wishing nor asking for anything, at any time, except what is pleasing to God, professing to desire no happiness other than the happiness of its most kind Father! No matter what happens, nor in what state it is, the soul is always very happy because God is. One must indeed be hard to please if he is not contented with the happiness of God. This is, therefore, the way in which one obtains from God all that he requests of Him, because he asks for nothing that is not pleasing to Him. Perfect conformity to God's will is paradise on earth."[16]

"In truth," he wrote elsewhere, "we should indeed be difficult to satisfy if we were not happy with what affords happiness to God, the angels and the saints, who rejoice not so much because of their own glory as on account of the accomplishment of the will of God within themselves, that is, because God is happy and pleased to glorify them. We shall have no reason to complain when we are in the paradise of the Mother of God, the Son of God and the Eternal Father."[17]

Finally, the Saint strove zealously to spread devotion to the divine will. To this end he compiled a hymn[18] from the psalms of David that mention the will of God, for use as a means of honoring daily the divine will. He also had little cards printed, which he distributed with the intention that they be worn over the heart. On one side of the card was printed: *Blessed be the most loving Hearts and the most sweet names of Jesus and Mary now and forever. May the Virgin Mary with her divine Child bless us.* He wanted those who wore the cards to make a pact with our Blessed Lord, offering Him their heartbeats as so many voices incessantly praising the loving Hearts and the sweet names of Jesus and

Mary. On the other side of this card were the words: *I beg, O Lord, and I desire with all my heart that Thy most adorable will be done in me and in all creatures according to Thy good pleasure.* It was his wish that each bearer of this card give himself with each breath to the divine will, imploring it to reign absolutely within him and in all creatures. This pact was to be renewed daily.

Such were the Saint's sentiments regarding the holy will, to which he had vowed and consecrated himself from earliest childhood. This was the path of grace traveled by him in attaining such a high degree of perfection. These were the means employed by divine providence to make such a great saint of him.

NOTES

[1] Jer. 31:35.
[2] Ps. 103:9.
[3] Isa. 62:3.
[4] Wisd. 3:9.
[5] Hebr. 10:7.
[6] Lk. 22:42.
[7] Jn. 6:38.
[8] Eudes, *Letters and Shorter Works,* p. 200.
[9] Eudes, *The Kingdom of Jesus,* p. 63.
[10] *Ibid.*, p. 67.
[11] The Congregation of Jesus and Mary, better known as the Eudist Fathers, founded in 1643, and the Order of Our Lady of Charity of Refuge established in 1641.
[12] 2 Mach. 1:3.
[13] Eudes, *Letters and Shorter Works,* p. 65.
[14] Mt. 6:10.
[15] Eudes, *ibid.*, p. 282.
[16] *Ibid.*, p. 218.
[17] This is another excerpt from a letter that was lost. It is found in *Oeuvres Complètes du Vénérable Jean Eudes,* vol. 12, p. 205.
[18] This hymn in honor of the Divine Will is found in *Manual of Piety for the Use of the Congregation of Jesus and Mary* (Quebec, Larose, 1948), p. 282.

Chapter 6. Manifestations of His Conformity to God's Holy Will

TO ACCOMPLISH GOD'S holy will, we must first clearly understand what it is. We cannot move eagerly toward a goal unless we have previously learned something about it. A person who knows the law well, and nevertheless violates it, brings a more severe sentence upon himself. Punishment or reward is in proportion to previous enlightenment. God always expects greater fidelity and effort from those to whom He has given greater light.

St. John Eudes came to know the will of God through incessant study, and he strove to carry it out faithfully in all things, great and small. He used to say that the divine will generally manifested itself in five principal ways: first, through the commandments of God and of the Church; second, through the counsels of perfection; third, through the rules and obligations of our state in life; fourth, through our lawful superiors; and fifth, through the various events of life.[1] The Saint proceeded in the light of this knowledge. He would rather have suffered every kind of torment than to act wilfully in the slightest way against the commandments of God and of the Church. He lived in the general disposition of accepting the evangelical counsels, according to the extent of grace granted him. He obeyed the Church laws with exactitude. It may be said of him, indeed, that he was a living book in which those called to the service of the Church might read the rules of their state in life. He honored his ecclesiastical superiors as representatives of Jesus Christ on earth, being as prompt to obey them as if their commands had come directly from the lips of the Saviour Himself. Not even Samuel had greater respect for the High Priest, Heli,[2] than St. John Eudes had for the prelates of the Church.

The Saint placed himself entirely at the disposal of the bishops through complete renunciation of his own judgment and will, that they might use him in the offices and functions which, in their judgment, would bring the greatest glory to God. His obedience was not limited merely to ecclesiastics of high rank, but also to those in lesser positions. He had learned to submit himself to every human creature, as advised by St. Peter;[3] and in accordance with the teaching of St. Paul,[4] he regarded himself inferior to all, and considered everyone as better than himself.

His dependence upon the divine will made him strictly faithful to the devotional practices of the community. As soon as he heard the bell for prayer, the divine office, or any other exercise, he would drop everything and obey. The bell was for him the signal of the great King, which did not permit him to delay for a moment, but impelled him to go promptly wherever he was called. His conscientiousness was the result of serious reflection, over a long period of time, on the perfect submission of Jesus Christ to commands given Him by His heavenly Father, by the Blessed Virgin Mary and St. Joseph, by the angel who guided Him into Egypt, by the Jews, Herod and Pilate. This submission of our Lord to His creatures for the glory of His eternal Father motivated St. John Eudes in the fight against self-will. He strove to destroy it completely in himself and in his spiritual children, thus rendering them more conformable to Jesus and Mary, who never sought personal satisfaction in anything.[5]

One of the strongest determinations of St. John Eudes, as we pointed out in the preceding chapter, was the reign of the divine will in his religious societies, and he felt deeply grieved whenever any members fell short in some point of obedience, which he wanted to be prompt and unhesitating. This may be seen in his letters. "Perfect obedience is prompt," he wrote to one of his spiritual sons, "and has no need of reasons to be convinced. If each one gave heed to his own temperament and inclinations whenever it was necessary to transfer a subject from one house to another, what would happen?"[6]

To Father John Dupont,[7] superior of the Coutances seminary, who was importuning the founder to be relieved of his duties, he wrote the following reproach: "Peace to men of good will, to men who have made a complete renunciation of their own will and have no other than God's, which is manifested to them through holy obedience. O my dearest brother, what a great delusion it is to maintain that we are quite sure that God does not desire something of us which obedience desires! Let us humble ourselves, dear brother, and not misrepresent our own inclinations and feelings as the will of God whenever they are contrary to true obedience, without which it is impossible to please His divine majesty, particularly in a congregation of priests who serve as examples for all types of virtue. You should consider yourself very fortunate even to die in your present position of responsibility. Let us ask our Lord to allow us to share in the divine obedience which brought about His death on the Cross, and for our part, let us strive to put our own will to death and follow our most kind Father, if we wish to be numbered among His children. I implore Him with all my heart to grant us this grace."[8] Such were the thoughts of St. John Eudes concerning submission toward those who rule in God's place on earth; they show how greatly he esteemed obedience, and how much he desired others to be faithful to its practice.

St. John Eudes was convinced that God desires and permits nothing save for His greatest glory, and derives it from all things. He permits matters to succeed as a blessing conferred upon those who love Him and submit to His commands. The divine will, always infinitely just and holy, deserves to be infinitely loved and adored. Thus it was the practice of the Saint under every circumstance to unite himself to the submission of our Lord Jesus Christ, by repeating with Him: "My Father, not my will but Thine be done; yes, Father, Thou hast so desired it."

This attitude can be observed in countless instances throughout the life of the Saint, especially in the face of illness or death of his friends, or of the members of his Congregation for whom he had so much esteem and affection. Once, after he had visited the house in Lisieux, he left when nearly all the community were ill. He later wrote to the superior of the seminary at Coutances: "All our brethren at Lisieux, clerics as well as laymen, were ill when I left, except two. However, that does not discourage me, thank God, because I see in it the divine will which does all things, and does them well, and because I have the greatest confidence that our Lord and His most holy Mother will not abandon us, but will provide for everything in the way most pleasing to them, which is, thank God, all that I desire."[9] When writing to Mother Frances Patin,[10] superior of Our Lady of Charity, who was in danger of death, he had this to say: "If I yielded to purely human feelings, your illness would move me deeply; but, aside from hoping that our Lord will restore your health, I am obliged by the sight of His most adorable will to say but one thing: 'Yea, Father: for so hath it seemed good in thy sight.' "[11]

When Father Peter Jourdan,[12] one of the best workers in his Congregation, was taken by death, St. John Eudes was deeply grieved, but the account of his sorrow shows clearly that his love for the divine will was incomparably greater than his attachment and affection for persons, however dear they were to him. This is how he expressed his grief: "May the divine will be our guide in all things and our sole consolation in our afflictions! Here is a cross that is very painful and has caused unwonted sorrow: it is the death of our most kind and beloved brother, Father Jourdan. But it is only right that God be the master, and His adorable will prevail over ours. If I gave way to my feelings, I should cry aloud with grief and tears: 'Doth bitter death separate in this manner?'[13] But when I consider the most holy, wise and bountiful will of God, I cry from the depths of my heart: 'Yea, Father: for so hath it seemed good in thy sight.' "

From what he wrote about the death of M. James Blouet, Lord of Camilly,[14] one of his dearest friends, we can also see the kind of submission and regret that he wanted us to have on such occasions with regard to the decrees of divine providence.

"May the divine will be our sole consolation in our afflictions! It does all things with such great wisdom and goodness that we have only to consider God's providence in all the misfortunes that befall us in order to be comforted. I must confess, however, that this consolation does not prevent my suffering a great sorrow, according to the senses, because of the death of our good M. de Camilly. We have lost a most sincere and faithful friend. But I speak from the human point of view in saying that we have lost him, for, after all, who does not lose God loses nothing. Then, too, we do not lose our friends when God calls them to Himself. On the contrary, they are all the more ours, and they are more useful to us in heaven than on earth. But we must help them to reach heaven quickly, for it often happens that one is a long time on the way there. I entreat all our dear brethren to be conscientious in rendering to God what we owe Him in this hour of sorrow; let us humble ourselves under the almighty hand of God and adore His divine will, submitting ourselves to it with all our heart, thanking Him for the crosses that He is pleased to send us, sacrificing to Him our lives and those of our loved ones. Above all, let us try to put ourselves in the state in which we should like to be at the hour of death, and to that end, renew our desire to fulfill all our obligations with the utmost exactitude."[15]

The Saint instilled similar sentiments of submission and abandonment in the Daughters of Our Lady of Charity when they suffered the loss of Sister Mary of the Child Jesus de Bois-David,[16] a professed religious of their Order. This is what he said to the Mother Superior on that occasion: "My good Mother, may the divine will be our guide in all things! The death of our dear Sister Mary of the Child Jesus shocked me somewhat at first; but having cast my eyes upon that most adorable will which arranges all things in the best possible way, my heart remained at peace and my lips could only repeat: 'Father, not my will, but Thine be done.' Ah, it is well that way, my dear Mother, since such is the pleasure of the Infant Jesus, who willed to take this dear Sister, consecrated to the Divine Childhood, at the very season dedicated to this great mystery. She has gone to take possession of heaven in the name of all the Sisters and to begin an eternal foundation of the Order of Our Lady of Charity. She has gone to paradise, there to adore, praise and love the most holy Trinity unceasingly and for all eternity, together with Jesus and Mary and all the blessed, in the name and on behalf of all her dear Sisters. These are the first-fruits of your house which you have offered to His divine majesty. It is your first sacrifice, which must have been very pleasing to almighty God."[17]

Such was the detachment of this great Saint, that he managed to remain as serene, in his innermost heart, when God permitted him to retain his friends as when divine providence took them away. He was equally indifferent to places. Having been obliged to undertake several journeys to Paris on business for his Congregation of priests, and for other reasons highly important to the glory of the divine Master, he remained in the great city for the time necessary for successful negotiations, even though it was singularly distasteful to him to be there. Courtly Paris, so exciting for most people, was not at all attractive to him, and if he had not discerned the holy will of God in his protracted stay there, he would no doubt have suffered much; instead he found joy in submitting himself to the sojourn.

"If I followed my natural inclinations," he wrote to one of his colleagues, "I can assure you that I should be extremely weary of Paris and would have left it a long time ago. But it is the holy will of God that is keeping me here, and I have neither hands nor feet to protect myself against divine providence. On the contrary, I allow myself to be bound to its most sweet hands, and its chains are so delightful to me that my captivity constitutes all my happiness and paradise. O my dearest brother, how happy is the soul who is detached from everything and adheres only to the most lovable will of Almighty God."[18]

Writing on the same topic to Sister Mary of the Nativity, a religious of Our Lady of Charity,[19] he informed her: "It is true, my dearest Sister, that my months are sometimes very long, and longer than I realize, but not longer than I wish. Through the infinite mercy of our Lord, it seems to me that I desire nothing, either in this world or in the next, except to abandon myself entirely to the sweet captivity of the most adorable will of God, so that it may lead me to Him. Hence I cannot tell you yet when I shall return to Caen. I am well aware that, with the grace of God, it will be when I wish, but I do not know yet when I shall wish to do so because I do not know when God desires it. . . ."[20]

"You ask me if I ever grow tired of Paris. That is like asking me if I ever grow tired of paradise, but this paradise is not Paris. What it is then? The divine will, which is detaining me here in Paris, that is my true paradise. . . . If I followed my own inclinations, I can assure you that I should prefer to be in Caen, where I could converse with you occasionally about the incomparable goodness of our most bountiful and adorable Saviour, rather than be here pacing the streets of Paris. But God keep us from ever doing our own will, and grant us the grace to acknowledge that we have no interest in this world save to accomplish His holy will everywhere and in all things with a great heart and a willing mind. Ah, what a joy it is to know that this is our sole concern, and that all the powers of earth and hell cannot prevent us for a single moment, with the grace of God, from performing this one duty if we wish to do so; the more they strive to hinder us, the more they help us to accomplish it."[21]

Similar sentiments he imparted to the Community of Our

Lady of Charity in a letter including the following: "When I left Caen, my dearest and most beloved Sisters, I expected to be away two months at the most, but my will was not in agreement with my thoughts, for it was my wish to be gone longer than eight months, although I was not aware of it. I willed it, since God did, for His will is mine. I did not know then that I should have this intention, because I was ignorant of God's will in the matter, just as I still do not know what divine providence intends for the future. It is quite evident that His holy mandate has brought me here, worthless instrument that I am, to accomplish what I can scarcely believe, but I do not know yet how He wishes to dispose of me later on. Pray, my dearest Sisters, that He will do whatever is most pleasing to Him solely for the glory of His holy name and without regard for my unworthiness and misery."[22]

Although enough has been said to demonstrate the love and attachment of St. John Eudes to the divine will, this chapter must include part of the letter he wrote to one of his priests who was giving a mission in the diocese of Coutances, where the Saint had planned to be present. "I was hoping all along," he wrote, "to join you in the Gatteville Mission, but our Lord does not find me worthy of it and is keeping me here in my Paris purgatory for my sins, longer than I had anticipated. Not that I fail to want it that way, for, thanks to His mercy, God gives me the grace to desire nothing in this world save to do His most holy will. And to tell the truth, everywhere that I find His will, there I am in my element and my paradise. And so Paris, my purgatory, is become my paradise, because I see clearly that the divine will has brought me here and is keeping me here yet a few days. . . . It makes no difference to me where I am nor what I do, provided I am serving God and accomplishing

His holy will. That is all we have to do in this world, and therein should we find all our happiness."[23]

One of our Saint's most frequent assertions was this: "I do all that I wish. In everything that I undertake there is no outcome except the one I desire, because I do not wish and shall never wish for anything except the holy will of God." If the saying of Cicero[24] is true, namely that men are known by the words they speak, we cannot form a more accurate idea of the virtue and holiness of St. John Eudes than by thinking over the things that he said and wrote concerning conformity to the divine will, the mark of true devotion, as St. Cyprian observes,[25] and after him St. Thomas Aquinas.[26] Indeed, it characterized our beloved Saviour, the Word Incarnate, during His life here on earth,[27] and it is the mark of the angels and saints, as it should be of all faithful souls, who aspire to union with God on earth and eternal possession of Him in heaven.

NOTES

1 Eudes, *The Kingdom of Jesus*, p. 59.
2 1 Kings 3:1.
3 1 Pet. 2:13.
4 1 Cor. 9:19.
5 Rom. 15:3.
6 Eudes, *Letters and Shorter Works*, p. 282.
7 *Ibid.*, p. 120, footnote 1.
8 *Ibid.*, p. 161.
9 *Ibid.*, p. 284.
10 In 1644 St. John Eudes asked the Visitation nuns of Caen to assist in the training of the first religious of the Order of Our Lady of Charity until his spiritual daughters would be able to choose from among themselves a sister qualified to govern them. On August 10, 1644, Mother Margaret Francis Patin, a Visitation nun, became superior of the Refuge of Caen. For twenty years she guided the nascent community and trained the first nuns of Our Lady of Charity. Mother Patin died the death of a saint on October 31, 1668. See Ory, *op. cit.*, p. 32.
11 Lk. 22:42; Mt. 11:26. The letter reference is *Letters and Shorter Works*, p. 187.

[12] Father Peter Jourdan (1608–1661) was one of the five companions of St. John Eudes when he founded the Congregation of Jesus and Mary on March 25, 1643. See Eudes, *ibid.*, p. 181, footnote 1.

[13] 1 Kings 15:32.

[14] James Blouet, Lord of Camilly, whose family had received the title of nobility for services rendered to France in 1610. One of his sons, John James, entered the Congregation of Jesus and Mary and succeeded John Eudes as superior general in June, 1680, two months before the death of the Saint.

[15] *Letters and Shorter Works,* p. 174. See also Sargent, *op. cit.*, p. 37.

[16] Sister Mary of the Child Jesus de Bois-David was born at Montmartin in the diocese of Coutances, Normandy, of a distinguished family. She married Simon de Bois-David, a Captain of the Guards. After the death of her husband, she entered the Order of Our Lady of Charity at Caen and took the habit on April 29, 1658. She died on January 3, 1660. See Eudes, *Letters and Shorter Works,* p. 119, footnote 1; also Ory, *op. cit.*, p. 83.

[17] Eudes, *ibid.*, p. 142.

[18] *Ibid.*, p. 157.

[19] His niece, Sister Mary of the Nativity Herson, religious of Our Lady of Charity at Caen.

[20] *Letters and Shorter Works,* p. 140.

[21] *Ibid.*, p. 154.

[22] *Ibid.*, p. 146.

[23] *Ibid.*, p. 61.

[24] Cicero, *De oratore,* Book I, chapter 27: . . . *quotiens enim dicimus, totiens de nobis judicatur.* "Judgment is pronounced upon us as often as we speak." See *On Oratory and Orators* edited by J. S. Watson (Philadelphia, David Mackay, 1897), p. 45.

[25] St Cyprian, *De habitu virginum,* No. 7: P.L. 4:447.

[26] St. Thomas, *Summa,* 2a 2ae, p. 82, art. 1.

[27] Mt. 26:42; Lk. 22:42; Jn. 4:34; 5:30; 6:38; Hebr. 10:9.

Chapter 7. Gratitude

ST. AUGUSTINE SAYS that one of the principal duties of a Christian is to be grateful to God.[1] The most conspicuous act of religion is sacrifice, and of all sacrifices, one of the greatest is the Eucharistic sacrifice, that is, the sacrifice of thanksgiving. There is nothing, therefore, so highly recommended as gratitude, in both the Old and the New Testament. God commanded the Jews always to keep in mind their deliverance from Egypt; to carry the marks of this favor in their hands in order not to forget it; to preserve its emotion in their hearts; to have it always on their lips, that they might praise it and tell their descendants about it.[2]

When Jesus Christ cured the ten lepers, He reproached the nine Hebrews for immediately forgetting the tremendous favor He had done them and for not taking the trouble to return to thank Him as the Samaritan did.[3] St. Paul would have us give thanks to God for all things, for it is the divine will, he tells us, that we do so in Christ.[4] To the duty of gratitude St. John Eudes was always extremely faithful. Sharing the sentiments of Holy Church, which gives thanks to God every day in the Holy Sacrifice of the Mass when the priest says: "We render thanks to Thee because of Thy great glory," the Saint would bless God for what He is in Himself and for the effects of His goodness in created beings, principally in those powerless to acknowledge Him, living in the total unawareness of His blessings, or actually spending their lives in base ingratitude.

St. John Eudes considered himself bound to the practice of gratitude for two reasons: first, because he was a priest; second, because he was bound to imitate the Divine Master. In his capacity as priest, he considered himself a representative of the whole universe, with the obligation of rendering to God all worship due to His infinite majesty. In imitation of Jesus Christ, the God-Man, who supplies for what is wanting in our religious duties toward the heavenly Father, the Saint voluntarily assumed the obligations of all created beings toward their sovereign Creator and Master.

Of all the months of the year, March[5] was the most important to him because of the many divine benefits conferred upon mankind during that month. The Creation, the Incarnation, the Redemption, the Institution of the Blessed Eucharist and of the Priesthood, the gift of Mary to be the Mother of men[6]—all these were so many mysteries that he honored in the course of the month of March. Many were the acts of thanksgiving that he offered to God who had so lovingly wrought these marvels of grace.

Since the Saint frequently expressed his gratitude for the favors granted by God to all created beings in general, he was no less aware of those he received personally. In testimony of his gratitude, he composed a *Magnificat to the Sacred Hearts of Jesus and Mary,*[7] recapitulating the graces bestowed on him by divine providence. He even requested to have a copy of this hymn of thanksgiving buried with him,[8] symbolizing thus his longing that the grains of dust to which his body would be reduced might become tongues and hearts continually blessing the most loving Hearts of Jesus and Mary, and through them, the most holy and august Trinity, primary source of all the blessings showered upon mankind. It was his way of returning to the Triune God, as to their origin, all the blessings he had received throughout his life. Not satisfied with his own private thanksgiving, he would also exhort others to share in his gratitude. He used to write to the superiors of his religious institutes, directing them to thank God and to stimulate gratitude in their communities. He also ordered novenas of Masses and rosaries for that intention.[9]

Whenever the Saint received good news about the societies he had founded, his reply would begin with these words: "Infinite glory to the Father, the Son and the Holy Spirit! Immortal thanks to our Blessed Mother, to St. Joseph and to the Holy Angels for the good news you have written me." He would then give the good tidings to his communities in words filled with thanksgiving, repeating countless times in his letters the beautiful word *Alleluia,* which means "praise God," since he wished the letters to preserve an everlasting memory of divine favors.[10] He also established certain devotional practices which are faithfully observed daily in his communities, giving ample proof of the nobility of his heart.[11] He would have Masses said, and would give his colleagues instructions so they could all profit well from these favors. He noted in Sacred Scripture, according to the Fathers of the Church, that the Lord always stressed and exacted this duty of gratitude from His people,[12] to be expressed by the commemorative feasts, sacrifices and offerings in acknowledgment of the blessings of God the Father.

Before the anniversaries of special favors granted by God to his new Congregation, he would remind his brethren of them, so that they might discharge their duties towards the divine majesty in acts of gratitude. He even had a calendar[13] printed on which those days were specially marked, to be remembered when the time arrived. It was hard for him to tolerate forgetfulness in anyone, and he would reprove his closest friends if they fell into error, as we can see from a letter written to a superior who had neglected to celebrate a day highly esteemed in his Congregation. "Is it possible, my dearest brother, that you have so little esteem and affection for a grace like that one, of which you are so well aware? I must confess that I felt, and do feel now, an inexpressible sorrow. I beg of you, and of all our brethren, too, to atone for this omission as best you can. To that end give the order that, on the first day open after the receipt of this letter, all the Masses be votive Masses: some of the Holy Spirit, some *de Cruce,* some *de Beata,* and have one *de Beata* High Mass—all of them in thanksgiving for the favors God has granted us and in reparation for our misuse of them. In the future, you will repeat this each year."[14]

Besides the calendar just mentioned, the Saint also directed that in each house a book must be kept by the superior, recording all the special favors received by the institution from God, the Blessed Virgin Mary and the Saints, together with the year and the day when they had been granted.

Gratitude is due not only to God, who showers His blessings upon us, but also to everyone who helps us in any way. That is why St. John Eudes was not satisfied simply to render testimony of his gratitude to the divine majesty. He did the same toward all charitable persons who showed him the least evidence of friendship; he would have considered it a grave injustice to act otherwise. He frequently offered to the Blessed Virgin Mary the founders, benefactors and friends of his Societies, beseeching her most humbly to preserve, bless and sanctify each one, to number them among the children of her Immaculate Heart, and to allow them to benefit from the prayer he said for them several times daily: "O Lord, grant eternal life to all our benefactors, for love of Thy holy name. Amen."

The superior of each house was instructed by the Saint to keep a second book, recording on one side of the page the names of benefactors, and on the other, the things they had contributed, so that, by reading the record from time to time, each member might know who the benefactors were, and when the occasion presented itself he might show his gratitude. Daily prayers were offered for benefactors, particularly for those who were deceased.

Finally, St. John Eudes went so far as to desire to do good, after his own death, to those who had given him assistance during his lifetime. In his last will and testament he remembered Brother Richard,[15] a lay brother of the Congregation of Jesus and Mary, from whom he acknowledged having received outstanding aid in all his material needs over a period of years. He implored his brethren, and particularly the priest who was his successor as superior general,[16] to continue to show the same charity toward this good brother as they would toward himself.

Such was this truly grateful heart of St. John Eudes, very different from that of King Ezechias of old, who failed to acknowledge fittingly his blessings from the Lord and who brought down divine wrath, as manifested by the ultimate destruction of his family, the city of Jerusalem and all its people.[17] The Saint resembled that land of which St. Paul speaks to the Hebrews, which is watered by frequent rains, produces abundant harvests for those who cultivate it and earns the blessing of heaven.[18] Having received much fruit of grace from the Most High, he strove to give thanks for it as much as possible, finding in his gratitude the secret of winning unreservedly the Heart of God, while conciliating the hearts of men.

NOTES

[1] St. Augustine, *De spiritu et littera*, chap. 11; P.L. 44:211.

[2] Exod. 12:1–27.

[3] Lk. 17:12–18.

[4] 1 Thess. 5:18.

[5] Eudes, *The Kingdom of Jesus*, p. 244. See also Cardinal de Bérulle, *Opuscules de piété* (Aubier, Editions Montaigne, 1943), p. 198.

[6] St. John Eudes based his assertions on the opinion of several Fathers of the Church. Cornelius à Lapide commenting on Matthew 27:35 says: "On what day was Christ crucified? I answer, on March 25, that day of his conception, on which day S. Dismas, the penitent thief, is commemorated. So say, too, S. Augustine (*de Civ. lib.* xviii, *ad fin.*), S. Chrysostom, Tertullian, S. Thomas, and others, whom Suarez follows (*par.* iii, *disp.* xl, *sect.* 5, *ad fin.*) This was the completion of His thirty-fourth year, the day too of the sacrifice of Isaac, and of the passage of the Red Sea (both eminent types of Christ on the Cross) . . ." *The Great Commentary of Cornelius à Lapide* translated by Thomas W. Mossman (Edinburgh, John Grant, 1908), vol. 3, p. 289. The same author explaining Luke 1:26 has this to say: "The Annunciation by Gabriel, and consequently the Incarnation of the Word, took place on the 25th of March; on which day likewise, Christ completing the thirty-fourth year of His life, was crucified. Many are of the opinion that the world was created on the same day; so that it was created by God on the same day on which it was afterwards recreated and restored by Christ in His Incarnation and Cross." Recent biblical scholars propose a later date for the death of Christ. For a study of the "Chronology of the Life of Christ," see F. Prat, S.J., *Jesus Christ* (Milwaukee, Bruce, 1951), vol. 1, p. 461.

[7] See Eudes, *The Sacred Heart of Jesus* (New York, P. J. Kenedy, 1946), p. 175.

[8] Herambourg is simply stating what he was told by the Eudists who had lived at the time of the death of St. John Eudes.

[9] Eudes, *Letters and Shorter Works,* pp. 115–118; 125.

[10] *Ibid.*, p. 86; 224 and 225.

[11] Each year a week of thanksgiving is observed in the Congregation of Jesus and Mary in order to give thanks to God, our Lord, our Lady and the saints. The week extends from January 31 to February 7. See Eudes, *Manual of Piety,* p. 159. In addition to the prayers offered on the death of benefactors, prayers are said daily for them and a number of Masses are celebrated for their intention in each community. See *Constitutions of the Congregation of Jesus and Mary,* p. 11. On February 9, after a special

conference on gratitude, the names of the benefactors of each house are read by the superior from the special book kept for that purpose. For the obligation of gratitude in the Order of Our Lady of Charity of Refuge and the Good Shepherd, see *Constitutions, Directory and Rule for the Order of Our Lady of Charity of Refuge* (1939), p. 39; *Constitutions of the Congregation of Our Lady of Charity of the Good Shepherd of Angers* (1956), p. 87.

[12] Lev. 7:12–13.

[13] The special days of thanksgiving in the Congregation of Jesus and Mary are indicated in *Manual of Piety,* pp. 141 and 293.

[14] See Eudes, *Letters and Shorter Works,* p. 278.

[15] *Ibid.,* p. 330. Brother Richard Le Moine, a lay brother of the Congregation of Jesus and Mary, died in 1722.

[16] The Saint's successor as superior general of the Congregation of Jesus and Mary was Father John James Blouet de Camilly. See Sargent, *op cit.,* p. 145.

[17] 4 Kings, 20:17–18.

[18] Hebr. 6:7.

Chapter 8. Love for Our Lord Jesus Christ

THE APOSTLE ST. PAUL threatened the Corinthians with anathema if they did not love our Lord Jesus Christ.[1] Everything that our Saviour accomplished and suffered on earth should be a powerful incentive to love Him. We owe Him this tribute of our hearts out of gratitude, in addition to the fact that the Son of God merits it infinitely because of His unsurpassed excellence. He is the throne of grandeur in whom the perfections of God glow with majesty. The fulness of the divinity is found in Him. The eternal Father has placed all His treasures in the hands of His well-beloved Son, in whom He is well pleased. Christ is the object of His delights, the goal of His glory and the subject of His divine thoughts. He is the infinite treasure, referred to in the Book of Wisdom, which renders men participants in all the blessings of heaven.[2]

Such was the synthesis that St. John Eudes made concerning the dignity of the Word Incarnate, who was his joy, honor and wealth, his refuge and life.[3] Although he always entertained a most profound respect for every word proceeding from the lips of Christ, he had a special reverence for the sentence, "Abide in Me,"[4] by which our loving Saviour invites men to find their rest and happiness in His Sacred Heart. This was a regular practice constantly recommended to souls under the guidance of our Saint. It was the counsel that he wrote to a Benedictine nun suffering from illness. "Take comfort, my dearest Sister," he said to her, "and rejoice in our beloved Jesus, for He is yours and you are His; He dwells in you and you dwell in Him. Therefore live always for Him, for there you will find your paradise. Withdraw your mind and heart from everything else so that they may be captivated and enclosed gently in this divine paradise. It is the paradise of the eternal Father in which He is well pleased. Seek all your happiness, too, in Jesus, for He alone is capable of satisfying your heart. Embrace willingly all the sufferings and afflictions that it may please our Lord to send you, since this is the most efficacious means of destroying ourselves and establishing Jesus in our stead."[5]

No matter what happened to bring him sorrow, St. John Eudes would console himself with the thought that Jesus is always Jesus, that is, always God, always great and admirable, always in perpetual delight and glory, and that nothing is capable of diminishing His joy and happiness. Frequently he gave voice to these beautiful words: "O Jesus! Truly we have cause for joy, beholding Thee so full of glory, of grandeur, of happiness and contentment! Surely we have very great reason to rejoice; there can be no one in the whole world with so great a cause for happiness. What have worldlings to motivate their joy? Mud, dust, wind and smoke; whereas the reason of our joy is the same which gives jubilation to the eternal Father, the Holy Spirit, the angels and the saints. Therefore rejoice, repeating with the Blessed Virgin Mary: 'My spirit hath rejoiced in God my Saviour.'[6] I no longer wish to find happiness in myself or in created things but in Jesus my Saviour. He is my all and I desire to belong wholly to Him. It is the most extreme folly and delusion to look elsewhere for any true happiness. Let us strongly and courageously renounce all other things and seek only Him."[7]

St. John Eudes did not only record these sentiments on paper, but he also bore them engraved in his heart. To him Jesus Christ appeared so great that he believed with St. Paul that heaven, earth and hell must bow before Him.[8] Everything that the Saint possessed in body and soul was made to render homage to the sovereignty of Christ. At the feet of his crucified Saviour he would annihilate his spirit, his will, his being and life, surrendering himself to the power of grace, that it might perform this blessed work of destruction. He would have liked to perform this exercise at every moment, but since weakness and the needs of the flesh, together with his activities, did not allow him to do so, he would implore our Lord to accept the will for the deed. He spared no effort to realize in himself these words: "I live, now not I; but Christ liveth in me."[9] Creatures were dead in his soul; he no longer considered or loved them in themselves, but rather in Jesus and Jesus in them. For him the world was crucified, just as he was with regard to the world. He sought nothing except to be completely happy in Jesus.

Living in continual dependence upon the grace of our Blessed Saviour, St. John Eudes would advise those who consulted him to do the same. It is a maxim which spiritual directors cannot impress too deeply on souls under their guidance. It is infallible; no one can go wrong with it, since this dependence is based on the conferring of all things on Jesus Christ by the eternal Father, on the Precious Blood which He shed to redeem souls, and on the blessings which He continually lavishes upon us. That is why, from morning till night, the Saint would offer to Christ the actions of the whole day, even the most trivial ones. He would dedicate himself anew to the service of our Lord, protesting to Him that he would never use his senses except for the glory of his Redeemer.

In his inability to love and honor Christ as much as His supremacy merited, and in his striving to satisfy the desire to do so, St. John Eudes used to present to our Lord several times a day the sum total of love and honor rendered Him by men and angels, and in general by all creatures, both in heaven and on earth. He would entreat the blessed, particularly those to whom he had a special devotion, to glorify our Saviour in his name. He would even call upon the Blessed Virgin Mary, and sometimes on the eternal Father, to beg them for an infinitesimal share in their all-surpassing love for this dear Son.

St. John Eudes learned by meditation that the supreme desire of the heavenly Father is to see His Son living and reigning in all men, that in all things He sees only His Son, that He seeks no other object to please and delight Himself; that in eternity itself His sole pursuit is to produce Him. That is why St. John Eudes devoted himself exclusively to forming Christ within himself, considering that this ought to be the special activity of priests and religious, who should not speak or write, publicly or privately, by their own lips or by their own works, except to make Christ live and reign in themselves and in the faithful.

The mystical doctors recognize three ways by which Jesus Christ is produced in souls: contemplation, love and annihilation. By the first, our Saviour is engendered in the bosom of the Eternal Father; by the second, in the womb of the most Blessed Virgin Mary; and by the third, in the most Blessed Sacrament of the altar. We, too, can make Him live within ourselves through contemplation, by accustoming ourselves to see Him in all things; through love, by frequently making acts of love and directing all our actions solely toward that end; and finally, through annihilation, by renouncing everything.

Subsequent chapters will show how St. John Eudes tried to form Christ in himself by means of the first and the third method, but at the moment we shall speak only of the second, of love. The Saint would invoke the power of the Eternal Father, the charity of the Holy Spirit, the prayers of the saints and the help of all creatures to destroy his ego, that our Lord might be established in the wake of that destruction. Often one heard ardent exclamations expressing his heart's desire: "O Jesus! O Good Jesus! O Possessor of my heart! O Beloved of my soul! O Thou only Necessary One! It is Thou whom I seek, it is Thou whom I desire, it is Thou whom I long for, it is Thou whom I need, my Jesus, who art in all things and beyond whom all is nothing. . . ."

> Jesus, without whom all is nothing, is my all.
> Thus, I want all things, though I want not one!
> For, having nothing, then will I have all,
> If you take all, and leave me Him alone![10]

He had engraved on his coat of arms other words which appeared often in his books and usually ended his letters: "Live Jesus and Mary!" He also ejaculated frequently: "Come, Lord Jesus,"[11] by which he desired that our Lord extinguish in him whatever might be contrary to divine love. "O Mother of Jesus," he would pray, "show me that thou art the Mother of Jesus by forming Him and making Him live in my soul!"

On the subject of the Holy Name of Jesus, his words let fly some sparks of the fire of love that burned in his heart.

"If I were to follow my own convictions," he wrote, "I should never speak or write any word but one, *Jesus,* for it seems to me that the tongue which has once pronounced, and the pen that has once written this adorable name and this divine word, *Jesus,* should never again be used to speak or write anything else. Besides, to say *Jesus* is to say everything, and after having said *Jesus,* there is nothing more to add, inasmuch as *Jesus* is an abridged word which in itself contains everything great that can be said and thought. *Jesus* is the name admirable above all names which, through its immense grandeur, fills heaven and earth, time and eternity, the minds and hearts of all the angels and saints; it even fills and possesses, from all eternity, the infinite capacity of the Heart of God, of the Father, the Son and the Holy Ghost. Even if I could write nothing, therefore, save the one word *Jesus,* and could go everywhere in the world crying out unceasingly and pronouncing no other name except this one *Jesus, Jesus, Jesus,* I believe that I should be saying and writing enough to fill to capacity the minds and hearts of all the inhabitants of the earth."

"What a holy and delightful language it would be," he continues, "if one could speak and make himself understood in this world without uttering anything except that sacred and lovable word, *Jesus! Jesus!* . . . As long as my heart beats in my breast, as long as I can move my tongue to speak and my hand to write, I will never preach or write anything but *Jesus.* I do not wish to have life, intelligence, tongue or pen except to proclaim verbally and in writing the wonders of that glorious name. . . .

"Who will give me a tongue and a pen that are seraphic and divine, that I may pronounce and write this divine name worthily? But I should like to possess a heart to love Him even more than a pen and a tongue to speak and write about Him. Lord, it is within Thy power to grant me both, and that is what I hope to receive from Thine infinite bounty! . . . The name of Jesus is so full of holiness that one needs to pronounce it worthily only once, as it should be pronounced, in order to make all holy. If all the sinners on earth and in hell could pronounce that glorious name as it should be pronounced, they would destroy the inferno of sin within themselves and establish in its stead a paradise of holiness."[12]

St. John Eudes believed that, in order to speak and write the Holy Name worthily, it was necessary to be all holy, celestial and divine. That is why he used to unite himself with the dispositions of all heaven and earth. Sometimes he would adore the infinite love of the three divine Persons in pronouncing that name when They chose it from all others to give to the Word Incarnate; or else he would try to capture the reverence and purity of the Blessed Virgin Mary, St. Joseph, St. Gabriel when they pronounced it. These practices showed the fire burning in his heart, with its sole passion of augmenting the kingdom of Christ. He would have surrendered everything for this end, even his own life, as he so often wished to do; actually he did everything possible during his lifetime to add to the honor and glory of Jesus Christ in a countless number of ways.

NOTES

[1] 1 Cor. 16:22.
[2] Wisd. 7:14.
[3] Eudes, *The Kingdom of Jesus*, p. 116 and 214.
[4] Jn. 15:4.
[5] Eudes, *Letters and Shorter Works*, p. 19.
[6] Lk. 1:47.
[7] Eudes, *ibid.*, p. 15.
[8] Phil. 2:10.
[9] Gal. 2:20.

[10] *The Kingdom of Jesus*, p. 119. This stanza is taken from an old French hymn published in *Recueil de plusieurs cantiques spirituels* (Paris, 1618) by Father John Le Jau, Dean of the Chapter of Evreux. See an article entitled "Sur une strophe d'un vieux cantique," by Reverend Charles du Chesnay in *Notre Vie*, a bi-monthly review of Eudist spirituality published in Paris, November-December, 1958, p. 173.

[11] Apoc. 22:20.

[12] The source of this beautiful passage on the Holy Name of Jesus is unknown. It may be an excerpt from *All Jesus*, a work left in manuscript form by St. John Eudes. Unfortunately this book was lost along with many other Eudist literary treasures at the time of the French Revolution. See *Letters and Shorter Works*, p. v.

Chapter 9. Devotion to the Mysteries of Our Lord

THOUGH ALL THE mysteries in the life of Jesus Christ are accomplished in His divine person, they are not yet completely fulfilled in His Mystical Body, the Catholic Church. It is our Blessed Lord's intention to extend and perpetuate them in His members by means of grace that He wills to communicate to them through these mysteries. St. Paul, writing to the Ephesians, teaches that we are contributing "to the measure of the age of the fulness of Christ,"[1] and he also declares in the Epistle to the Colossians that he is completing in his body the things that are wanting in the Passion of our divine Redeemer.[2] Life is given to us only that we may cooperate with our Lord in the divine work of the consummation of His mysteries, by which God is so highly honored. This is the intention of the Church in bringing the mysteries of Christ to our attention successively throughout the liturgical year, as well as in commemorating them daily in each part of the Mass and of the Divine Office. Thus do we glorify Jesus Christ, who beholds His life renewed in mankind as He has always desired.

St. John Eudes was constantly amazed to witness how little these divine mysteries were known and loved by people professing to be Christians, who should find true happiness nowhere except in this knowledge and love. Such are the very words of the Son of God Himself. "Now this is eternal life," He testifies to His heavenly Father, "that they may know thee, the only true God, and Jesus Christ, whom thou hast sent."[3] The Saint believed that in the divine mysteries alone is found happiness on earth as well as in heaven. He emphasized the fact that we would have to render an account of them at the hour of death. He frequently pointed out that our scanty attention to these mysteries would be one of the most serious charges brought against us, that the Last Judgment would take place only to make the divine mysteries recognized by all creatures, and that hell was created to compel those who did not honor these mysteries through love while on earth to honor them in suffering for all eternity.

Hence the special devotion of St. John Eudes to the sacred mysteries of Christ's life according to the various times of the year.[4] He devoted October and part of November to rendering homage to the divine life of our Blessed Lord in the bosom of His Eternal Father. During the last two weeks of November he recalled the grace of our Saviour at work in the world for thousands of years before the Incarnation in the hearts of the angels, patriarchs, prophets and all just men.

During Advent he honored the Incarnation and the dwelling of our divine Saviour in the womb of His holy Mother. From Christmas to the Purification he honored all the mysteries of the Holy Childhood, and from the Purification, the hidden life of labor in the company of His Blessed Mother and St. Joseph up to the age of thirty. Ash Wednesday and the following days were dedicated to the baptism of Jesus in the Jordan, and to His manifestations as the Christ through the voice of the eternal Father, through the descent of the Holy Spirit and through the testimony of St. John the Baptist. During the first week of Lent, St. John Eudes would honor the solitary life of our Lord; during the second week, His public life of preaching; and for the rest of the Holy Season of Lent, His life of humiliation and suffering. On Holy Thursday he adored our Lord in the institution of the Blessed Eucharist and in the ceremony of the washing of feet; from Good Friday to Easter Sunday, His agony, passion, death on the cross, His descent into limbo and His burial.

The entire season of Easter he devoted to the glorious mystery of the Resurrection, Christ's entrance into a life of glory and His last days on earth. From the Ascension to Pentecost he would contemplate the triumph of Christ in heaven, a practice that he also carried out every Sunday of the year. Pentecost week was consecrated to the Holy Spirit, with meditation on the sanctifying mission, the grandeurs and the mysteries of the Third Person of the Blessed Trinity.

On the Feast of the Holy Trinity he adored the life of the three divine Persons in our Lord as well as the human soul of Christ united to the three divine Persons. The following Monday he dedicated to the Father, Tuesday to the Son, and Wednesday to the Holy Spirit. The days after Corpus Christi and all the Thursdays of the year he devoted to the mystery of the loving Real Presence of Jesus Christ in the Sacrament of the Altar.

St. John Eudes divided the time remaining until August to the honoring of our Saviour's public life, which he had not had sufficient time to commemorate during Lent, and to the glorious second coming of Christ as judge of the living and the dead at the end of the world. The month of August he devoted to the contemplation of our Blessed Lord in His essence, His person, His soul with its powers and His body with all its members. September brought homage from the Saint to the seven empires of Christ: the first in the natural world; the second in the Church Militant; the third in the death of each individual; the fourth in the particular judgment which He pronounces each day and at every moment upon every soul departing from this life; the fifth in purgatory; the sixth in hell; and the seventh in heaven.

All Saturdays and feasts of the Blessed Virgin Mary were consecrated to honoring the life of Christ in His Holy Mother with all its mysteries. He would observe the same practice on the feasts of the angels and saints. By following this procedure there remained nothing in the life of Jesus Christ to which St. John Eudes did not pay special honor. It might be said of him, therefore, as David said of all just men, that his days were full[5] because there was not one when he failed to devote himself to the perfections, virtues and mysteries of the Incarnate Word.

In addition, the Saint dedicated the years of his own life to those of the life of the Saviour. Each year he chose as many days as the years he had lived thus far to make a firm resolution to lead a better life, to put on the new man while casting off the old, and to concentrate on loving and serving God as if he were just beginning to live or as if he were about to die. On each of these days he used to do what he should have done during the corresponding years. On the first day he would adore our Blessed Lord in all that occurred in His person during the first year of His divine life on earth, accusing himself and asking pardon of our Lord for the time when he had lost his divine orientation through the state of original sin. In satisfaction he would offer all the glory rendered to the eternal Father during the first year of the life of our Lord and of His Blessed Mother.

Then the Saint would offer to the Most High all that had taken place in himself during the first year of his own life, earnestly beseeching the most Blessed Trinity, the Blessed Virgin Mary, the angels and the saints to supply for his deficiencies in it and to change whatever he had suffered at that time into blessings and gratitude to Jesus Christ in honor of His first year on earth. He would finish the exercise by offering our Lord all the actions of the day, uniting them with the love and praise bestowed upon Christ during His first year by the eternal Father, the Holy Spirit, His Blessed Mother, His angels and His saints, asking them all to render a hundredfold the homage that he should have paid during his first year.

St. John Eudes followed almost the same practice on the remaining days corresponding to the subsequent years of his life, and when his age exceeded the temporal life of Jesus, he continued the same exercise not only on his own behalf, but also on behalf of those with whom he had special ties, uniting the years of each one's life with his own.

Each year at the beginning of January,[6] St. John Eudes took time to cast himself at the feet of our Lord in order to adore Him in the first moment of His mortal life; to honor the thoughts, sentiments and dispositions of His soul in that first moment with regard to the heavenly Father and to mankind; to bless and thank Him, acknowledging Him to be the eternal King of ages, who purchased at the price of His blood all the days given him on earth. He would also make several promises to Christ: the first, to use that particular year to glorify Him and to make reparation for his past offenses toward the holy love of the Saviour; the second, to avoid placing any obstacle in the way of the divine plan for him, to do and suffer for its fulfillment whatever was pleasing to God; the third, to accept gladly whatever sufferings of body and mind God's providence might send; the fourth, not to use a single moment of his life for anything except to serve God. To that end the Saint would unite himself with the tribute of love that would be rendered to the Incarnate Word in heaven and on earth throughout the year, and he would beg most earnestly, through the intercession of the Blessed Virgin Mary, the angels and the saints, for the graces most necessary to carry out faithfully his good intentions.

St. John Eudes also set aside some time to pay honor to our Lord at the end of each year.[7] He would adore all that had taken place in Christ on the last day, during the last hour and moment of his life. The Saint would thank our Lord for the glory that He always rendered to His heavenly Father, for the graces that Jesus Christ had granted in turn to himself, unworthy creature, and for those our Lord would have communicated to him if he had not placed an obstacle in the way. He would ask pardon for all the sins which he had committed and for those to which he had been accessory. He would abandon himself to Christ, seeking to perform in this world and in the next whatever penance was pleasing to the divine will.

Next the Saint would bless Jesus Christ for His intentions in his regard on the last day of His mortal life, wishing with all his heart for their fulfillment, desiring to die rather than to oppose them in any way. He would offer his own last day and final hour, protesting that he had no longing save that of dying in the exercise of His holy love.

The devotion of St. John Eudes was not satisfied even with these practices. On each day of the week he honored some phase of the life of Jesus Christ by meditation and imitation. He consecrated Sunday to the divine life of the Son of God in the bosom of His Father from all eternity, and to the glorious life of the God-Man in heaven after the Resurrection and Ascension. Monday was consecrated to the Incarnation and the Nativity; Tuesday, to the Holy Childhood; Wednesday, to the hidden secluded life of toil; Thursday, to the public life on earth and to His present life in the most Blessed Sacrament of the altar; Friday, to the Sacred Passion and Death of our Lord; Saturday, to His life in the most Blessed Virgin Mary. It is impossible to express the devotion with which he carried out these practices. To realize it we must study the meditations that he made daily.[8]

Another devotional exercise practiced by St. John Eudes consisted in adoring our Blessed Lord each day in one of His virtues or various capacities,[9] for example, as Son of God, as the principle of the Holy Spirit with His Father, or as the Redeemer of mankind; and from each standpoint the Saint would render homage of thanksgiving, oblation, love, trust, humility and any other tribute to which he was inspired at the moment.

Besides these exercises so pleasing to our Lord and so salutary to the souls who practice them and seek to bind themselves more closely to our divine Saviour, St. John Eudes always took some time during the day to offer his love to Christ by various acts of devotion. During these happy moments he longed to be transformed along with all creatures into adoration and praise of that sole object of his heart's desire. He gave himself wholly, absolutely, solely to Christ for time and for eternity, in virtue of His grace, the power of His spirit, the strength of His charity. The Saint accepted whatever God's most holy will decreed for him, and exhorted all creatures to love Jesus and to atone, by their love, for the treason of the fallen angels and of so many human beings who never discharge their duties toward their loving Saviour.

This singular devotion to the sacred mysteries of our Blessed Lord prompted St. John Eudes to seek various means of realizing them in his life. No phase of a divine mystery escaped his reflection and devotion.[10] Sometimes he meditated on the exterior facts of the mystery, or on the interior thoughts, intentions and dispositions of our Saviour and the effects of grace that He communicates to us every day through this mystery. At other times, he would consider the part played by the Blessed Virgin Mary, the angels and the saints in a particular mystery. He would often enter into sentiments of joy at the sight of our Blessed Lord, who is so holy, perfect and lovable, in the mystery which he was contemplating. He would experience intense happiness in considering the honor rendered to the Blessed Trinity by the Son of God made man, and the reciprocal honor that the Son of God made man received from the Father and the Holy Ghost. He would humble himself at our Lord's feet, begging pardon for his negligence and his opposition to the intentions that Jesus had when He fulfilled this mystery in His own life. Acknowledging his unworthiness, the Saint would humbly beg our Lord to use His might and love to honor Himself in him, to imprint in the hearts of all Christians a great zeal for His glory, to destroy in their souls anything that might prevent him from making the loving Saviour better known throughout the world as he so ardently desired, to complete these mysteries in His Church, abandoning himself at the same time completely into God's hands to do and suffer anything that He desired.

There was nothing in St. John Eudes that was not completely devoted to the mysteries of our Lord. He used his mind to consider them, his heart to love them, his tongue to speak about them, his hands to perform actions in their honor. The aim of all his exercises was to imprint in himself a likeness of the mystery on which he was meditating by practising the virtues associated with it, and by conforming to them as much as possible. If the birth of Jesus formed the subject of his meditation, he would renounce everything and desire to possess nothing so that he might actually imitate the poverty of the Divine Infant in the manger. If he were contemplating the hidden years, he would make a retreat to honor the secluded life of our Saviour. If he made the Passion the object of his cult and devotion, he would joyfully embrace the cross and all mortifications.

Thus St. John Eudes could say in truth as did St. Paul: "I live, now not I, but Christ liveth in me."[11] He belonged to the number of those happy souls destined to live in conformity with the image of the Son of God,[12] so that having become one with Christ through imitation of His mortal life, he might also be united to the mysteries of His glorious life. It would be difficult indeed to find a man more enlightened than the Saint with regard to the Word Incarnate. His actions were done in conformity with his knowledge. The unveiled countenance of our Lord reflected its glory in him as in a mirror; he was transformed into the likeness of our Saviour and became a living book teaching the sublime knowledge of Jesus Christ.

NOTES

[1] Eph. 4:13.

[2] Col. 1:24.

[3] Jn. 17:3.

[4] On the sequence to be observed in honoring the mysteries of our Lord's life, see *The Kingdom of Jesus,* p. 255.

[5] Ps. 72:10.

[6] *The Kingdom of Jesus,* p. 295.

[7] *Ibid.,* p. 289.

[8] *Ibid.*, p. 195.
[9] *Ibid.*, p. 36.
[10] *Ibid.*, p. 260.
[11] Gal. 2:20.
[12] Rom. 8:29.

Chapter 10. Special Devotion to Some Mysteries of Our Lord

ST. JOHN EUDES had a singular veneration for all the mysteries of our Blessed Lord's life on earth. Each year on Ascension Thursday he chose the mystery that he would honor during the ensuing year,[1] commemorating each one in turn. Nevertheless, he had favorite mysteries that were the principal objects of his devotion throughout his entire life. The Incarnation of the second divine Person of the Blessed Trinity drew special honor, not only by reason of the humiliations which the Son of God willed to endure in this mystery and the glory received from it by the Blessed Virgin Mary, but also because of the great blessings communicated to all men through this mystery, which constitutes the origin and beginning of their salvation. This also applied to his Congregation in particular, which took birth on the Feast of the Annunciation,[2] the day chosen by the Church to celebrate the mystery of the Incarnation.

The captivity of Jesus in Mary moved the Saint profoundly, and he ardently desired that the Infinite God who had become enslaved out of love might make captive his own mind and heart, his thoughts and all his affections. He considered the mystery of the Incarnation the most important in the life of the Saviour, although at the same time one of the most neglected by Christians. St. John Eudes concentrated on the Incarnation by considering the ardent love for us shown in this sacred mystery by our divine Redeemer, the profound humiliations that He suffered in it and the signal graces that He earned for us. During the holy season of Advent the Saint lived in union with the devotion of the Church to this divine mystery, using the aspirations by which the patriarchs of old had expressed their fervent longing for the coming of the Messias. He repeated the same supplications so that our Lord might renew in him, too, the virtues and the spirit of the Incarnation and of His life in the Blessed Virgin Mary. To this sentiment of entreaty he would join admiration, thanksgiving, delight and love.

The divine Childhood was the second mystery particularly dear to St. John Eudes. A number of his contemporaries[3] had been favored by special devotion to it, enabling them to attain a very high degree of sanctity. This served as an indication of the benefits he would reap by devoting himself to it.[4] Convinced as he was that if we do not become like the Child Jesus, we shall not enter the kingdom of heaven, he contemplated and imitated, insofar as he was able, the dispositions and virtues of the Divine Child during the first period of His life. He frequently knelt in spirit before the Child Jesus with all humility, that he might adore His divine Saviour in this state and pay Him whatever other homage his piety would suggest.

The Saint was not satisfied to do these acts himself; he urged all his spiritual children to do the same, particularly during the time consecrated by the Church to honoring the Holy Childhood, as may be seen from a letter dated January

13, 1660, to the superior of one of his seminaries: "I beseech all our brethren," he wrote, "to make a daily visit to the Infant Jesus in the stable at Bethlehem, as also to His most Holy Mother and St. Joseph, to render them homage and to ask for a share in the spirit of the Holy Childhood, which is a spirit of innocence, purity, humility, obedience, simplicity, charity and forbearance."[5] He wrote in the same vein to the Daughters of Our Lady of Charity.[6] He strove to spread the devotion and compiled a booklet containing various practices to develop it.[7]

St. John Eudes also cultivated devotion to the hidden life of our Lord, which he wished his friends to share, as is revealed in a number of letters. As for the public life of our Lord, which he tried to imitate perfectly, and in honor of which he composed a beautiful office,[8] we shall not say anything here, so that we may dwell more at length on those mysteries which caused his piety to glow still more splendidly.

The mystery of the Sacred Passion of our Blessed Lord was esteemed by our Saint as the principle of salvation and the perfection of Christians, the most effective means of implementing the remission of our sins and the sanctification of souls in compliance with the will of God. St. John Eudes was convinced that whatever might be the merit of the sufferings of our Saviour, however efficacious they might be before the throne of the Most High on behalf of mankind, most persons, even the most spiritual ones, do not derive all the advantages that they should from these sufferings because they lack a deep devotion to the Passion. For this reason he dedicated several days toward the end of Lent to honoring our Lord in His sufferings, and on Good Friday[9] he would gather his community at 2:30 in the afternoon, that they might render our Saviour in His agony and death their homage of adoration, thanksgiving, atonement and declaration of their willingness to die with Him and for His sake.

If our Saint did not set aside much time during the course of the year to devote himself to the mystery of the Passion, it was simply because he made it the regular subject of frequent meditations. Indeed, he never spent a day without practicing devotion to the Five Wounds, as he has revealed in his work, *The Kingdom of Jesus,*[10] making an act of love for Christ crucified as he kissed each wound. It may even be said that he renewed this devotion from moment to moment, frequently pronouncing the holy name of Jesus in his heart or with his lips in honor of the Five Wounds. He also carried a crucifix, which he set before him while he studied or held in his hand while hearing confessions, constantly glancing at it with love, compassion and thanksgiving. Thus St. John Eudes obeyed the command of the Apostle Peter to keep Christ crucified always in mind.[11]

The mainspring of the life of St. John Eudes, however, was devotion to the continuing mystery that our Lord effects daily in the Church, that is, the adorable Sacrament of the altar. The Saint taught and practiced frequent visits to the Blessed Sacrament, remaining as long as he could in Its presence and finding there great joy and happiness. The dignity, power, light, holiness and fulness of perfections hidden under the appearances of mere bread were, for him, reasons to feel profound humility. Contemplating the nature, attributes and person of Christ, the dignity and excellence of His holy humanity, all that He is, all that He has done and all His intentions for His Church in this mystery of the Holy Eucharist, the Saint would adore His Saviour for the whole world, longing that the entire universe might be transformed into adoration and praise. He would unite himself with the love of all the angels and the saints. He would give testimony of his most humble gratitude for the divine favors toward mere creatures. He would beg pardon most humbly for his shortcomings in gratitude and fidelity. He felt deeply moved by the outrages Christ suffered in the tabernacle at the hands of unbelievers, heretics and bad Catholics. He would offer in reparation all the glory that had ever been given the God-Man in heaven and earth, with the most ardent desire to obtain honor for Christ in every way that he could contrive.

During these happy moments at the foot of the altar the Saint used to open his heart to his Eucharistic Lord. He was heard to utter fervent words like these: "O Love, Love, who shall not love Thee? O Jesus, would that there were no heart, no love, save for Thee! O Furnace of Love, warm, inflame, enkindle, consume my heart, my soul, my mind and my body in Thy divine flames!" Considering our Lord in this sacrament as a great king to whom one should not present himself empty-handed, the Saint would give himself wholly and permanently to Christ, expressing the positive desire to sacrifice to Him all created beings if it had been in his power. Reflecting on the virtues that the only-begotten Son practiced so admirably in this state of abasement in the Blessed Eucharist, St. John Eudes would humble himself because of his lack of conformity to that glorious example and renew his resolve to imitate Him, asking the grace to do so, and imploring the help of the Blessed Virgin Mary and the saints.

Whenever there was exposition of the Blessed Sacrament in the neighborhood, he made it a point to send two of his colleagues each day to offer adoration and honor on behalf of the community. He would exhort them earnestly to observe that custom and to be most faithful to it whenever there was exposition in their churches and chapels.

Let us listen to the Saint's words on this practice: "If

someone asked a great king to do him the honor of dining at his house, he would invite all his friends as guests in order to give a reception worthy of his royal majesty, and he would prepare the most magnificent banquet possible. In such a way would he gain the good graces of this prince, obtaining from him whatever he desired. But if he were not at home when the king came, and had prepared neither reception nor repast, would he not justly deserve the king's indignation?

"To expose the Blessed Sacrament in our church is to invite the King of kings to our house to dine with us. Therefore we should give Him the most honorable reception and prepare the most magnificent banquet possible, asking all our friends to assist at it. The food and drink of this feast are the adoration, praise, thanksgiving and other similar acts of religion and piety that we ought to offer Him and induce others to offer Him."[12]

One can see from this analogy, at a time when kings were very powerful, how zealous the Saint was for the glory of our Eucharistic Lord dwelling upon our altars. In the opinion of St. John Eudes, failing to honor our Blessed Lord in the tabernacle was to render oneself guilty of a great crime and unworthy of the blessings of heaven. He believed that in this exercise of devotion to the Eucharistic Heart of Jesus more than in any other, man's interests were inseparable from the honor paid to God, and that the best means of becoming rich in grace was to have recourse to its very source, Christ dwelling in our midst, that He might bestow eternal life on us more abundantly.

It was this same reason which prompted him, whenever he had to make a decision, to enter the sanctuary to consult our Blessed Lord as his oracle. He never arrived at any decision without having first implored the guidance of his

Eucharistic Lord. Most particularly did he urge the members of his Congregation to follow this practice in every decision. "Let us often have recourse to our Lord in the Blessed Sacrament," he wrote to the Superior of one of his seminaries, "that we may ask Him to guide and direct us along all our paths. Let us acknowledge that we dwell in darkness and ignorance, that we have infinite reason to live in perpetual distrust of our own intellect and of everything within us, and that we must rely on the assistance of divine light and grace."[13]

Indeed, the mystery of the Real Presence meant all things to St. John Eudes. In it he found the solution to his difficulties, consolation in his sorrows, support in his reverses, abundance in his needs, rest in the midst of the distracting business which took up so much of his time; in a word, the remedy for all his ills. Jesus Christ hidden upon our altars was his all-powerful, his ever-accessible treasure. We shall continue to study his devotion to the Blessed Eucharist in one of the following chapters, which will deal with his esteem and preparation for the Holy Sacrifice of the Mass and for the reception of Holy Communion.

NOTES

[1] In addition to the sections on the devotion to the mysteries of our Lord in *The Kingdom of Jesus* St. John Eudes also wrote *All Jesus, or Exercises on the Mysteries of Jesus,* which was never published and was lost at the time of the French Revolution. The manuscript of this work was available in Herambourg's day. See Reverend C. Lebrun, *The Spiritual Teaching of St. John Eudes* (London, Sands & Co., 1930), p. 56.

[2] March 25, 1643.

[3] Cardinal de Bérulle, Father de Condren, Father Oliver and Baron de Renty had spread the devotion to the Child Jesus with zeal.

[4] Devotion to the Holy Childhood was long established in the Church, but it was revived and transformed in the seventeenth century by Cardinal de Bérulle who made it entirely his own. Both de Bérulle and de Condren thought less of introducing a particular devotion to the Child Jesus, than

of diffusing a particular *spirit,* the spirit of Christian Infancy, or as they generally called it, the spirit of Infancy. The devotion in the strict sense of the word, that is, the totality of devotional acts intended to honor the Infancy did not take shape nor was it organized until after de Bérulle's death. It was a Carmelite nun of Beaune, Sister Margaret of the Blessed Sacrament, who renewed and diffused, more than any other person, the Devotion, properly so called, to the Child Jesus. St. John Eudes met Sister Margaret while he was preaching a mission at Beaune in 1648. To spread this devotion, the Saint wrote *The Divine Childhood of Jesus,* which was lost during the French Revolution. He composed a complete office for a Feast in honor of the Divine Infancy of Jesus to be celebrated on February 6. See *Oeuvres Complètes,* vol. 11, p. 241. He also had printed a special exercise in honor of the Child Jesus, which he distributed among his friends. See *Manual of Piety,* p. 264. Another exercise in honor of the Child Jesus is found in *The Kingdom of Jesus,* p. 237. For the history of the devotion in France see Henri Bremond, *A Literary History of Religious Thought in France* (New York, The Macmillan Company, 1936), vol. 3, pp. 434–496.

[5] This letter is not found in the editions of the letters of St. John Eudes. Since quotation marks were not used by Herambourg, this fragment was overlooked by the editors of *Oeuvres Complètes.*

[6] *Letters and Shorter Works,* pp. 139 and 141.

[7] *The Divine Childhood of Jesus,* referred to in note 4.

[8] The only part of this office that is now extant is a hymn in honor of the public life of our Lord. See *Oeuvres Complètes,* vol. 11, p. 660.

[9] See *Manual of Piety,* p. 185.

[10] *The Kingdom of Jesus,* p. 238.

[11] 1 Pet. 4:1.

[12] *Manual of Piety,* p. 205.

[13] *Letters and Shorter Works,* p. 277.

Chapter 11. Practices of Love for Our Lord

TRUE LOVE NEVER says: "It is enough." A lover is not content unless he is constantly giving his beloved new marks of his affection. Such was the love of St. John Eudes who in his unceasing efforts to honor our Blessed Lord devised many devotional practices to stimulate his own love and to encourage others to love the Divine Master.

The Saint adored Jesus Christ in irrational and inanimate creatures, uniting himself with their testimony, according to the Psalmist: "His work is praise and magnificence."[1] He also used this other aspiration: "O dear creatures of God, bless Him, praise and exalt Him in my name forever." He tried to compensate for those created things that are without knowledge and love by loving our Lord in their stead, thanking Him for all favors granted to them, sacrificing to Him their lives, being and natural perfections. He would also unite himself with all the praise offered Him in heaven and on earth.

It was the custom of St. John Eudes even to descend into hell in spirit,[2] and there, in the midst of the enemies of

Jesus Christ, he would adore the divine Redeemer for all that He is in Himself and in His creatures, in union with the great love of the Father and of the Holy Spirit, and would bless the Son of God for His justice toward the demons and the damned. He desired the strength and the capacity to love that these accursed creatures had once possessed, but had lost through their malice, in order that he might use it to love our Saviour and to be as attentive in praising Him as they are in blaspheming Him. He would offer the being, the life and the potentialities that they once had, laying them at the feet of their Creator and sacrificing them to His glory. In this way the Saint honored our Lord in the lost souls in spite of their refusal.

Meditating on his shortcomings and weaknesses, St. John Eudes wanted to do during his lifetime what he ought to do but could not do after his death. He transported himself in spirit to purgatory to pay homage to our Saviour in that holy place where almighty God purifies souls. He would accept the pains that he would undergo there by divine command, overlooking no means by which he might give testimony to his love for Christ. He would unite himself with the glory that Jesus had received and would receive from the just souls that had passed and were to pass through Purgatory. But realizing that all the praise of creatures cannot in any way conform to the infinite grandeur of the Son of God, he also used to beg the Blessed Trinity to share their love with God made man in his name and to atone for his sins, beseeching them to allow him to love the Incarnate God in union with them. Gratitude alone for the triune God would have motivated his devotion to their service, even if he had no other incentive. Addressing himself to our Blessed Lord, the Saint would implore Him to use all the powers of His divinity and humanity to praise the Godhead, saying the verse of the Canticle of the three children: "O, all ye powers of the Lord, bless the Lord."[3]

St. John Eudes left in writing several practices[4] that he often used to excite and preserve the love of Jesus in his heart and in the hearts of others. He composed a rosary[5] of thirty-four beads in honor of the thirty-four years of Christ's life on earth,[6] saying on each small bead three times, in imitation of St. Peter, these words taken in part from the Gospel[7] and in part from St. Augustine:[8] "I love Thee, most loving Jesus; I love Thee, Infinite Bounty; I love Thee with all my heart, with all my soul and with all my strength, and I wish to love Thee more and more." On the large beads the Saint would say: "O Fire that burns perpetually and never cools, O Love that is always ardent and never diminishes, inflame me, inflame my whole being, that I may love Thee without reserve."

Another rosary of love[9] that the Saint would say began with the words: "Come, Father of Jesus." Then on the small beads he would address himself to the Eternal Father, begging Him to glorify His Son: "Father, glorify thy Son that thy Son may glorify thee."[10] On the large beads, he said the stanza: "All honor, praise and glory be, O Jesu, Virgin-born, to thee; all glory, as is ever meet, to Father and to Paraclete."[11]

St. John Eudes also devised a third rosary[12] which he called the rosary of the glory of Jesus. He began it with the words: "Come, Lord Jesus," repeating them three times, with the intention of drawing Jesus into his soul, that He might live and reign there. On each small bead he would say the stanza: "All honor, praise and glory be . . ." When he recited these words on the first bead, he would present to our Lord all the honor rendered Him during the first year of His life by His Father, His Holy Spirit, His Blessed

Mother, His angels and His saints, in reparation for his failure to honor the Incarnate God during the first year of his life. He would do the same thing on the other beads in connection with the remaining years, and on the large beads he would say the "Glory be to the Father . . ." as devoutly as he could, in order to pay homage to the most Blessed Trinity.

In addition, the Saint composed thirty-four acts of love[13] for Jesus, sparks of sacred fire which burned in his heart, and each month he would choose a day to recite them. However, all that he said, did or undertook for the glory of our Divine Lord was little in comparison to the offering and consecration of his religious societies to the Sacred Heart of Jesus. He understood the excellence of the perfections of the Sacred Heart, sanctified through the unction of the Word and the uncreated holiness by which His human body and soul are sanctified. The Saint taught that the Sacred Heart lives a supereminent life, one moment of which is worth more than the lives of all the angels and of all men, since it represents the full scope of the fruitfulness of the Holy Spirit. He regarded the Sacred Heart as supremely pleasing in the eyes of God, since it is the object of the tenderest feelings of the eternal Father, who loves the Divine Heart which sacrificed itself and is still sacrificing itself daily to appease the justice of the Most High.

St. John Eudes used to say that through the Sacred Heart the angels praise God, the Dominations adore Him, the Powers honor Him, the saints bless Him and all men atone to His divine majesty for their deficiencies. The Sacred Heart is like to the sun from which all the other planets borrow their light, or like to a great river which rejoices heaven and earth with the flow of its graces, or again like to a vault in which devout souls experience that mysterious inebriation referred to in the Canticle of Canticles.[14] The Heart of Jesus is the boundless treasure in which sinners find remedy for their troubles, payment for their debts, relief for their spiritual poverty, remission for their sins and fulfillment of their obligations, while those who are striving to serve God find in the Divine Heart inspiration to exercise their faith, to sustain their hope, to establish their love and assure them of paradise.

We shall not enumerate here the other foundations of this saving devotion to the Sacred Heart which St. John Eudes inaugurated in the Church.[15] All holy as it is, the devotion was first condemned by some critical minds and rejected as an innovation.[16] We shall merely explain that what made St. John Eudes resolve to devote all his energy to the spreading of devotion to the Sacred Heart was the beauty of this devotion which our Lord had revealed to St. Gertrude,[17] St. Mechtilde[18] and St. Teresa,[19] particularly the declaration to St. Mechtilde that His Divine Heart is the inexhaustible source of all kinds of graces, favors and blessings, the immense treasure of all virtues. Our Lord made it known that if any soul needs humility, meekness and patience, it should seek them in the rich treasury of His Sacred Heart where it will find all things in abundance.[20] Jesus ardently loves souls that place their trust in Him, so much so that if, through the impossible, He lost the power to give them blessings or to grant what they ask of Him, it would cause Him such sadness that all the joys and delights of heaven could not console Him. The loving Heart of Christ so desires to unite Himself with souls that if He did not do so in Holy Communion, the sorrow it would cause Him would be capable of bringing death to Him, if He were still able to suffer.

In gratitude for the inestimable bounties of the Sacred Heart and in veneration of its grandeur, St. John Eudes devoted himself wholly to its service, working and planning to have it honored in every way within his power. He composed several prayers reflecting the depth of his affection.[21] Through the Sacred Heart he adored the eternal Father and implored Him for the favors he sought to obtain. He always regarded the Divine Heart of Jesus as the perfect model of the virtues he must practice, and being unsatisfied with his personal efforts, he united himself to the sentiments of St. Paul, who wrote in his Epistle to the Philippians that he longed to see them all in the bowels of Jesus Christ,[22] which is interpreted by St. Anselm[23] and St. Thomas[24] as meaning that he longed fervently to see them dwelling intimately in the Heart of our Lord and in His love. For that reason St. John Eudes dedicated his newly-founded Congregations to the Sacred Heart.[25] We may say that his religious societies were conceived, born, nourished and reared in the Divine Heart so that all their members must dwell perpetually in that Heart as in the place where they were born and where they will find the means necessary to work for their own perfection and for the sanctification of others. They must devote themselves to the contemplation of the grandeurs of the Sacred Heart, the admiration of its marvels, the recognition of its bounties and the imitation of its virtues.

That is why St. John Eudes, having chosen the Sacred Heart to be the chief patron[26] of his Institutes, worked to obtain permission and approbation from the Bishops[27] to establish the Feast of the Sacred Heart. He even urged his spiritual children[28] to prepare themselves for the feast by fasting and good works, such as giving dinner to twelve poor persons who would afterwards receive alms, accompanied by a brief spiritual instruction. He composed a special Mass and Office for the first Feast of the Sacred Heart.[29] The mere reading of these liturgical works is sufficient to set hearts on fire, so replete are they with light, grace and unction. He also composed a litany[30] incorporating all the beautiful qualities of Sacred Scripture and of the Fathers of the Church on the love of Christ's Sacred Heart. To spread the devotion more widely and to make it public, he instituted a confraternity[31] in honor of the Sacred Heart of Jesus and of the most Pure Heart of Mary, which Pope Clement X confirmed, approved and enriched with a number of indulgences,[32] including a plenary indulgence granted to its members on the day of their enrollment, at the hour of death and on the twentieth of October, when the feast was solemnized.[33] In short, the Saint's great zeal for the Sacred Heart of Jesus, the glorious object of his affections, constantly revealed itself throughout his long, arduous and busy life.

These are the practices of love by which St. John Eudes strove to honor our Blessed Lord and to have him honored. He devoted all his energy to seeking them; he found all his joy in thinking about them, and he deserved great merit in devising them, since in Sacred Scripture God says that He will shower the happiness of heaven upon those who glorify Him on earth, while He will condemn for all eternity those who have nothing for Him in this world but indifference, aversion and contempt.[34]

NOTES

[1] Ps. 110:3.

[2] Eudes, *The Kingdom of Jesus,* p. 217.

[3] Dan. 3:61.

[4] Eudes, *ibid.*, p. 223. See also *The Sacred Heart of Jesus,* p. 78.

[5] Eudes, *The Kingdom of Jesus,* p. 241.

[6] The exact duration of Christ's public life is uncertain. St. John Eudes follows the opinion of St. Jerome that the ministry of Jesus lasted three years and a half. Assuming, as do many authoritative writers, that our Lord began His public life at the age of thirty, St. John Eudes concludes that the entire life of the Savior extended over a period of thirty-three years and six months. Our Lord therefore died in His thirty-fourth year. This

accounts for the fact that St. John Eudes asks us to honor the thirty-four years of our Lord's life on earth. For the chronology and duration of Christ's life, see L. C. Fillion, S. S., *The Life of Christ* (St. Louis, B. Herder, 1944), vol. 2, p. 8 and *The Catholic Encyclopedia,* vol. 8, "Jesus," p. 379.

[7] Jn. 21:15–17.

[8] St. Augustine, *Manuale,* chapter 10; P.L. 40:956.

[9] Eudes, *The Kingdom of Jesus,* p. 221.

[10] Jn. 17:1.

[11] Hymn of Matins in the Office of the Common of Feasts of the Blessed Virgin Mary.

[12] Eudes, *The Kingdom of Jesus,* p. 285.

[13] See *The Kingdom of Jesus,* p. 223. Also note 6 of this chapter.

[14] Cant. 5:1.

[15] Eudes, *The Sacred Heart of Jesus,* p. 179, "Appendix" where excerpts are given from the papal documents concerning St. John Eudes and the Devotion to the Sacred Heart of Jesus.

[16] Three classes of persons opposed to preaching of the Devotion to the Sacred Heart of Jesus: the first, because it was a new devotion in the Church; the second, because they misinterpreted the meaning of the devotion; and the third, because they found in it the negation of Jansenistic rigidity and coldness in piety. See Rev. D. Boulay, *Vie du Vénérable Jean Eudes* (Paris, Haton, 1907), vol. 3, p. 216.

[17] See *The Exercises of St. Gertrude* translated by a Benedictine nun of Regina Laudis, Bethlehem, Conn. (Westminster, The Newman Press, 1956), Seventh Exercise, "Atonement for Sin and Preparation for Death," p. 162. Also *Love of the Sacred Heart Illustrated by St. Gertrude* (London, Burns, Oates & Washbourne, 1921), p. 80, and St. John Eudes, *The Sacred Heart of Jesus,* p. 74.

[18] St. John Eudes found in the works of St. Mechtilde ten salutations to the Sacred Heart of Jesus beginning *Ave, Cor sanctissimum.* To these he added three other invocations as well as the second part of the prayer, which contains the principal acts of Christian worship according to Sacred Scripture and the liturgy. The complete prayer as composed by St. John Eudes was recited from their very inception by the two religious societies that he founded. It is still a daily prayer in all communities that claim St. John Eudes as their spiritual father. See Sargent, *op. cit.*, p. 75; Rev. J. Arragain, *Le coeur du Seigneur* (Paris, La Colombe, 1955), p. 26.

[19] See Alice Lady Lovat, *The Life of Saint Teresa* (St. Louis, B. Herder, 1912), p. 566.

[20] See Eudes, *The Sacred Heart of Jesus,* p. 49, footnote 6.

[21] The *Ave, Cor sanctissimum,* the *Magnificat, A Hymn of Praise and Thanksgiving to the Sacred Heart of Jesus and to the Holy Heart of Mary,* and the *Litany of the Sacred Heart.* See Eudes, *The Sacred Heart of Jesus,* pp. 169, 173 and 175.

[22] Phil. 1:8.

[23] St. Anselm, *In epistolas beati Pauli* (Paris, 1533), f° 160 r°.

[24] St. Thomas, *In epistolam ad Philippenses,* chapter 1, lectio 2 (Paris edition, L. Vives), vol. 21, p. 346.

[25] The Eudist Fathers and the Religious of Our Lady of Charity.

[26] See *Constitutions of the Congregation of Jesus and Mary,* p. 1.

[27] The Bishop of Coutances, Bayeux and Evreux in Normandy and the Bishop of Rennes in Brittany approved the Feast of the Sacred Heart of Jesus in the Saint's day. It was first solemnly celebrated on October 20, 1672. See Sargent, *op. cit.,* p. 240. Also Rev. Charles Lebrun, *Le Bienheureux Jean Eudes et le Culte Public du Coeur de Jésus* (Paris, Lethielleux, 1917), p. 29.

[28] In a letter to the priests of his Congregation dated July 20, 1672, the Saint requested that his spiritual sons should observe a day of fasting on the vigil of the Feast of the Sacred Heart to be celebrated on the following October 20. He also asked that twelve poor persons should dine in the community refectory on the eve of the feast and that a Solemn Mass should be celebrated on the feast day in all communities to which episcopal permission had been granted.

[29] See Eudes, *The Sacred Heart of Jesus,* p. 139.

[30] *Manual of Piety,* p. 123.

[31] This was the first Confraternity established in honor of the Sacred Hearts of Jesus and Mary. Its official title was *Confraternitas sub invocatione ejusdem Cordis Jesu et Mariae.* See Boulay, *op. cit.,* vol. 4, p. 293.

[32] Pope Clement X granted these indulgences in 1674. See Boulay, *ibid., loc. cit.*

[33] The Feast of the Sacred Heart, which was set for October 20 by St. John Eudes, is still kept on that date in the Congregation of Jesus and Mary and in the Order of Our Lady of Charity of Refuge and of the Good Shepherd.

[34] 1 Kings, 2:30.

Chapter 12. Devotion to the Blessed Virgin Mary

ST. JOHN EUDES used to say that Jesus and Mary are so closely bound together that whoever beholds the Son beholds the Mother, and that whoever loves the one cannot help loving the other. We should not separate what God has so perfectly joined together. Jesus and Mary are the primary foundations of the Christian religion, the two living sources of all the blessings showered upon us, the two objects that we should perpetually consider in all our devotional exercises.

In the preceding chapters we have studied the love of St. John Eudes for our Lord. It is not difficult for us to conclude from such evidence that he was similarly devoted to the Blessed Virgin Mary. Both had established the throne of their love in his heart. In his spiritual exercises he always rendered to the Mother, in due proportion, of course, whatever he rendered to the Son. He believed that Christians ought to perpetuate the life and sentiments of Jesus Christ on earth, particularly in regard to our Blessed Lord's devotion to Mary as manifested in the way He honored her through His choice of her to be His mother. His obedience to her, His outward behavior toward her during the time of His childhood and His hidden life, and the glory and authority which He invested in her in heaven and on earth were the chief manifestations of Christ's deep filial respect and love for His Blessed Mother. For these same reasons, St. John Eudes frequently begged Mary to let him share in the love of the Sacred Heart of her Son for her, in the conviction that, since Christ has associated us with Himself in His capacity of Son of Mary, He will also wish to share with us His sentiments toward so devoted a Mother.

The Saint would often adore God in the infinite love He bears the Blessed Virgin Mary, the noblest of creatures, and in the wonderful plans He had for her from all eternity. He would thank God most humbly and rejoice within himself because of the signal privileges granted to Mary; or else, looking upon her solely in connection with Jesus Christ and considering her as his sovereign lady, second only to her divine Son, he would place himself frequently in her hands, dedicate himself wholeheartedly to her service, unite himself completely with her virtues and constantly implore her help. He would pay homage to her in every way possible as befitted her dignity. Finally, in honor of the choice that our Lord had made of her as Mother, he also chose her to be his own Mother.

Mary was the frequent object of the Saint's thoughts. In order to make him happy it was necessary only to speak of her glories to him. No matter how great was his suffering of mind or body, to speak to him about Mary was sufficient to ease his pain. No one was more eloquent on the subject of our Lady than St. John Eudes. He was delighted whenever he found occasion to say something in praise of the Mother of God, and he always did so with such fervor that he would enkindle the hearts of all those present. One of his spiritual sons paid this tribute to him after his death: "We never heard him preach a sermon without showing some evidence of his devotion to Mary. I do not know whether, during the three years that I had the happiness of living with him, he held a single conversation without speaking of her, and whenever he did so, it was always with exclamations of enthusiasm. 'Oh, how good she is!' he used to say from time to time. 'How lovable she is! How worthy of our honor! Oh, how happy are they who devote themselves to her service, who are truly devoted to her!' Then it would become quite obvious, from the change in his face and demeanor, and from his protracted sighs, that his words were but sparks of the fire burning in his heart, and that his ideas and feelings regarding this 'Mother of Fair Love,' as he so often called her, far surpassed the strongest expressions that he could use to reveal them."[1]

The holy name of Mary[2] was like delicious honey on his tongue; he always pronounced it with deep respect, and never without adding some beautiful epithet. He usually called her "our admirable Mother." One day he wrote the following advice to a nun who, having great love for Mary, wished to honor her under the title of our Lady of Protection: "The name of our Lady of Protection," he said, "is a very good one, but if I were to give one to Mary, I should call her our all-bountiful Lady."[3]

St. John Eudes inspired everyone with his devotion to Mary, especially priests because of their close alliance and special ties with her. Just as she is the Mother of Jesus Christ, priests can glorify themselves as being, in a certain manner, His father, since each day they bring Him down upon the altar and engender Him once more in the hearts of Christians through the administration of the sacraments. He would exhort pastors, catechists, confessors of religious, college professors, schoolteachers, fathers and mothers, those who had servants, to do the same. He used to tell them that devotion to Mary was the true means of contributing to the salvation of many souls and of assuring their own happiness, in conformity with these words of the Holy Spirit in Sacred Scripture, attributed by the Church to the Blessed Virgin Mary: "They that shall explain me shall have life everlasting."[4] He himself never went into the pulpit without saying something in praise of Mary, so that he might incite his listeners to place their trust in her.

The deep filial love of St. John Eudes for the Mother of God is also apparent in his letters. The priests of his Congregation once received this injunction from him when they were giving a mission: "I urge you in particular, my beloved brethren, to honor and have others honor in every possible way our most bountiful and lovable Mother, the most holy Mother of Jesus, the beloved of God and the consoler of the afflicted."[5] And in giving advice on good administration to his niece, Mother Mary of the Nativity Herson, a religious of Our Lady of Charity, who had been sent to the Convent of Bayeux as Superior by order of the Bishop, he concluded with this counsel, as the most important one to be heeded above all others: "Over and above everything else I exhort you, my dear daughter, to implant deep in the hearts of all your daughters a tender and cordial devotion to the most holy Mother of God, who is an inexhaustible source of every kind of blessing and an infallible means of attaining eternal salvation."[6]

On another occasion, when writing to Reverend Mother St. Gabriel,[7] Religious of the Royal Abbey of Montmartre, he had this to say: "I thank you with all my heart, my dearest daughter, for the great love you bear our most lovable Mother, Mary, the Mother of Jesus. Grow unceasingly in this holy love and strive to make her loved by all. Fear not; the all-bountiful and all-powerful Mother of God has never failed and will never fail those who love and serve her, after God, and who place all their trust in her incomparable goodness. But she acts in her own good time, and we must wait patiently and obediently for the will of her Son, which is also hers, to manifest itself."[8]

His zeal for the honor of the most Blessed Virgin Mary is evident, then, from the excerpts of his letters, as well as from many similar ones which we omit for fear of tiring the reader. The heart of our Saint longed unceasingly for her glory. He came to be considered one of the most devoted servants of Mary of his age. It was a glory that his enemies could never take away from him though they ironically called him and his confreres the "Children of Mary." His friends, on the contrary, exhorted him to grant them a small share of his great love for the Mother of God.

An outstanding example of this is found in a letter from a saintly Jesuit missionary who was laboring in Canada, with great blessings, for the salvation of souls. Burning with love, too, for the most Blessed Virgin Mary, he wrote this letter to her worthy servant, St. John Eudes, of whom he had heard with much joy in the far distant country of Canada.

PAX CHRISTI

I was comforted, Reverend Father, to hear from Father Torcapel[9] about your holy ambition to surpass everyone, no matter whom, in loving our Lady. Would to God that you could communicate your spirit to all the ambitious people of the world!

May I take the liberty of asking you, for the love of Mary, the Virgin Mother, whom you love so much, to procure for me the blessing of being admitted as the least of your co-servants into the service of this sovereign Queen, or if you prefer, as the youngest of all your brethren, through the adoption of this

Mother of mercy. I beg of you the signal favor that if you die before me to bequeath to me, to whatever extent you can, a measure of your devotion to her so that you may continue even after your death to honor her on earth in my person.

Father Torcapel will tell you himself of my displeasure on seeing so many persons receive our Lord in the Blessed Sacrament, with the immense gifts that He brings with Himself, without showing the least sign of gratitude to her who has given Him to us. Now, in order to remedy this ingratitude or to compensate in some way for it, I should like to form an Association of Chaplains of our Lady. By that I mean a number of zealous priests who will make a mutual agreement never to say a Mass in which they do not have, among other intentions, that of honoring the Blessed Virgin Mary and of offering to God His adorable Son through her hands so that He may ascend to His Father, in His capacity of victim, through the mediation of the same person who brought Him to us when He was made man. I should not want this devotion to limit itself merely to the above intention, but I should also like to include a special mention of the Blessed Virgin during and after Mass and Holy Communion. For example, on the evening preceding our Communion, let us entreat her to come and take possession of our hearts in order to prepare them to receive her Son, and after Mass or Communion, let us thank her for having given us such a loving Shepherd of our souls.

I beg you, Reverend Father, to consult our Lady about this, and if she tells you that it is pleasing to her, get this work under way, start the Association and grant me the favor of admitting me to it. However, since few persons flock to devotions if they do not offer some attraction of spiritual interest, I leave it to your prudence, together with your extraordinary desire to increase the devotion to the Blessed Virgin, to put down in writing the means of attracting souls to this devotion, and to have the charity of writing out a copy of it for me. Let your love for the Blessed Virgin apologize for my taking the liberty of writing you so familiarly, I who am but a poor missionary unknown to you. I recommend myself to your prayers and holy sacrifices as well as to those of all your fervent co-workers.

Your most humble servant in our Lord,
JOSEPH MARY CHAUMONOT, S.J.[10]

Quebec, October 14, 1660.

This letter brings out the intense ardor and devotion of the writer for the worthy Mother of God. Although Father Chaumonot himself was enkindled with zeal for our Lady, he sincerely acknowledged, nevertheless, from what he heard about St. John Eudes that there was even more love and fervor in the latter's heart than in his own. We do not know for sure just what reply the Saint made to this holy Jesuit with regard to the Association of Chaplains referred to in his letter, but we do know from a second letter of thanks, written from Montreal, Canada, on September 27, 1661, that St. John Eudes gladly granted the favor requested of him. We think that it may be well, for the reader's satisfaction, to offer an excerpt from it here, which may help considerably to arouse devotion to the Blessed Virgin Mary by noting the sentiments of this humble son of St. Ignatius.

PAX CHRISTI

If the greatest monarch in the world, Reverend Father, had adopted me as his son, with the intention of making me his heir, I should not have felt a thousandth part of the joy that I experienced upon receiving your promise to bequeath to me all the devotion, veneration and zeal that our good Jesus has given you for the glory of His amiable and admirable Mother. "Whence does this come to me, poor beggar? Whence does this come to me, uncultured son of the earth?" . . . if not from the immense goodness of this Mother of mercy, who is pleased to grant her greatest favors to the most unworthy.

Oh, how I should like all Christians henceforth to solicit and pursue these spiritual benefices and heritages from the servants and handmaids of God, instead of running after those of the world! Would to God that I might have ideas and words worthy of such a subject to give to the public, in order to urge everyone to love them! . . . It is you, dear Father, and those like you, on whom our good Master bestows this honor of using your writings to enkindle the world with love for Him and for His Blessed Mother. Persevere, venerable Father, in this holy work. If God has intended to instill in me any new sentiments that may help to procure additional honor for our good Queen and Mother, I beg Him in all sincerity to favor you instead with them, knowing that you will make much better use of them than I. What I should like to obtain from His infinite bounty, through your holy sacrifices, is the grace to make good use of my knowledge of the languages of the poor Hurons and Iroquois in order to convert them, and to persevere until death in this task to which God called me more than twenty-four years ago. I ask you to be so good as to recommend me to the prayers and sacrifices of all your fervent missionaries, whom I embrace *in visceribus et in osculo Christi,*[11] as my brethren and joint heirs of the reverence of the dear Mother of our Saviour with which He has endowed you. Adieu, Reverend Father.

I remain your most humble and obedient son in our Lord.

JOSEPH CHAUMONOT, S.J.

If we were to record all the testimonies of various persons regarding the devotion of St. John Eudes to the most Blessed Virgin Mary, we would need volumes to do so. It will suffice to repeat that his was a noble ambition not to allow anyone to surpass him in honor, trust and love for the Mother of God, although he freely made way for everyone where natural talents were concerned. Whenever he exhorted anyone to love her, he always did everything possible to honor her more, not through any motive tinged with secret and intellectual pride, but through his deep attachment and profound esteem for the holy person of the Blessed Virgin Mary.

NOTES

[1] St. John Eudes did not live continuously at Caen except during the last three years of his life, 1677–1680. Father Andrew Esnouf, who was Father Herambourg's superior at Rennes when he wrote this book, had resided at Caen from 1675 to 1680. He may be the spiritual son referred to here. See P. Costil, *Fleurs de la Congrégation de Jésus et Marie,* vol. 1, pp. 375–378.

[2] St. John Eudes, *The Wondrous Childhood of the Most Holy Mother of God* (Peekskill, Convent of the Good Shepherd, 1915), p. 150.

[3] This is a fragment of a letter that was lost.

[4] Ecclus. 24:31.

[5] Eudes, *Letters and Shorter Works,* p. 283.

[6] *Ibid.,* p. 240.

[7] Mother St. Gabriel, Charlotte de Chaulnes, was sub-prioress of the Benedictine Abbey of Montmartre between 1661 and 1667. In *Letters and Shorter Works* there are nine letters from St. John Eudes to Mother St. Gabriel. See Reverend Ange Ledoré, *Les Sacrés-Coeurs et le Vénérable Jean Eudes* (Paris, Lamulle et Poisson, 1891), vol. 1, p. 253.

[8] Eudes, *Letters and Shorter Works,* p. 275.

[9] Father John Torcapel, not Forcapel as it is misspelled by Boulay, came to Quebec with Bishop Montmorency de Laval on June 16, 1659. He was in charge of the first parish at Quebec for one year until his return to France on October 20, 1660. He entered the Congregation of Jesus and Mary at the age of 35 and died at the Seminary of Evreux on September 19, 1668. See *Livre qui contient les noms de ceux qui sont du corps de la C. J. M.,* Archives départementals de Calvados, série H, Eudistes; *Nécrologie de Rouen,* Archives des Eudistes à Paris; Auguste Gosselin, *Henri de Bernières, premier curé de Québec* (Quebec, 1902), pp. 41, 44, 45.

[10] Father Peter Joseph Mary Chaumonot (1611–1693) was born at Chatillon-sur-Marne, France, March 9, 1611 and died at Quebec on February 21, 1693. A Jesuit missionary, Father Chaumonot was "venerated by the holiest apostles of Canada as a marvel of sanctity." He worked among the Huron Indians on the outskirts of Quebec and built a chapel dedicated to Our Lady of Loretto, which still exists, Indian Lorette. See *La Vie du R. P. Pierre Joseph Marie Chaumonot, de la Compagnie de Jésus, Missionnaire de la Nouvelle France, écrite par lui-même, par ordre de son supérieur, l'an 1688.* (New York, Presse Cramoisy de Jean Marie Shea, 1858). Also Sargent, *op. cit.,* p. 197.

[11] Rom. 16:16 and Phil. 1:8. Father Chaumonot's expression is a combination of two of St. Paul's greetings in his epistles: *in osculo sancto* and *in visceribus.*

Chapter 13. Practices of Devotion to Our Lady

MEN OF THE WORLD spare no effort to win the favor of those whom they seek in marriage. Even in Sacred Scripture we see that the Patriarchs of old did everything possible to ingratiate themselves with those whom God had destined to be their wives.[1] St. John Eudes, belonging to the most Blessed Virgin Mary by virtue of so many ties, and particularly through his choice of her during his tenderest years,[2] overlooked no practice by which he might show his devotion and love for her. Imitating the zeal of St. John whose name he bore[3] and to whom Jesus Christ had entrusted her at the time of His death,[4] he was completely devoted to her service.

In order to be more faithful to this duty, the Saint bound himself by a vow to honor her and to look upon her from that time forward as His Mother and Queen. He never let a day go by without giving her some proof of his dependence on her, in which he desired to live and die. He considered the "Hail Mary" to be the most pleasing prayer that one could address to her, since it contains the most wonderful tidings that she ever received. The recitation of the rosary was a habit with him; it was his daily exercise. He even wore a rosary from his girdle, being happy to let everyone know that he was glorifying her by this devotion. He used to say that he was afraid that Jesus and Mary might reject those at the point of death who did not have this mark of piety, deeming them unworthy to share in their mercies. He always strove to recite the rosary with the greatest possible attention and devotion.[5] He would first offer himself to our Lord, while saying the Creed, begging that he might shed his blood for the glory of His mysteries, in union with the sentiments in which Jesus had shed His own. He would also humble himself profoundly before the Son and the Mother, giving himself to their reciprocal love for each other and uniting himself with all the praises that would ever be rendered them in heaven and on earth. Then he would say each decade in honor of a particular virtue they had practiced, in which he would ask to share: the first decade in honor of their humility; the second, in honor of their purity of heart; the third, in honor of their meekness and charity; the fourth, in honor of their submission to the will of God; the fifth, in honor of the most pure love of Jesus Christ for His Father, and that of Mary for Jesus.

St. John Eudes used to follow approximately the same practice whenever he recited the Little Office of the Blessed Virgin, honoring in each part a portion of the life of Jesus in Mary and of Mary in Jesus, or else uniting himself at each psalm with all the praise given her by the eternal Father, the Son and the Holy Spirit, and by the angels and saints, both collectively and individually.[6]

The Saint never said any prayers nor performed any exercise without asking Mary's blessing at the end for himself and for others, using these words which also served as a conclusion to most of his letters: *Nos cum prole pia benedi-*

cat Virgo Maria.[7] This practice he left to his Congregation of priests and desired its members to observe it faithfully.[8] In order to merit this grace and to constrain the Blessed Virgin Mary not to refuse it, he established the practice of always reciting this verse from the *Ave Maris Stella:*

Monstra te esse Matrem,
Sumat per te preces,
Qui pro nobis natus
Tulit esse tuus.[9]

John Eudes loved and honored all holy images of Mary, but he preferred those which united the Son and the Mother. He was convinced that, since they had always been so closely united, it was a mistake to depict the one without the other; he even believed that the Blessed Virgin Mary herself disapproved of it. He was often heard in that regard to repeat this beautiful couplet:

Pingenti solam sine nato mater aiebat
Me sine me potius pinge, dolebo minus.[10]

The Saint never wanted Jesus and Mary to be separated in any devotion paid to them. When the plague was scourging the inhabitants of Caen, he had statues of the Mother of God placed at the gates of the city and at the St. Peter Bridge, and from that time forward no casualty befell it.[11] Whenever he encountered an image of her on the streets, he would stop, face it and say the "Hail Mary," with devotion that touched those who heard or saw him do so. It was a practice that he always observed when entering or leaving his room, and one that he recommended to his spiritual sons and daughters. On his rosary there hung a medal which bore her likeness, and during a conversation he always had it in his hand; he would kiss it frequently with inexpressible tenderness. The love of St. John Eudes for Mary was stronger than death, since he requested in his last will and testament, to have buried with him one of the images of her which he kept in his room.[12]

This great lover of Mary reopened chapels which had formerly been dedicated to Mary but had fallen into ruin, either because of troubled times or the negligence of men. There was a chapel near Valognes, completely abandoned, which was opened only once a year, on the feast of a holy apostle whose statue was within. St. John Eudes made every effort to recover its titles. He had it put in order again and procured a number of ornaments to beautify it, calling it Our Lady of Victory. It became celebrated for its throngs of pilgrims and numerous miracles, which revealed that the Blessed Virgin Mary was truly victorious and that the glory of this second house, repaired by her faithful servant, was far greater than that of the first one. "Great shall be the glory of this last house more than of the first."[13] He went to the same trouble for a poor chapel of Our Lady of Solace, in the parish of Vesly, in the diocese of Coutances, which was reconsecrated under the name of Our Lady of Consolation, in memory of the first appearance of her Risen Son to her.[14] His zeal moved people to contribute to it through almsgiving, and the signal favors received by many persons in that place of piety were sufficient proof that the Blessed Virgin was most pleased with the restoration of the chapel.

St. John Eudes had the greatest esteem for the confraternities erected in Mary's honor, especially those of the Holy Rosary and the Holy Scapular. He highly recommended these devotions to the faithful, and he himself wished to be buried with these two pledges of salvation.

The Saint paid singular honor to all the feast days of our Lady. He used to say that these feasts ought to be days of rejoicing for us because of the abundant graces that she obtains for us from her divine Son, if we love her like true children. He wished his Congregation to celebrate, with the permission of the Ordinaries, those feasts which take place in various dioceses in the Church: for example, the feast of the Holy Heart of Mary, of her virginal marriage with Saint Joseph, that of her Sorrows, that of the visit she received from her Son as soon as He had risen, those of her joys, of her holy name, of her victories, of her holy childhood and of her expectation.[15] He looked upon this practice with which he had been inspired as a special grace.

The zealous missionary was delighted whenever he learned that these feasts had been solemnized with great ceremony in one of his houses. This may be noted in a letter that he wrote to the Superior of the Seminary of Coutances on the occasion of the Feast of the Most Holy Heart of Mary. "I thank you," he said to him, "for the great consolation afforded me by your letter. It filled me with joy to learn that the Feast of the Most Holy Heart of Mary was celebrated so solemnly, and that His Excellency the Bishop of Coutances assisted at it and has promised to do so again next year. I give boundless thanks to our Lord and to His most Holy Mother."[16]

He exhorted persons whom he knew intimately to celebrate Mary's feast days with special devotion. Writing to a Benedictine nun on the subject of the Feast of the Nativity of Mary, he gave her this counsel: "Pay full honor today to the first moment of the life of the most Blessed Virgin on earth. O moment! O life! O moment worth more than all the centuries that preceded it since the beginning of the world! O life dearer and more precious to God, in that single moment, than all the lives of the angels and of the greatest saints! Ah, who could ever comprehend the relationship of

God with this little child Mary who had just been born! What an abundance of graces and blessings did He diffuse in the soul of this child! What zeal and love of God, what union with Him! She gave Him more love and honor at that moment than had been rendered Him during the preceding five thousand years! O holy Virgin, let all the moments of my life, all my eternity, pay homage to that first instant of thy life! At this very moment, my dear Sister, let us begin a holy and celestial life with the Blessed Virgin in honor of her own holy and celestial life."[17]

The Saint would prepare his soul for Mary's feasts through special spiritual acts, such as fasting, almsgiving and prayer. He used to avail himself of various practices in connection with the different mysteries that the Church celebrates, and the graces contained in them. Although he honored them all to the fullest extent, he was particularly attracted by the mysteries of her Holy Childhood. In its honor he wrote an admirable book[18] in which he showed forth the truth of the Immaculate Conception.[19] This mystery, so advantageous to the Blessed Virgin Mary and so contested by the enemies of her glory, was the mystery dearest to his heart. He composed a Little Office of the Immaculate Conception[20] which can easily be recited by anyone. He solemnized the feast on December 8th with exceptional devotion, having it preceded by a fast which he ordered to be observed in his Congregation. He looked upon this feast in honor of Mary Immaculate as the feast of purity.

St. John Eudes tried, for his own part, to render himself as pure as possible, that he might not be unworthy to share in her spirit and graces. Later on we shall describe another practice[21] which he instituted in honor of this most holy mystery of the Immaculate Conception.

On the Feast of the Presentation he would renew his clerical promise[22] in union with the offering that Mary made of herself to God, reconsecrating himself as a priest to His Divine Majesty under the patronage of the Mother of God and protesting that, from that time forward, he would neglect nothing that might render his life more conformable to the dignity and sanctity of his sacerdotal state. On the Feast of the Annunciation, when Mary had been chosen to be the Mother of all men by becoming the Mother of the Word Incarnate, he always renewed the vow of perpetual servitude he had made to her previously on that same day.

On the eve of her triumphant Assumption into heaven he used to pay his respects to her before her departure from the world to take possession of heaven.[23] He would kneel before her in the name of all mankind, paying homage to the various states of her life, asking pardon of her for his negligence in honoring her during the year and for the little he had profited from her mysteries, and offering her in reparation the praises rendered her by the angels and saints in heaven and on earth. He would thank her for the things that she had thought, said, done and suffered in this world in order to cooperate with her Son for our salvation. He would make amends to her for the injuries she had received and for the sorrows she had endured on earth, offering in atonement the adorable Heart of her Son and all the homage of the Church Triumphant and Militant. He would present himself to her in order to suffer whatever she wished for that intention, and to obtain glory for her in every way possible. He would give her his heart wholly and irrevocably, imploring her to destroy in it whatever was displeasing to her, to separate it completely from creatures, to unite it closely with her own, to enrapture it and bear it up to heaven. On that feast of Mary's triumph it was his custom to choose one of the mysteries of her life to be the special object of his veneration during the year.

Of all the days of the week he had a particular devotion to Saturday because it is consecrated by the Church to honoring the life of Jesus in Mary and of Mary in Jesus. On that day he used to honor her with special care and affection, endeavoring to atone for all the faults he believed himself guilty of having committed toward her during the week. At the end of that day he would honor her in her last hour and at the last moment of his own life.

Another indication of his affection for Mary is found in the books[24] that he wrote in her praise. It made him supremely happy to use his tongue and pen to make the Mother of God known and loved. The offices that he composed for several of her feasts—among others, that of her Holy Heart—are still another proof of his love.[25] After his death a salutation was discovered which begins with these words, written in his own blood: "Hail Mary, Daughter of God the Father."[26] He had it printed during his lifetime, and we know from experience that those who have used it and recited it have greatly benefited from it.

There is no doubt, however, that the two religious societies, the Congregation of Jesus and Mary and the Order of Our Lady of Charity, established by the Saint to honor her and to have her honored in a more special manner, will be the eternal monuments of his piety toward her. He dedicated all churches of his community to her Most Pure Heart. He established in them a number of practices in her honor which his spiritual children have performed with great blessings, and on countless occasions during his lifetime he offered them to that Mother of Love who never refuses such devotional acts when they are presented to her.

Besides the Confraternity[27] that he erected in her honor, he also founded a third order that he called the Society of the Children of the Heart of the Admirable Mother.[28] It is intended for persons living in the world who have not the health, the means and the vocation to join religious societies, and who, nevertheless, wish to lead a life still more perfect than that of members enrolled in the Confraternity of the Sacred Hearts, which accepts anyone, provided he is leading an exemplary Christian life. He established this Society of the Heart of the Admirable Mother for the same ends as the two Congregations of which we have spoken, namely, to honor and imitate the most Blessed Virgin Mary more devoutly and to have her honored and imitated by others. He desired that the men and women received in it be above reproach, that they practice a true and unwavering devotion to Mary, that they have a really filial affection for the Mother of Love, and that they live in perfect continency and chastity. It was also his wish that they wear underneath their usual clothing, a small habit made up of three parts: the first, a white tunic in honor of the Immaculate Conception; the second, a white silk girdle in honor of her virginity and maternity; the third, a red silk cross, fastened inside the tunic opposite the heart, in honor of her sorrows. The early members of this society found, through the special favors they received from it even in this life, that it was most pleasing to her. It is still daily apparent how advantageous it is for some souls who, living in the world without subscribing to its spirit and maxims, which they renounce in an open profession, generously participate in this society. The credit for its glory then goes to its worthy founder, St. John Eudes, who wore for many years this holy habit in which he wished to be buried.[29] By this means and many others, he succeeded in making the Blessed Virgin Mary known, honored and loved. It was one of the principal and noblest works of his life while he was on earth, and it remains one of the brightest jewels in his eternal crown, since it is true, according to the opinion of the Fathers of the Church,[30] that our Lord is pleased to grant a magnificent reward in heaven to the servants of His holy Mother.

NOTES

[1] Gen., chap. 28 and 29.

[2] "Memoriale Beneficiorum Dei," in *Letters and Shorter Works,* p. 287.

[3] Herambourg asserts that St. John the Evangelist was the patron saint of John Eudes. Father Denis Boulay in *Vie du Vénérable Jean Eudes,* vol. 1, p. 15, stresses the fact that people in country places of France always make a distinction between *John* and *John the Baptist.* Furthermore, according to Father Boulay, St. John Eudes does not seem to have had a special devotion to St. John the Baptist, whereas he chose St. John the Evangelist as one of the patrons of the Congregation of Jesus and Mary. On the other hand, we find in the correspondance of the Saint a letter from the Religious of Our Lady of Charity with their feast day wishes for June 24, the Feast of St. John the Baptist. See *Letters and Shorter Works,* p. 63. Also *Notre Vie,* September-October, 1951, p. 365.

[4] Jn. 19:27.

[5] Eudes, *The Kingdom of Jesus,* p. 184.

[6] *Ibid.,* p. 181.

[7] "May the Virgin Mary with her Divine Child bless us." This is the blessing for the first lesson of Matins for the Office of the Blessed Virgin Mary.

[8] All public devotional exercises in the Congregation of Jesus and Mary conclude with this blessing. It is recited while making the sign of the cross.

[9] Show thyself a Mother;
Offer Him our sighs,
Who for us incarnate,
Did not thee despise.

[10] "The mother would say to him who paints her alone without her child: 'Paint me without myself; it will grieve me less.'" Maurice Vloberg, *La Vierge et l'Enfant dans l'art français* (Paris, Artaud, 1954), p. 157, refers to a couplet quoted by the theologian John Caramuel y Lobkovitz (1606–1682), a contemporary of St. John Eudes:

Cur sine Prole mea Me pingis? Pingere, quaeso,
Me sine Me potius quam sine Prole velis.

[11] See Sargent, *op. cit.,* p. 39.

[12] In his "Last Will and Testament" St. John Eudes mentions ". . . the

holy image (of Mary) which is fashioned in part from holy relics and is kept in a small niche of gilded copper." *Letters and Shorter Works,* p. 327.

[13] Agg. 2:10.

[14] Eudes, *ibid.,* p. 298.

[15] The Feast of the Holy Heart of Mary was first celebrated at Autun in Burgundy on February 8, 1646, at the close of a three months' mission preached by St. John Eudes. The feast is still kept on February 8 in the religious societies founded by the Saint. The marriage of Mary and Joseph was observed on January 23. The other feasts mentioned here were observed on the following dates: Our Lady of Sorrows, Friday after Passion Sunday; Visit of the Risen Saviour to His holy Mother, first free day after the Octave of Easter as double of the second class; Feast of the Joys of Our Lady, July 8; Feast of the Holy Name of Mary, September 25, now kept by the Church on September 12; Our Lady of Victories, October 7; Feast of the Childhood of Mary, October 12; Feast of the Expectation of Mary, December 18. See *Oeuvres Complètes,* vol. 9, p. 135.

[16] *Letters and Shorter Works,* p. 276.

[17] *Ibid.,* p. 16.

[18] *L'Enfance Admirable de la très sainte Mère de Dieu* published at Paris, 1676. It was translated into English and published by the Sisters of the Good Shepherd at Peekskill, N.Y., in 1915. The English title is *The Wondrous Childhood of the Most Holy Mother of God.*

[19] *Ibid.,* pp. 46–90. In the eighth chapter of *The Wondrous Childhood* St. John Eudes explains the privilege of Mary's Immaculate Conception and meets current objections against this teaching before it was actually defined by the Church. The Saint was always an ardent and staunch supporter of the dogma of the Immaculate Conception.

[20] See *Oeuvres Complètes,* vol. 12, p. 88.

[21] The practice referred to here is the singing of the *Inviolata* on Saturday evening by the Eudist Fathers. See *Manual of Piety,* p. 132, also chapter XXXI of this work, p. 275.

[22] On the Feast of the Presentation it is still customary for priests to renew their clerical promises made on the day that they were tonsured. For the ceremony as prescribed by St. John Eudes, see *ibid.,* p. 254.

[23] *Ibid.,* p. 219.

[24] *The Admirable Heart of the Most Holy Mother of God* and *The Wondrous Childhood of the Most Holy Mother of God.*

[25] Ten complete offices for various feasts of Our Lady were written by St. John Eudes. See *Oeuvres Complètes,* vol. 11, p. 135.

[26] This salutation will be found in *The Admirable Heart of Mary* (New York, P. J. Kenedy, 1948), p. 359.

[27] See Chapter XI, note 30.

[28] This Society is often called the Third Order of St. John Eudes. It is for laymen and laywomen who wish to strive after a high degree of Christian perfection in the world. Its members take a private vow of chastity.

[29] In his "Last Will and Testament" St. John Eudes requested that he

be buried in the habit of the Third Order of the Heart of Mary. See *Letters and Shorter Works,* p. 327.

30 This thought is frequently found in French spiritual writers of the Seventeenth Century. It is the topic of a conference in a book written by a friend of St. John Eudes, Father Louis Francis d'Argentan, *Conférences théologiques et spirituelles sur les grandeurs de la très sainte Vierge Marie.* The patristic basis of this thought is developed in P. C. Dillenschneider, *Marie au service de notre rédemption* (Hagueneau, 1947), pp. 186–200.

Chapter 14. His Mystical Marriage Contract with Mary

THE GRANDEUR AND glory of the Blessed Virgin Mary deserves such high honor that it is always a great favor for her to admit us into the ranks of her slaves and servants. She is so good, however, that, as if forgetting all the illustrious prerogatives that raise her infinitely above us, she wants to accept and receive us on the grounds of love, as her children and chosen spouses.

Mary Immaculate honored with espousal saints characterized by special devotion to her. The life of St. Robert, founder of the Cistercians,[1] states that our Lady placed a ring on his mother's finger as a sign of the mystical marriage she intended to contract with him later. In the biography of St. Edmund, Archbishop of Canterbury,[2] it is narrated that, as a small boy, he told his aunt that he had found a spouse with whom he was in love. He was speaking of Mary, the Queen of Heaven, whom he had chosen as his beloved, making a vow of perpetual virginity before a statue on whose finger he placed a gold ring engraved *Ave Maria.* The example of the saints encourages Christians to take Mary as spouse. This is not presumptuous because Jesus Christ, her divine Son, fervently seeks souls to be His spouses, being well pleased when they cooperate and choose Him. It is related that Christ our Lord sought to enter into marriage with St. Catherine[3] in the presence of His Blessed Mother and the court of heaven.

Charmed with the beauty of our Lady's perfections and her great goodness, St. John Eudes consecrated his affections to her, chose her as his spouse, and imitated the devotion of the saintly Archbishop of Canterbury. He wrote out a marriage contract many years after the marriage had been consummated, which he signed with his blood. It reveals his feelings of tenderness and love toward Mary Immaculate. Following is a copy of this contract. The original he ordered to be buried with him.[4] We have made no changes in order to preserve all its forcefulness.

JESUS MARY JOSEPH

CONTRACT OF HOLY MARRIAGE WITH THE MOST BLESSED VIRGIN MARY, THE MOTHER OF GOD

O admirable and most lovable Mary, Mother of God, only Daughter of the eternal Father, Mother of the Son of God, Spouse of the Holy Spirit, Queen of heaven and earth, it is no wonder thou art willing to be the spouse of the least of all men and greatest of all sinners, who had the boldness to choose thee from his tenderest years to be his most unparalleled spouse, and to consecrate his body, heart and soul wholly to thee. The truth is that thou dost wish to imitate the infinite goodness of thy Son Jesus who is willing to be the spouse of a sinful and wretched soul. May all the angels, saints, creatures and the Creator Himself praise and bless thee eternally for it, and atone for all my countless acts of ingratitude and infidelity toward thee.

Since thou hast already shown such great kindness, O most charitable of all creatures, be pleased to accept the conditions of our holy union which I am about to write down on this paper.

It will serve as the contract, or rather, as a copy of the contract of which I implore the Holy Spirit to be the notary, that He may write it in thy Heart and in mine in the golden and indelible letters of His pure love.

Whereas the husband is the head and superior of the wife, and whereas she is subject to his authority, I wish to respect and honor thee as my Queen and Sovereign Lady, and I desire my whole being, with all its dependencies and appurtenances, to be fully subject to thy power, that thou mayest dispose of them all according to thy pleasure.

Whereas a portion of the wife's dowry remains in the hands of her husband—that which is popularly known as a changeable gift—who uses it as he deems best, I desire to appropriate and retain nothing of the dowry thou hast brought me, that is, the numberless graces and favors which the heavenly Father has granted me through thy intercession. I willingly surrender all claims to any advantage for my private interests, placing them all in thy hands, together with all the fruits they have yielded, so that thou mayest return them to Him who is their primary source, and to whom alone may all glory for them be eternally rendered.

Whereas the wife, after her husband's death, retains only a portion of his wealth as her marriage settlement, it is my intention, O my most honored Lady, that all that I am, all of which I am capable, all that I have in body and soul, nature and grace, all that I hope for in glory, and in general, all that belongs to me in either the spiritual or temporal order, or that depends on me in any way whatsoever, be thine entirely and without reservation, that thou mayest do with them what thou wilt. But all that is nothing. Oh, if I had a hundred million worlds, how gladly would I give them to thee, O my holy Mistress, truly, if through the impossible I were a divine being, like thy Son Jesus, I would give myself to thee with the utmost happiness, in union with the same love with which He gave Himself to thee!

Whereas the wife must conform to her husband and become

like him, according to these divine words, "Let us make man a helper like unto himself,"[5] I desire with all my heart to strive to become like thee, O my Queen, through constant imitation of thy holy life and eminent virtues. I beseech thee to use thy God-given power to destroy in me whatever may prevent my doing so, and to impress upon me a lively image and perfect likeness of thyself.

Just as husband and wife must live together in the same house, so also do I desire to dwell with thee in the most lovable Heart of Jesus, which is also thy Heart. Grant that I may never leave it, I beg of thee, but that I may have no other dwelling in time and in eternity.

Just as the wife is inseparable from her husband and is obliged to follow and accompany him everywhere, so also do I beseech thee, my all-good, to be ever with me, in all places, at all times and in all my actions, that thou mayest guide and govern me in all things, according to the most adorable will of thy Son.

Just as the honor of the wife, which is her husband's glory, must be very dear and precious to him, so do I declare my desire to be especially fervent in honoring and having honor paid thee in every way I can, with the help of the grace of thy Son.

Just as husband and wife must love each other with a love that is sincere, constant and cordial, so have I every imaginable proof, O my all-lovable one, of thine incomparable affection for me; thou seest, too, the fires and flames, the sincerity and tenderness of my heart in thy regard. O my all-desirable one, what do I wish, what do I love, in heaven and on earth, after thy Jesus and mine, other than thee? O thou sole object of my affections, second only to my God, what would I not do and suffer for love of thee? I know there is nothing more pleasing to thy Son and thee than labor for the salvation of souls. Surely thou art aware of my feelings on that subject. Oh, that I had all the hearts of men and angels, with all the capacity to love that ever was and ever shall be, that I might avail myself of them to love Jesus, the Son of Mary, and Mary, the Mother of Jesus! But even then I should not be satisfied. One must have the heart of God in order to love worthily the God-Man and the Mother of God. Thanks be to God, I have such a one, because Jesus has given Himself wholly to me, so His Heart is consequently mine. Yes, the Heart of Jesus is my own heart. It is in the love of this Heart that I wish to love my most kind Saviour and His most lovable Mother, and that I desire to love them deeply, ardently, tenderly, solely and eternally. I wish to love only what they love, hate only what they hate, rejoice over nothing save what gives them happiness, grieve over nothing except what displeases them. And I wish to find all my consolation and pleasure in thinking of them, conversing with them, speaking of them and hearing them spoken of, acting in their service, suffering for love of them, and dying ten thousand times, were it possible, for Jesus and Mary.

Just as husband and wife have a mutual obligation to aid and console each other in infirmities, illnesses and afflictions, it is my desire to serve, aid and console thee according to the power God has given me, in the person of the poor, sick and afflicted, in whom I shall see thee as the mother in her children, beseeching thee, too, my all-gracious one, to help, protect and sustain me in my spiritual and corporeal needs.

Just as husband and wife should have but one heart and soul, grant, O Queen of my heart, that I may have with thee but one soul, one mind, one will and one heart. To that end, deprive me of my own heart and give me thine, according to thy word, that I may sing for all eternity

O qualis haec benignitas:
Ardens Mariae charitas,
Meum sibi cor abstulit
Suum mihi cor praebuit.[6]

May the Immaculate Heart of Mary be the soul of my soul and the spirit of my spirit; may this lovable Heart be the principle of my life and all my thoughts, words, actions, feelings and affections; may I perform all my actions and bear all my trials and afflictions in the love, charity, humility, submission, patience and the other holy dispositions and intentions of this most holy Heart.

Just as the wife should redouble her care of her husband and affection toward him during his last days and at the hour of his death, so also do I ask of thee, O beloved of my soul, to be present and near me personally on my last day and during my final hour, according to thy promise, to defend me against the enemies of my salvation, to strengthen and comfort me, to prepare me for a holy death, to give me a share in the holy dispositions of thy death, to receive my soul when it leaves my body, to lodge it within thy bosom and thy maternal Heart, for thou art the Mother and Spouse of my Jesus; to elevate it unto thyself in heaven, that there I may love, praise and glorify forever the most Blessed Trinity, together with thee and with all the angels and saints.

Just as the wife should care for the children that her husband leaves her after his death, so do I beseech thee with all my heart, O my all-charitable one, to take very special care of all the spiritual children God has given me; they are thy children, too, since He has given them to me through thee. I place them all in thy care from this moment on, beseeching thee to preserve them so well that not a single one may be lost. I also place in thy blessed hands the Communities that divine providence has given me in charge, or with which He has granted me a special bond of unity; and all those persons who have any friendship and charity toward me, or who have recommended themselves to my prayers, or to whom I have any obligation whatsoever, without forgetting those who have felt any hatred or aversion toward me, for whom I pray thee to ask pardon of divine mercy. But above all else, I recommend to thee most earnestly, O my all-good Spouse, the small Congregation of Jesus and Mary that thy Son and thee have given me, entreating thee, O my Queen, by all the kindness of thy most benign Heart, to atone for all my omissions toward it; to annihilate anything that may obstruct the designs of God for it; to protect, bless and govern it in all things.

Remember, O most kind and powerful Virgin, that thy Son Jesus is its founder, superior and father; that thou art its foundress, superioress and mother; and that it is wholly dedicated and consecrated to thy most Holy Heart. Grant then, I beseech thee, that all the children of this Congregation may be true children of thy Heart, and with this objective in view, that each may make a complete renunciation of his own will to comply everywhere and in all things with the most adorable will of God. Expel all those who seek to live according to the desires of their own hearts, and do not allow anyone of that character to enter. Bless and favor in every way those who faithfully observe the rules established in this Congregation. Bless too with thy holiest blessings all who love and protect it. But most of all do I ask of thee, O my holy Princess, that thou grant it a Superior pleasing to thy Heart, one who will make amends for the countless mistakes that I have made in its regard and rule it in thy spirit, which is the spirit of thy Son.

Those are the conditions of the contract of holy marriage which thou hast desired me to enter into with thee, O Queen of heaven, as with the most holy spouse of my spirit and heart. Once again I entreat thee to find it pleasing and to sign it with the blood of thy virginal Heart, just as I am going to sign it with my own blood. Grant that it may be accepted and signed by thy adorable Father, who is also my Father; by thy Son Jesus, my Redeemer; by thy Spouse, the Holy Spirit; by thine own father, St. Joachim and thy mother, St. Anne; and by thy spouse, St. Joseph. Grant that thy good guardian angel, St. Gabriel, my own guardian angel, St. John the Baptist, St. John the Evangelist, all the saints particularly devoted to thee during thy life on earth, and all the other angels and saints, may sign it as witnesses; and that the Holy Spirit may imprint thereon the eternal seal of His divine love. Amen, amen! So be it!

Drawn up at Caen, in the house of the Congregation of Jesus and Mary, on Saturday, this 28th day of April, 1668. Signed in his own blood by John Eudes, missionary priest of the Congregation of Jesus and Mary.

After reading this mystical marriage contract, one may indeed say that Mary has seldom had a servant on earth so closely united to her as St. John Eudes. The Spouse of the Canticle of Canticles[7] found glory in no longer belonging to herself since she belonged entirely to her Beloved and He belonged wholly to her. Similarly St. John Eudes could also say that he no longer belonged to himself, because the glorious Virgin Mary was entirely his and in consequence he was all hers. This mystical marriage accomplished a union even more intimate than that of marriage partners in the world; the contracting parties had thereafter but one mind, one heart and one will, because the husband had completely resigned everything within him into the hands of his most holy and beloved spouse.

NOTES

[1] See *Acta Sanctorum* (Paris, Apud Victorem Palme, 1866), April, vol. 3, p. 677; Father M. Raymond, O.C.S.O., *Three Religious Rebels* (New York, P. J. Kenedy, 1944), p. 20.

[2] See *St. Edmund, Archbishop of Canterbury: His Life as Told by Old English Writers* (London, Sands & Co., 1903), arranged by Bernard Ward, p. 14.

[3] The reference is to St. Catherine of Alexandria. See *Les Petits Bollandistes* (Paris, Bloud et Barral, 1878), vol. 13, p. 590. Also Rev. Berchmans Bittle, O.F.M. Cap., *A Saint a Day* (Milwaukee, Bruce, 1957), p. 308. *The Catholic Encyclopedia* has a picture of a painting depicting the mystical marriage of St. Catherine of Alexandria. It is interesting to note that St. Catherine of Siena also took Christ as her bridegroom when she was still a child, in imitation of her patron, St. Catherine of Alexandria. See Johannes Jorgensen, *Saint Catherine of Siena* (New York, Longmans, Green, 1938), p. 19.

[4] See "Last Will and Testament," in *Letters and Shorter Works,* p. 327.

[5] Gen. 2:18.

[6] "O what a rich blessing is this! The ardent charity of Mary removes my own heart and gives me hers instead." See Sargent, *op. cit.,* p. 216.

[7] Cant. 6:2.

Chapter 15. Favors Received Through Mary

"I LOVE THEM that love me." These words from the book of Proverbs[1] the Church usually applies to the Blessed Virgin Mary, and their truth asserts itself daily. Her love, as she says, is an active love that delights in revealing its tenderness to all who love her. "Come over to me, all ye that desire me, and be filled with my fruits."[2] Several passages of the Old Testament, as applied by the Church, compare Mary to the olive ripe for the oil-press.[3] Never yet has anyone been found who can say that, having invoked her and served her faithfully, he was not rewarded with some mark of her goodness and mercy.[4]

In the person of St. John Eudes we have an example of one whom our Lady treated with special affection. We shall not attempt to mention all the favors that she obtained for him, but only those indicating superlatively the loving caresses of the Mother of Fair Love. His humility kept most of these blessings a secret, upon which speculation should not intrude. We shall leave aside the special favors that he received from Mary at the time of his conception and birth as well as those granted during his childhood and at the time of his reception into the Sodality of our Lady as a student with the Jesuit Fathers.[5] These graces the Saint revealed in a handwritten memorandum[6] in which he acknowledged that our Lord extended particularly great mercies to him during that time through the mediation of His most holy Mother. As for the other special favors, we shall merely say in a general way that the Blessed Virgin Mary cared for him as a real mother; hers was the fidelity of a true spouse; she cherished him as the apple of her eye, and guided him in all things in conformity with God's plan for him.

Mary, Mother of Jesus, was indeed his oracle in times of doubt, the guiding star of his travels, his refuge in danger, his consolation in trouble, and the beloved who quickened every beat of his heart. He did nothing without her guidance.

Our Lady used to communicate inwardly with St. John Eudes, and sometimes very perceptibly. He became so completely absorbed in her influence on his soul that he gave little thought to the things that happened to him externally, even though they were harsh and painful. Once, on the eve of the Assumption, several hostile individuals circulated a libel about him, filled with shameful invectives.[7] He read it with so little natural resentment that later he frankly admitted to some close friends who knew of the outrage committed against him, that the joy he experienced concerning the ineffable glory of the Blessed Virgin did not permit him to give thought to the scandalous pamphlet or to dwell upon such trivial affairs.

Whenever St. John Eudes encountered hardened and stubborn sinners, he would pray to our Lady, refuge of sinners, to obtain their conversion. He had learned that, even as Ruth of old[8] obtained permission from Booz to glean the ears of corn which slipped through the hands of the harvesters, so too the Blessed Virgin Mary finds access to the divine majesty of God on behalf of sinners when the zeal of preachers and other evangelical workers is unable to penetrate their obstinacy. The extraordinary number of souls converted by St. John Eudes is testimony to our Lady's love for him. He learned by experience that her intercession was all-powerful. In fact, he had proof of this on all his missions. We shall cite only one instance of her many favors in his great apostolic work.

Laboring on one occasion in a large city with his co-workers, he learned that there was an atheist who acknowledged neither God nor devil. All efforts to convince him of the unhappy state into which he had fallen had been unsucessful. He scorned all proffered admonitions. Then the Saint called upon him, conversing with the man for a considerable length of time and speaking strongly to him about the most moving truths of religion with apostolic zeal but without success. Seeing that he was vainly storming a hardened heart determined to resist, St. John Eudes drew from his pocket a picture of the Blessed Virgin that he always carried with him, and while giving it to the atheist, he began to speak again with such forcefulness and energy that the man, coming to himself as from a daze, asked: "Father, what do you want me to do?" The Saint answered gently: "I want you to become converted." No sooner had he said these words than the atheist, acknowledging the crime of his bitterness of heart, asked pardon of God and did penance for the godless conduct of his life. The picture of the Blessed Virgin had produced this wonderful change. The Blessed Mother became for this sinner a sun that dispelled his darkness by its rays and softened his hardness by its warmth. The Saint realized once again that not only heaven and earth, but even hell and sin itself, are obliged to bow in the name of Mary, and that it is always advantageous, no matter how deeply involved in sin a person may be, to have recourse to her.

This devout servant of the Mother of God had always longed to die on a day consecrated to her glory, and to surrender his soul into her blessed hands. She obtained his heart's desire, for he died on the nineteenth of August, four days after the feast of her glorious Assumption, with an inward peace and consolation affording visible proof that she had granted his wishes.

Great are the privileges of those sincerely devoted to the service of the Mother of Christ. It is indeed desirable, for the conversion of sinners and the spiritual advancement of the faithful, that those who labor for the salvation of their neighbor foster this devotion to our Lady, particularly in the souls under their spiritual guidance. Never did St. John Eudes, the zealous missionary, let a week pass on his missions without preaching a sermon in honor of Mary. And this is one of the main reasons why he and his spiritual children have always succeeded so well in their undertakings, and have brought down upon themselves the blessings of heaven.

NOTES

[1] Prov. 8:17.

[2] Ecclus. 24:26.

[3] Ps. 51:10; Ecclus. 24:19; Joel 2:24.

[4] St. Bernard's *Memorare.*

[5] Eudes, *Letters and Shorter Works,* p. 287.

[6] *Ibid.,* p. 289.

[7] A priest by the name of Charles du Four, Abbé of Aunay, Canon of Rouen, published a libel entitled *Letters to a Doctor of the Sorbonne,* in which he accused St. John Eudes of heresy in his doctrine on our Lady. The Saint refused to reply, but a friend, Father de Launay-Hué, strongly and convincingly rebutted, turning against the author the accusation of heresy that he had brought against the Saint. *Ibid.,* p. 246, footnotes 1 and 2; also Sargent, *op. cit.,* p. 269. A note in *Notre Vie,* September-October, 1951, p. 366, points out that the spelling of the Abbé's benefice is Aunay, not Aulnay as found in most biographies of the Saint.

[8] Ruth 2:2–10.

Chapter 16. Special Devotion to Some Saints

SINCE THE SAINTS are the friends of God, we are obliged to venerate them. We cannot love God perfectly without also loving those whom He loves. Because He is pleased to honor the saints in heaven, allowing them to share in His glory, it is eminently reasonable that we honor them on earth by singing their praises, imitating their virtues and imploring their aid.

The honor that the saints give to Jesus and that Jesus renders them reciprocally formed the double incentive for St. John Eudes' devotion to them. It was his practice[1] to adore our Lord in the saints, to thank Him for the abundance of their graces, to offer Him all their love and to ask to be allowed to share in the virtues they practiced. Such were his intentions whenever he undertook a journey, celebrated Holy Mass or performed good works in their honor. It was also his custom, whenever he addressed the saints, to humble himself profoundly at the sight of his own unworthiness and to thank them for their loyal services to our Blessed Lord. He also offered himself to them that they themselves might present him to our Lord; he prayed to them to obtain in his favor the destruction of whatever the divine majesty of God found displeasing in his person; he begged for graces similar to theirs, and besought them to love and honor Jesus in his name. Lastly, he humbly asked them to associate him with the praises they gave God in heaven, and to make use of him to glorify Christ on earth.

Although he honored all the saints and the blessed in heaven, naturally there were certain saints to whom he had a special devotion. Each year, on All Saints' Day, he would choose a definite group of saints to honor, and on the Feast of St. Michael, a choir of angels.

His love for our Lady inspired a particular devotion to the Archangel Gabriel, whom God chose to be the guardian of His most holy Mother and employed in all things pertaining to the mystery of the Incarnation.[2] God appointed St. Gabriel to inform the Prophet Daniel of the time when the Son of God was to come into the world.[3] He also sent the Archangel down to earth to tell Zachary and Elizabeth that the precursor of Christ would be born to them; and to advise Joachim and Anne that they were to have a daughter who would be the honor and blessing of heaven and earth. It was Gabriel who announced to the Blessed Virgin Mary the happy news of her election to divine motherhood.[4] It was also the same Archangel that revealed to St. Joseph in a dream that he was not to be afraid to take Mary as his spouse.[5] Moreover, it was Gabriel who consoled and strengthened the agonizing Saviour in the Garden of Olives the night before He suffered the torments of His Passion.[6] The Saint used to teach that the Archangel Gabriel had special power to help and guide souls in the love of our divine Saviour, because he participated so directly in the mystery of the Incarnation, which is a mystery of love. He would often think of the holy relationship existing between this great archangel and the most Blessed Virgin Mary. He would ask St. Gabriel to obtain for him a share in the spirit of Jesus and Mary, to bring him into association with their states and mysteries, and to let him share in the love he bore them.

The sentiments of St. John Eudes toward his guardian angel were also very devout. He honored his heavenly protector because of the excellence of his angelic nature, and loved him tenderly because of the constant usefulness of his services. He often conversed with his angel guardian, and in this holy intercourse he learned how to avail himself properly of the help of such a noble and faithful friend. He always longed to have lived on earth at the time of our Lord, that he might have paid Him honor in the midst of the ignominious treatment He had received, but being unable to fulfill this wish, he sought to do it through his guardian angel, for he used to say: "This angel was mine, even at that time, in the mind of God, and consequently I can appropriate what he was then doing and offer it to Jesus as something belonging to me."

Looking upon his angel guardian as an auxiliary given him to help him honor and love the divine Majesty, the Saint would offer the respect and love of this heavenly spirit to the most Blessed Trinity, beseeching him to atone for his shortcomings, particularly whenever he was unable to devote himself directly to God. Furthermore, he would deliver himself to this dear guardian of his soul, praying him to make use of him for the glory of his Master, to destroy anything in him offensive in the sight of God, to let him share ever so little in angelic enlightenment, love and zeal, to stimulate, preserve and strengthen the union and friendship which existed between God and his soul. In the practice of this devotion, he devised several pious exercises in honor of his guardian angel. He also had a special devotion to the guardian angels of his father and mother, to those who were the protectors of the places where he lived or of the persons whom he frequented. He would address himself to them from time to time, praying to them, uniting himself to them and neglecting nothing in his power to show his respect. He also paid similar honor to the angels who were protectors of the places he visited.

First among the saints John Eudes venerated the members of the immediate circle of the family of Christ. Since St. Joachim and St. Anne[7] had been chosen by God to be the parents of the Blessed Virgin Mary, he honored the grace, holiness and all the other dispositions with which God had endowed them for their great dignity. He used to say that if divine Bounty had wrought such wonderful effects in St. Elizabeth and St. Zachary through St. John the Baptist, how much more admirable were those wrought in St. Joachim and St. Anne through their blessed daughter. He regarded St. Joseph as an object of delight for the three divine Persons of the Blessed Trinity. He honored the humble carpenter of Nazareth as the head of the Holy Family, the foster father of Jesus Christ, and the faithful spouse of the Virgin Mary. St. John Eudes was extremely devoted to St. Joseph, both because of his great holiness and because of the signal favors received through the foster father of Christ for himself as well as for his Congregations. He would urge his spiritual children to have recourse to St. Joseph in their needs. He composed several prayers in his honor; among others, a salutation beginning with the words, "Hail, Joseph, image of God the Father,"[8] which included the principal virtues that St. Joseph practiced. He ordered this prayer to be recited daily after the evening meal by the members of his communities, that they might be reminded of their duties toward the foster father of the Word Incarnate and the spouse of the Blessed Virgin Mary.

Among the apostles the Saint greatly esteemed his heavenly patron, St. John the Evangelist.[9] He regarded the Apostle as the beloved saint of Jesus Christ because of the great privileges with which our Lord had honored him, when He allowed him to rest upon His sacred breast and against His divine Heart,[10] and when He gave His holy Mother to him as to the one whom He loved the most tenderly.[11] St. John Eudes called the Evangelist the seraphic St. John, the seraph of the apostles and the apostle of the seraphim. He regarded St. John as the Apostle of Charity who had imparted better than any others this beautiful lesson of love, drawn from the very Heart of the Saviour. It was especially because of this characteristic that St. John Eudes wished St. John to be honored in his Congregation of priests, and that he wanted its members to have recourse to him particularly on any occasion of strife. To this end he ordered them never to allow a day to pass without praying to the disciple whom Jesus loved.

St. John Eudes likewise developed special devotion to all holy priests, reading their lives, trying to live his own life in conformity with theirs. Their shining examples of virtue served as precepts to him and there was nothing they had done that he did not believe himself obliged to do in order to fulfill the duties of his vocation worthily. For him there was no topic of conversation more pleasing than the narration of the lives of saints who were priests. In the Congregation of Jesus and Mary he established the Feast of the Holy Priesthood to be celebrated on the thirteenth of November[12] and he composed a special office and a Mass[13] that reveal his esteem for the divine priesthood. The Saint devoted this feast day to thanking our Lord for instituting the Sacrament of Holy Orders in His Church and for calling him to such a noble vocation. He also renewed his resolution to live like a true priest in the worthy exercise of all his sacerdotal functions.

Another very special practice of St. John Eudes was to honor all the saints who are unknown on earth.[14] He would speak with the greatest esteem of the unnoticed lives that they led, and, adoring the intentions of God in allowing them to remain in oblivion, he would implore them earnestly to obtain for him the grace to conform to these words of the devout Thomas à Kempis: "Love to be unknown and to be esteemed for nothing."[15] He also emphasized special devotion for the saints venerated in the places where he was living, extending his respect to the things that pertained to them.

It was his wish that the holy relics of the saints be held in very high esteem. He looked upon them as a portion of Jesus Christ, and as the very precious remains of His Mystical Body. The scars which they had the honor to suffer for His sake, the illustrious testimony which they bore to the glory of His name, the brilliant enlightenment which clothed them in heaven, the teachings they left to mankind by their deaths in fulfillment of their obligations toward God, the honor which they will receive from His divine majesty for all eternity, the respect and submission which the demons are forced to render them, the noticeable protection which we receive daily from them—all these were the basis and incentives of his veneration. He established a feast in his Congregation in honor of the relics preserved there.[16] He ordered the Office of the Holy Relics to be recited, and on the eve of the Feast, in the presence of all, he would read the obligations to honor them.[17] He would carry relics with him in union with the love with which God has preserved His saints in His bosom from all eternity, and with the honor they have rendered and will eternally render His divine majesty. He used to recommend this same devotion to the souls under his guidance.

Each month, furthermore, St. John Eudes chose a saint[18] to be honored daily in some special way; he strived to imitate the virtues of that saint, acknowledge his favors and obtain graces through his mediation. He would ask for the destruction of self, for the love of Jesus Christ, and for a participation in all the good accomplished by his patron saint of the month. If, at the end of the month, he realized that he had omitted one of his duties, he would offer the divine Heart of our Lord in reparation. He overlooked no means of testifying to these blessed citizens of heaven, how full of respect and love was his heart for them. He believed himself to be secure under their protection. He would publicize their merits at every opportunity and never was he happier than when occasion arose to speak of their glory. Thus did they obtain for him the good graces of the Prince whose favorites they are. The blessings that the Saint received through their intercession reveal that God takes a singular delight in the veneration of those who have honored Him on earth and continue to honor Him in heaven.

NOTES

1 Eudes, *The Kingdom of Jesus*, p. 276.

2 See *The Wondrous Childhood of the Most Holy Mother of God*, p. 288, where St. John Eudes quotes St. Bernard (*Epist.* 67) to the effect that St. Gabriel was the Guardian Angel of Mary. The Saint chose St. Gabriel as one of the secondary patrons of the Congregation of Jesus and Mary because of the prominent part that the angel played in the Mystery of the Incarnation. See *Constitutions of the Congregation of Jesus and Mary*, p. 1.

3 Dan. 9:21 ff.

4 Lk. 1:26.

5 Mt. 1:20.

6 Lk. 22:43.

[7] See *The Wondrous Childhood of the Most Holy Mother of God,* p. 377. St. John Eudes composed a special litany of St. Joachim and St. Anne. See *Manual of Piety,* p. 215.

[8] St. John Eudes also wrote a special litany of St. Joseph. *Ibid.,* p. 156. His prayer beginning *Ave, Joseph, imago Dei Patris* is found in the *Manual of Piety,* p. 75. St. Joseph is a secondary patron of the Congregation of Jesus and Mary. See *Constitutions,* p. 1.

[9] This is the second time that Herambourg asserts that St. John the Evangelist was the patron saint of St. John Eudes. See Chapter XIII, p. 118 and p. 122, note 3.

[10] Jn. 13:25.

[11] Jn. 19:27.

[12] The Feast of the Priesthood was celebrated in the Congregation of Jesus and Mary on November 13. The full title was "The Feast of the Divine Priesthood of our Lord Jesus Christ and of all Holy Priests and Levites." See Rev. Charles Lebrun, *The Spiritual Teaching of St. John Eudes* (London, Sands & Co., 1934), p. 255.

[13] The special Office and Mass composed by St. John Eudes for the Feast of the Priesthood may be found in *Oeuvres Complètes,* vol. 11, p. 513.

[14] In the Congregation of Jesus and Mary, November 13 is dedicated each year to all unknown saints. See *Manual of Piety,* p. 251.

[15] *Imitation of Christ,* Book I, chapter 2, verse 3.

[16] The Feast of the Holy Relics was first observed on November 27. In 1652 it was transferred to November 13. At the present time it is kept in the Congregation of Jesus and Mary on November 5. The Office and the Mass for the Feast are found in *Oeuvres Complètes,* vol. 11, p. 557. See also *Manual of Piety,* p. 244.

[17] See *Manual of Piety, loc. cit.*

[18] *Ibid.,* p. 137.

Chapter 17. The Virtue of Religion[1]

THE VIRTUE OF religion comes next in excellence after the theological virtues of faith, hope and charity. St. Thomas Aquinas teaches that religion brings us nearer to God Himself than the other virtues, directing us to pay Him due honor and reverence.[2] Arnobius, in the seventh book of his treatise, *Against the Nations,* clearly defines religion as "a proper attitude in respect to things divine."[3] There were few persons in the seventeenth century in whom the knowledge of God, as Salvianus calls it,[4] and of the things of God, were found in a higher degree than in His venerable servant, John Eudes. It was this spirit of religion that inspired him with such lofty and devout thoughts on the Church. He looked upon the Church as the beloved daughter of the eternal Father, who had given her His only Son to be her spouse and His divine Spirit to be her guide. For St. John Eudes, the Church was the sister and spouse of Jesus Christ, His Mystical Body, His heritage, state, kingdom, house, treasure, crown, glory and delight. Those were the views of the Saint on the Catholic Church with reference to our Lord.

With reference to himself, St. John Eudes honored Holy Church as the mother who had conceived him through the power of God in holy baptism, who still bore him in her bosom, who nourished him with the heavenly bread of the divine word and with the body and blood of the Saviour. He looked upon the Church as his queen, his governess and his guide along the path to heaven; as his teacher who taught him the truths of heaven, being herself the pillar of truth;[5] as the one to whom he was indebted for the holy orders which conferred upon him all the privileges and powers of the priesthood. These lofty considerations aroused an ardent longing to serve the Catholic Church and incited him to consecrate all his love to her.

St. John Eudes was even more attracted to Holy Mother Church when he reflected on the charity of Jesus Christ toward her, to whom He had so nobly testified by His suffering on the Cross, by the shedding of His blood and the bestowal of His graces. These considerations obliged the Saint to abandon himself completely to Christ so that he might share in His sentiments toward her, beseeching Him to impress them deep in his heart. This faithful disciple of the divine Master could truthfully say with Him that his zeal for the house of God had devoured him.[6] He frequently reflected, too, on the ardent love of the Apostles and of holy priests for the Church and on what they had done and suffered for her sanctification and growth, for the ornamentation and veneration of her temples, for the defense of her ceremonies, the observance of her laws, the administration of her sacraments, the spreading of the divine word, the worthy exercise of her religious functions, and above all, for the salvation of her children. He looked upon priests as men who did not belong to themselves but had dedicated themselves wholly to the service of this Spouse of our Saviour, for whom they should use all their efforts, thoughts, words, actions, good, strength and time, their intellects, bodies, souls and lives, all that they owned, all that they knew and all that they could do. With these things in mind, he was ashamed of his own shortcomings and strove to imitate all saintly priests, recommending himself to their prayers.

Noteworthy was the zeal of St. John Eudes for all the interests of Holy Church. He had a sincere affection for her honor and service, total submission to her doctrine, strict obedience to her commandments and a singular veneration for her customs. He used to thank our Lord in her name for the graces He had bestowed upon her. He would implore Christ earnestly to preserve, increase and sanctify the Church more and more, and above all, to give her pastors and priests pleasing to His heart.

St. John Eudes regarded all bishops and priests with a profound feeling of esteem and respect, as men whom God had elevated, in His incomparable goodness, to the highest dignity in heaven and on earth after that of the Mother of God. He used to say that they were the glorious conquest of the Saviour, the first fruits of His labors, the most worthy price of His blood, His chief portion and richest inheritance, the most noble officers of His house, the governors, judges, princes and kings of His empire. He called them the eyes, mouth and heart of Jesus Christ:[7] His eyes because it is through them that our Lord watches over, enlightens and guides the faithful and weeps over the loss of souls; His mouth, since through them He speaks and continues to bring to men the same Gospel that He Himself preached; His Heart, since they communicate, in His virtue and by His authority, the life of grace and glory to all the members of His Mystical Body on earth.

The Saint considered priests as the associates of the Eternal Father in the generation of His Son, closely united to our Lord in His capacity of Mediator, Judge, Saviour and in the power of offering with Him the same sacrifice to the Father as He Himself offered. He regarded priests as persons discharging the duties of the Holy Spirit, which are to enlighten minds and warm hearts, establish the Church and apply to souls the fruits of the passion and death of Christ. If he held these lofty ideas of priests in general, what could not be said of his feelings toward pastors in particular? He showed every mark of esteem and affection in all his dealings with them. He was always ready to do them favors and ever willing to offer himself to help lighten their labors. Among pastors he particularly honored all prelates, especially our Holy Father the Pope. He could not bear to hear anyone speak disrespectfully of their anointed persons. He never wished anyone to miss an opportunity to show them submission and deference. He even commanded his spiritual children to neglect no means to implant these same sentiments, by word and example, in the hearts of all the faithful.

The spirit of religion also helped St. John Eudes to conceive great and exalted ideals of the majesty and sanctity of our churches.[8] He often compared the house of God to the bosom of the Eternal Father. He used to say that Jesus Christ delighted in dwelling there among the children of men, as in the bosom of Him who is their common father. He looked upon church buildings as a true paradise in which is found all the glory of God, *caelum in angustum redactum.*[9] He never entered the church except with fear, and he would hesitate at the door of the sanctuary. His reflections on the humiliation of our Lord in the Blessed Sacrament of the altar and on his own sins would make him shudder in the presence of the divine majesty. The disrespectful behavior of many Catholics in the holy place caused him a great deal of suffering. He could never witness without grief and resentment the useless conversations and unworthy conduct common among people of the world. He would confront such profaners of the temple with a stern countenance, addressing these words to them: "How terrible is this place!"[10] In *The Kingdom of Jesus* he included a treatise on the honor and veneration due to churches.[11] His zeal still unsatisfied, he said a great deal more on the subject in several other of his books.

St. John Eudes never spoke more eloquently than when it was a question of crying out against irreverences committed in the house of God. During the time of a mission that was being given in the diocese of Coutances, a nobleman had badly beaten a peasant in church. Thereupon St. John Eudes prophesied from the pulpit that God would take vengeance on that crime before the year had passed. It happened just as he predicted; the nobleman was killed some time later, and all the inhabitants of the district, filled with greater esteem for the prophetic missionary, henceforth entered the church with fear of the holy place, after witnessing the punishment that divine justice deals out to those who profane it. Thus they made the same confession as Heliodorus of old, one of the chief officers of King Seleucus.[12] Seeking to violate the temple of Jerusalem, Heliodorus was thrown to the ground and stricken by two angels.

In order to impress upon the faithful their duty to respect the temple of God, St. John Eudes had notices printed regarding the way one should behave in church. It was his desire that these rules be posted on the doors, in a place where they could easily be read by everyone. He could not tolerate seeing children playing in church. He opposed the entrance of women into the sanctuary,[13] particularly giving them seats reserved for priests. In this matter he was following the laws of several councils that forbade this practice under pain of very severe penalties.

Likewise, St. John Eudes wanted marked respect to be shown cemeteries and sacristies as places sanctified by the episcopal blessing, the relics of the saints and the prayers offered there. In short, he was the faithful servant in his Master's house, who made every effort to see that it was honored. He opposed, through the spirit of religion, and as much as he could with prudence, the vanity of benefactors who wanted their personal shields, arms and heraldry engraved on the tabernacles, ciboria, chalices, decorations, seats and walls of the churches. This vanity he compared to that of the Pharisees who boasted everywhere of the good that they were doing. An aristocrat once offered to pay the expenses of building a church for the seminary at Caen on condition that he would be allowed to display his coat of arms in it. St. John Eudes refused unequivocally and vowed never to accept anything for the construction or decoration of the church on such a condition. He believed that God looked unfavorably upon offerings made Him for publicity's sake, and he deemed that such actions robbed Christ of a portion of an offering sacrificed to Him.

The zeal of St. John Eudes for the Church developed very deep veneration for all the sacraments, which to him were admirable instruments of the power, wisdom and goodness of the eternal Father by which He forms and causes Jesus Christ, His Son, to live in Christians. Through the sacraments the Holy Spirit of God strengthens, perfects and sanctifies souls, according to St. Peter, the prince of the apostles.[14] St. John Eudes regarded the sacraments as divinely instituted to extend the ranks and broaden the empire of Christ the King in order to effect its perfect consummation in each soul. The Saint described the sacraments as fountains of the Saviour to which those who aspire to salvation may come to draw with joy the waters of grace; the instruments by which the fruits of His life and death are applied; the treasures of the house of God which contain an infinity of riches hidden from the wise and prudent of this generation but revealed to the meek and humble; the sacred vessels in which Holy Mother Church preserves the Precious Blood, the divine spirit and the holy grace of her Spouse, that she may nourish, sanctify and beautify her children. He tried to foster this attitude in the minds and hearts of all the faithful.[15]

It was for that reason, on his missions and elsewhere, that he strove particularly to show Christians the dignity of the sacraments in their original source, which is the goodness and mercy of God; in their secondary source, the Passion and Death of Jesus Christ; in their effects, which are the fulfillment of the sufferings of the Saviour, the destruction of sin and the establishment of the reign of God. He stressed the dispositions of body and soul which the individual should have in order to receive the sacraments well, as also the various ways in which one may profane them, so that all might learn to avoid these profanations.

The example of St. John Eudes inspired even greater respect than his words. He treated the sacraments with singular devotion. He was careful that the objects used to administer them were always very clean, and whenever he conferred a sacrament, he would act with such exact deference that he greatly edified those assisting him. From this we may judge that he belonged to the ranks of those blessed and faithful dispensers of the sacraments of whom St. Paul speaks: ". . . here now it is required among the dispensers that a man be found faithful."[16] Since priests are in charge of the finances of the King of kings, they must acquit themselves so well in their task that they all have hopes of one day being abundantly rewarded for it, since our Lord, in the holy Gospel, promises a rich reward to those who have been faithful in little things.[17]

NOTES

[1] The virtue of religion is a moral virtue by which we render to God due honor and worship. It is a moral virtue because acts of religion do not have, as their direct object, God, but rather the reverence which is due to Him. The various acts of worship which man is capable of offering to God are prayer, sacrifice, adoration, vows and oaths.

[2] St. Thomas Aquinas, *Contra Gentiles,* part 3, q. 96.

[3] Arnobius (c. 225–327), a Christian apologist, who flourished in the third century. He wrote an apologetic work in seven books that St. Jerome calls (*De vir. ill.,* 79) *Adversus gentes.* In the only ninth century manuscript that has reached us, it is entitled *Adversus nationes.* Arnobius was a vigorous apologist for the Christian faith, but he was more earnest in his defense of Christianity than correct in his tenets. Father Herambourg's reference is to *Adversus gentes,* l. 7, n. 51; P.L. 5:1288.

[4] Salvianus was a Latin writer of Gaul, who lived in the 5th century. His two important treatises are *Ad ecclesiam adversus avaritiam* and *De gubernatione Dei* or *De praesenti judicio.* The reference here is to *Adversus avaritiam,* l. 2, n. 9; P.L. 53:199.

[5] 1 Tim. 3:15.

[6] Ps. 68:10; Jn. 2:17.

[7] See Eudes, *The Priest,* p. 6.

[8] *Oeuvres Complètes,* vol. 2, p. 9. "Traité de l'honneur dû aux lieux saints."

[9] This phrase is substantially the same as the sentence from St. Jerome: *caeli nomine significare Ecclesiam noverimus in qua caelorum mysteria celebrantur. In Job,* chapter 25: P.L. 26:689.

[10] Gen. 28:17.

[11] See note 8 above. When editing *The Kingdom of Jesus* in 1648, St. John Eudes included this short work on the respect that we ought to have for churches. The treatise is omitted in all modern editions of *The Kingdom of Jesus* and is published apart by the editors of the *Oeuvres Complètes* in vol. 2, p. 9.

[12] 2 Mach. 3:7–30.

[13] This abuse, unheard of today, was common in Catholic countries in the seventeenth century. See Eudes, *ibid.,* pp. 20, 21.

[14] 1 Pet. 5:10.

[15] Eudes, *The Priest,* pp. 43–44.

[16] 1 Cor. 4:2.

[17] Mt. 25:21–23.

Chapter 18. The Divine Office

THE RECITATION of the Divine Office is, after the celebration of Holy Mass, the greatest and most important action that a priest has to perform.[1] It is the most worthy occupation in heaven and on earth, the unending chant of praise of the angels and saints. It is, therefore, of paramount importance that all priests reflect frequently on the dignity of their vocation, which renders them, in a certain sense, participants in the blessed life of the heavenly host, as St. Basil says in a letter to St. Gregory Nazianzen: "What is more blessed than for man to imitate on earth the choirs of the angels in heaven and to pay homage to the Creator in hymns and canticles."[2]

St. John Eudes was assigned to this function of the Divine Office by his state in life. Knowing its merits and excellence, he made the recitation of the breviary a major occupation. No sooner had he received the subdeaconate than he applied all his attention and devotion to the perfect fulfillment of this duty. He asked God most earnestly for the necessary graces and had others pray for the same intention. His prayers were indeed heard. It may be said that he became a perfect adorer of the heavenly Father in spirit and in truth, as God desires and as Jesus Christ asks of us in the Gospel.[3]

The Saint was admirably disposed for the fervent recitation of his breviary by his lofty ideas on the excellence and holiness of the Divine Office, which he recorded for posterity in the beautiful book[4] that he composed on the subject. He never recited the Office without first making a thorough preparation. Following the advice of Ecclesiasticus,[5] he would carefully prepare his soul, devising several practices[6] which he used alternately.

First, he humbled himself profoundly at the sight of his nothingness and his sins. He recognized, even as the Patriarch Abraham, that he was but ashes and dust when speaking to the Lord.[7] Like David he confessed that his faults rendered him unworthy of being heard by the most high God.[8] He had learned from Sacred Scripture that praise is not well received by God when it comes from the tongue of a sinner.[9] Wishing to avoid the terrible reproach which divine justice makes to the guilty, "How darest thou sing my praises with thy heart soiled with crimes?"[10] he swept away, like the Psalmist, all the dross that could spoil his inward beauty.[11] He purified his soul by acts of contrition and drove far from his mind all things that could distract him.

Next St. John Eudes reflected seriously on his reasons for praising the Creator. The grandeur of the Divine Being, the excellence of God's perfections, the extent of His mercy, the exactitude of His justice, the dignity of His operations and the number of His works were divine motives that prompted him to offer to God the sacrifice of his lips. This he did all the more gladly because he saw himself charged, in his capacity of priest, with the obligation shared alike by all creatures to bless their Author. It was his conviction that, since the Lord is infinitely great and infinitely worthy of praise, as the Psalmist sings,[12] since a priest represents all mankind in his person, just as the High Priest of the Old Testament represented the twelve tribes of Israel, he was responsible for the failings of mankind, for which he himself would be punished if he failed to make reparation. He therefore felt impelled to discharge this obligation of the Divine Office so conscientiously that he would invite the whole world to unite with him, and he would make all the effort necessary to correspond with the duty as he should.

His third practice was to recall that he was going to present himself before the same God who inspires fear and trembling in the powers of heaven, who keeps the minds of the angels and saints continually absorbed, and fills Jesus Christ Himself with a profound respect at the sight of His glory. This thought prompted the Saint to discipline his inward and outward person, to keep them both in a state that proclaimed his complete detachment from all the things in the world and absorption in those of heaven. Like the Psalmist, his lips were filled with praise for the Creator,[13] and he was always seeking occasions and places to recite the Divine Office with unhurried dignity, attentively and without distraction, distinctly and without omission, faithfully observing even the smallest ceremony prescribed by the Church. His mind and heart were admirably elevated and completely detached from external objects which intrude themselves at every moment. He placed no reliance on his own personal dispositions, but humbling and offering himself at the feet of Jesus Christ, he would request our Lord to recite the Divine Office for him.

St. John Eudes was convinced that nothing is pleasing to God unless it is offered through His well-beloved Son, that it is necessary for man to clothe himself with the garments, that is, the intentions of Christ, the Elder Brother, in order to be heard favorably by the heavenly Father.

As a fourth exercise he would give himself to the zeal, love and holy dispositions with which the Word Incarnate incessantly praises the all-glorious Trinity in heaven through Himself and His saints; on earth through the Blessed Sacrament, and through the co-operation of righteous souls; and throughout the whole universe which, as the Church sings, is filled with the glory of the Most High: "Heaven and earth are full of Thy glory."[14] During the recitation of the Divine Office he would renew these acts, and realizing that he must always pray in union with Jesus Christ, he would exalt the majesty of the Father through the benedictions of the Son, meditating on His grandeur and marvellous perfections.

We must explain, however, that the particular inclination of St. John Eudes in all his exercises was to honor the Word Incarnate, the divine focus of his thoughts.[15] He made it a practice to glorify the Son of God, especially in the mystery of His Incarnation. He set forth the life of Christ according to the different parts of the Divine Office. The first nocturn of Matins he offered to honor the divine life of the Son of God in the bosom of the Father from all eternity, before the creation; the second nocturn was in honor of His life in the world before the Incarnation; the third nocturn honored His life for nine months in the womb of the Blessed Mother. Lauds was recited for the glory of the Holy Childhood up to the age of twelve years; Prime, for the glory of His hidden life as a carpenter; Tierce, for the glory of His public life of preaching. The Saint would say Sext in memory of the passion, death and burial; None, in memory of His resurrection, ascension and glorious life in heaven since the Redemption; Vespers, in memory of the state in which He has remained on earth since the ascension, in the Holy Eucharist and in His Church; Compline in honor of His universal empire in heaven, or earth, in purgatory and in hell, and of all that He is and will ever be toward God and His creatures.

Thus in each part of the Divine Office St. John Eudes would consider the mystery of Christ's life that he wished to honor. He would meditate on the thoughts, feelings and dispositions of Christ in that particular phase of his life and on the union of the Son of God with the Eternal Father, the Holy Spirit, His Blessed Mother, the angels and saints; on the love of God the Father for Jesus in this mystery; the sorrow and joy that He experienced and the blessings that He wished to bestow upon us. Next he reflected on the lack of conformity between his life as a member of the Mystical Body and that of its Head, and he would humble himself profoundly, asking pardon, abandoning himself to all the designs of grace, praying earnestly for the total destruction of whatever could hinder him. He would also unite himself with the sum-total of praise rendered to our Lord during that portion of his life, wishing to be wholly transformed into homage for the increase of His glory.

Another method[16] of reciting the Divine Office which the Saint sometimes used was to dedicate each psalm and lesson in honor of our Lord. Considering the holiness of the dispositions with which the well-beloved Son of God is praised in heaven and on earth, he would say the first psalm in union with the honor that the eternal Father bestows upon His divine Son made man and with all the love that the Father bears to the Son; the second, in union with the honor the Son renders Himself; the third, with that which the Son receives from the Holy Spirit; the fourth, with that which the Blessed Virgin offers Him; and so on with the others, uniting himself at every psalm to the blessings given Christ by each individual order of angels and all the blessed in heaven, the faithful in the Church, the holy souls in purgatory and all created beings in the universe. He would present this honor and love to Jesus Christ in fulfillment of his obligation to praise Him during his lifetime, to atone for his personal sins, as well as to make reparation for the abuse heaped upon our Saviour and the terrible sins committed against His goodness.

St. John Eudes devised so many methods of meditation while reciting the Divine Office that he became an authority on the subject: witness his book on *The Divine Office* already mentioned.[17] Wishing to instruct others, he explained the various dispositions of his soul during the period of the fifty-six years that he used these methods. No matter how conscientiously he strove to recite the Office fittingly, he never finished without offering it to the Sacred Heart of Jesus,[18] in which he hoped to find reparation for any negligence of which he had been guilty in this holy exercise.

St. John Eudes recommended further that the Divine Office be recited holily, outwardly as well as inwardly, never in public places unless absolutely necessary, and that the whole act be carried out without carelessness or haste. He frequently wrote to that effect to his spiritual sons. In a letter to them he said: "I beseech you above all things to see that those exercises which directly concern God, such as the Holy Sacrifice of the Mass, the Divine Office, morning and night prayers, the *Benedicite* and thanksgiving after meals, are never performed in haste, under any pretext whatsoever, but carefully, distinctly and devoutly."[19] He energetically denounced the irreligion of priests who celebrated the Divine Office with so little reverence that from their chanting one might believe that they were engaged in mocking God and causing others to dishonor Him.

It was the wish of the Saint that the entire ritual of the

breviary be strictly observed, even the least ceremony. He knew from the pronouncements of the Church councils that the ceremonies are the images of our faith, the spurs of our piety, the signs and symbols of our religion. He recalled that under the Old Law, which was but a figure of ours, God had commanded many ceremonies, using dire threats to keep them intact and punishing most severely those who would not submit.[20] He was always mindful of the fact that St. Charles Borromeo[21] had never allowed any detail of the Divine Office to be omitted, no matter what the time or place, regardless of the ruggedness of the mountain country through which he had to travel while making his diocesan visitations, the type of persons with whom he found himself, or the weariness resulting from the many difficult labors he had undertaken during the day. All these considerations moved St. John Eudes to be faithful to each observance, and we may say that he did not disregard a single iota of the church ceremonies that he had to perform.

St. John Eudes was convinced that the chanting of the Divine Office is a sacrifice of praise which we offer to God, who is present at the Holy Office that we sing in the company of the angels. He insisted that the use of chant was inspired in the Church by the Holy Spirit in order to attract people, to make stronger impressions on their hearts, and to impart feelings of devotion in order to dispose them to receive His graces. Therefore he always wished to have as much singing as possible, in conformity with the intentions of the Church, but he did his best to avoid all chant and music prompted by self-love and vanity to please worldlings. It was his desire that the singing be plain and simple, performed with the pure intention of pleasing God alone and not others, with attention paid more to the words being sung than to the satisfaction of singing, as St. Bonaventure counsels: "Seeking, above all, what glorifies God better and what is more beneficial to ourselves and our neighbor."[22]

Such were the sentiments which the spirit of God implanted in the mind of St. John Eudes with regard to the Divine Office. The virtue of religion, in which he excelled, inspired his lofty ideas about the infinite majesty of God and gave him a singular respect and devotion for everything associated with divine worship. It endowed him, furthermore, with the dispositions of the angels in exercising the function of praising God performed by them throughout eternity.

NOTES

1 See *The Kingdom of Jesus,* p. 175.

2 St. Basil, *Letters,* P.G. 32:225.

3 Jn. 4:24.

4 This book, *The Divine Office,* was left in manuscript form by St. John Eudes. It was lost at the time of the French Revolution. See *Oeuvres Complètes,* vol. 1, p. xii.

5 Ecclus. 18:23.

6 Eudes, *The Kingdom of Jesus,* p. 176.

7 Gen. 18:27.

8 Ps. 50. This is the theme of the penitential psalms.

9 Ecclus. 15:9.

10 Ps. 49:16–17; Isa. 29:13–16.

11 Ps. 76:7.

12 Ps. 95:4.

13 Ps. 70:8.

14 From the *Sanctus* of the Mass.

15 Eudes, *ibid.,* p. 176.

16 *Ibid.,* p. 178.

17 See note 4 above.

18 Eudes, *The Sacred Heart of Jesus,* p. 178.

19 Eudes, *Letters and Shorter Works,* p. 61.

20 Lev. 14; 26:18.

21 St. Charles Borromeo (1538–1584) inspired St. Vincent de Paul, Venerable Father Olier and St. John Eudes to establish seminaries and to introduce into the priestly life in France the regular devotional exercises that he used in his diocese of Milan. St. John Eudes cultivated a special devotion to St. Charles. In reference to St. Charles and the recitation of the divine office, see John Peter Giussano, *Life of St. Charles Borromeo*

(London, Burns & Oates, 1884), vol. 1, p. 90; vol. 2, pp. 292, 310; Cesar Orsenigo, *Life of St. Charles Borromeo* (St. Louis, B. Herder, 1943), p. 323.

[22] This text attributed to St. Bonaventure is from *Stimulus amoris*, part 2, chapter 7. The author of this work is another Franciscan, James of Milan, who wrote it towards the end of the 13th century. The text as found in the works of St. Bonaventure, *Opuscula* (Paris, 1647), vol. 2, p. 223, is as follows: *In omnibus quaeras facere quod sit magis honorificum Deo, conformare Christo, utile tibi et proximo.*

Chapter 19. The Holy Sacrifice of the Mass

THERE IS NOTHING greater and more excellent in the world than the Holy Sacrifice of the Mass. The Mass is the most sublime of our mysteries and the Holy Eucharist the most admirable of our sacraments. Holy Mass is the most important action in the universe, embodying all the interests of the glory of God and the salvation of souls. It is the masterpiece of the power of the eternal Father, of the wisdom of the Word Incarnate and of the goodness of the Holy Spirit. It is the extension of the mystery of the Incarnation, the continuation of the mystery of the Cross, the renewal of the Passion and Death of the Saviour. It is the joy of heaven, the treasure of earth, the consolation of purgatory and the terror of hell.

St. John Eudes wrote an admirable book on the all-important subject of the Mass.[1] We shall merely note certain details, demonstrating the extent of his devotion to this supreme act of religion. One of the divine favors he besought most earnestly was to be able to offer Holy Mass every day of his life. How different he was from priests who, appearing most fervent when they first celebrate the Holy Sacrifice, gradually allow their ardor to cool. Whether he was suffering from troublesome illness, undertaking difficult journeys or transacting a heavy volume of business, he was rarely prevented from offering the Holy Sacrifice. He was convinced that there was too much of the glory of God, usefulness to the Church and personal spiritual benefit involved in this duty to neglect it. He declared that the Holy Sacrifice was something so great that three eternities would be necessary to offer it worthily: the first, to prepare for it; the second, to celebrate it; and the third, to render adequate thanksgiving.[2] He looked upon this act as the most important of any that he had to perform; he never undertook to celebrate without making careful preparation, and afterwards offering a most humble thanksgiving. He would do both in the sanctuary for the edification of the faithful, and with so much recollection that those present were themselves deeply moved to devotion.

Knowing full well the purity of the divine Victim that the priest offers at the holy altar, he also realized that the hands which present it must be without stain, and the heart that receives it without blemish. That is why, before saying or hearing Mass, he would make in the presence of the angels and saints, an inward confession of all the sins of his life, the sight of which overwhelmed him with shame. In the Garden of Olives, before offering the sacrifice of His lifeblood to the eternal Father, Jesus Christ assumed the burden of the crimes of all mankind, and in this St. John Eudes strove daily to imitate Him, begging pardon for his past sins. In addition, he would take time to meditate on the greatness of the action he was about to perform, to thank God for divine permission to present the Sacred Victim to Him. He would declare that he neither desired nor sought anything save the glory of God, and would give himself to the three divine Persons, beseeching Them to annihilate in him whatever was displeasing to Them and to grant him the virtues he needed. Lastly, he would surrender himself completely to our Lord, entering as much as possible into the sentiments of our Saviour on the tree of the Cross.

Here is the method that St. John Eudes followed in saying Holy Mass.[3] He offered it first in honor of the most august Trinity, in honor of what Jesus Christ is in Himself, in His various states, mysteries, virtues, actions and sufferings, and in honor of all that He is and all that He does, whether through mercy or justice, in His holy Mother, His angels, His Church Militant, Triumphant and Suffering and, in general, in all the creatures of heaven, earth and hell. Secondly, he celebrated Mass in thanksgiving to God for the temporal and eternal blessings that He had bestowed upon the sacred humanity of His divine Word, upon the Blessed Virgin Mary, the angels, mankind and all creatures, and particularly upon himself. Thirdly, he aimed to satisfy divine justice for his own sins, for those of the whole world and especially for those of the suffering souls in purgatory. Fourthly, he offered Mass to fulfill God's plan for him and for others; and fifthly, he begged God for the graces needed by him and by all mankind, so that each one might serve and honor the heavenly Father according to the perfection that He requires.

These things he did as a priest. In his capacity as host he used to offer himself with Jesus Christ as a victim.[4] He would implore the all-lovable Saviour to come within his soul or to draw him near to His Sacred Heart in order to sacrifice him to the glory of His Father. As the immolation of the victim is required for perfection of a sacrifice, he would implore Christ to let him die to himself, to his passions and his self-love, to consume him in the sacred fire of divine love throughout his whole life. He would strive toward this end, to enter into the dispositions of our Lord offering Himself on the Cross, and continuing to offer Himself daily upon our altars. He would cast himself at the feet of the Queen of Heaven, of all holy priests and all the blessed, that he might share in the sentiments with which they perpetually offer the God-Man in paradise to His eternal Father. It was his desire to possess the fervor of the angels themselves. He would have liked to be a seraph, filled with love for our divine Saviour.

At the altar, the whole interior preoccupation of St. John Eudes consisted in praying earnestly to our Lord that, just as He changed the lowly and earthly nature of bread and wine into His Body and Blood, He would also change and transform any apathy, coldness or indifference of His servant, Eudes, into the ardor, tenderness and lively affection of the Sacred Heart. The Saint inspired many people to follow the same practice. He used to say that Christians, being united with Jesus Christ as members with their Head, should share in His qualities of priest and victim; that as priests, in their own way, they should offer with Him the same sacrifice, but as victims, they must be immolated with Him, too, for the glory of the eternal Father.

It is difficult for us to realize the extent of the fervor of St. John Eudes at Holy Mass. It was then his desire to become all inflamed with love. The most fitting symbol of his devotion is the burning bush of Moses, on fire but never consumed because the majesty of the Lord was present to preserve it.[5] Then would his heart heap fuel upon its flames, as we may note from the words preserved in his own handwriting with regard to participation in this divine mystery. They are like arrows flying from his soul, capable of making an impression even on hard hearts.

"O Abyss of love," he wrote, "O infinite Bounty, O immense Charity, why am I not all love for Thee! O most beloved, most loving and most lovable Jesus, when shall I love Thee perfectly? O, who will grant that all the parts of my body and soul be changed into the hearts of seraphim? O, who will grant me this blessing, to be completely transformed into a blazing fire and pure flame of love for Thy sake? O angels, O saints of paradise, grant me your love, that I may use it to love my Jesus! O men, O creatures capable of loving, grant me your hearts, all of you, that I may sacrifice them to my Saviour!

"O most sweet Saviour, would that it were possible to have within myself all the love of heaven and earth! O, how very gladly would I offer it all to Thee! O Beloved of the Eternal Father, O Treasure and Delight of heaven and earth, in what manner art Thou now adored, loved and glorified on this altar by millions of angels who surround Thee on all sides? O, in what manner shouldst Thou be revered, praised and loved by men, since it is not for the sake of the angels but for the love of mankind that Thou art present here? Ah, let all angels and men, all creatures of heaven and earth, be transformed into adoration, praise and love of Thee!"[6]

Such were the interior dispositions of St. John Eudes during the Holy Sacrifice of the Mass. He recommended them most urgently to all his spiritual sons. "Above all, I implore each of our dearest brethren," he wrote to them, "to say Mass with careful attention of mind and heart to such a great and divine mystery, never to be in haste and to pronounce distinctly every word he says at the altar."[7] He was indeed right, for God is displeased with the priest who performs his duties carelessly, as the Prophet Jeremias records.[8] A priest celebrating Holy Mass has everything to fear if he does so without due respect and devotion, since it is God's supreme achievement.

After Mass, the Saint used to kneel at the feet of our Lord, whom he bore within his breast, in order to pay homage to Him. Then only adoration, praise, thanksgiving and love existed in the sanctuary. Knowing that during these happy moments when Jesus Christ was dwelling in him, His Eucharistic Lord was accomplishing in His Father's regard what He does in heaven and on our altars, the Saint would unite himself with the divine dispositions and implore once again to be immolated with Him for the glory of the most Blessed Trinity. He would offer himself eagerly to suffer all the privations and sacrifices necessary for the accomplishment of that end, asking Christ to use His power to separate Eudes from himself and from whatever was not God, to annihilate in him the old Adam and to clothe him with divine desires.

A practice that St. John Eudes recommended to many other priests, for whom he tried to obtain the same graces as for himself, was to recite after Mass a salutation that he composed in honor of the Divine Heart of Jesus and of the most Pure Heart of Mary, beginning with the words: "Hail, Hearts most holy."[9] At the same time he would beseech our Lord to imprint on him a perfect likeness of the holiness and the other virtues contained in His Heart and mentioned in this salutation, and to destroy completely in him whatever might hinder it. In much the same sentiments he would say the prayer of St. Augustine: "Soul of Christ, sanctify me." He made a devout paraphrase of it, which he used to recite after Mass.[10]

It is true that St. John Eudes continued to experience the same love the whole time that he possessed within himself our glorious Saviour as he did during the celebration of Holy Mass. At thanksgiving he was heard to pronounce ardent words of love, giving ample evidence of the great fire that burned in his soul: "O most sweet Jesus, dearest, most desirable, most lovable Jesus! O sole desire of my heart, O object of my love, O my dear soul, my dearest heart, my treasure and my glory, all my happiness and my only hope! I love Thee, O most loving Jesus, I love Thee, O infinite Bounty! I love Thee with my whole heart, with my whole soul, and with all my strength, and I wish to love Thee ever more and more!" By his heart, his soul and his strength he meant the heart and soul of Jesus Christ, all the powers of the divinity and humanity of our Lord that were in him and belonged to him through Holy Communion and were his to use.

We have learned from one of his spiritual sons, to whom he sometimes revealed his interior dispositions and devotional practices, that he would recite in thanksgiving this invocation in psalm 102: "Bless the Lord, O my soul: and let all that is within me bless His holy name,"[11] which he would say after each verse of the *Magnificat*, which he made the canticle of his gratitude, just as it was that of the Blessed Virgin Mary with whom he was so closely united. The words, "my soul and all that is in me," the Saint interpreted to mean Jesus Christ, the Son of God, who is the praise of the eternal Father, and the most Blessed Trinity which had taken possession of Him. Finally, he would conclude with a "Hail Mary" for the intention of uniting himself with everybody at that moment on pilgrimage to shrines consecrated to the Mother of God, that he might share in their good works and he besought the Mother of goodness to grant the requests of all who had recourse to her if they were for the greater glory of God and the accomplishment of their salvation.

St. John Eudes taught these practices to souls under his spiritual guidance, whom he invited to assist frequently at our holy mysteries. He wanted them to receive Holy Communion daily or at least to make a spiritual Communion, in order to satisfy the ardent desire of Jesus Christ to dwell in the hearts of men and give Himself to them. He gave this direction particularly to persons whose interior life he knew well, as his letters show. For example, he wrote to a lady[12] who was afraid to approach the Blessed Sacrament because she did not feel sensible devotion. "Rejoice, dearest sister," he told her, "and have no fear of receiving Communion as usual, for every soul clothed with divine grace is always prepared for Holy Communion, even though the senses may not be garbed in the beautiful garment of devout feelings and divine consolations, but remain instead in great dryness and poverty of devotion."[13] He used to call this lady his eldest daughter. Her daily food was the Bread of heaven because she understood so well how to profit by it.

If St. John Eudes exhorted the faithful to frequent Communion, he was also most willing to be available for its administration. He would give Holy Communion in union with the infinite charity with which the eternal Father sent His divine Son to men. He would also unite himself to the boundless love with which the Son of God gave Himself to us, with which the Holy Spirit formed Him in the womb of the Blessed Virgin Mary and with which that same Virgin Mother offered Him so often in sacrifice for love of them during her life on earth. Sometimes he would unite himself with the devotion and sanctity with which the glorious Apostles and so many holy priests have administered this divine Sacrament. Again, while giving Holy Communion to any person he would ask our Lord to accept, as a preparation for the recipient and in satisfaction for his sins, the infinite love of the eternal Father for the Son and God's own love for Himself, or else the purity of our Lady, the ardor of the seraphim or the merits of all the saints in heaven and on earth.[14]

St. John Eudes had profound esteem for the duty of serving Holy Mass. He used to say that to serve Mass was to perform the office of the Mother of God, of St. Joseph and of St. Gabriel, all of whom rendered so many services to Jesus Christ on earth.

The Saint served Mass as often as possible, and always with inviolable fidelity to the ceremonial of the Church, profound recollection—an obvious sign of his faith—deep humility at the thought of his unworthiness, and intimate union with the devotion of St. Thomas, St. Bonaventure and other great saints in performing this action. Like these saints he had extreme horror of whatever might displease God, overwhelming desire to be associated with the praise and adoration of all the angels present and particularly his own guardian angel, immense gratitude for all that our Lord was accomplishing for him at the altar, and a sincere resolution to live no longer for himself but entirely for Him from whom he received so many favors. Before serving Holy Mass, the Saint would put on the surplice which is the distinctive garb of clerics. He knew that the wedding garment was an adornment necessary for any one seeking to enter the banquet hall and seat himself at the King's table.[15] Keeping always in mind that he was acting as the representative of our Lord Jesus Christ, the New Man, whom the Christian and especially the priest, should put on, he usually knelt to don his surplice and said these words: "May the Lord put on me the new man, who according to God is created in justice and holiness of truth."[16] He instructed all his priests and seminarians to carry out the same practice.

St. John Eudes frequently counseled his missionaries to teach children to serve and answer Holy Mass well, and to instruct them in the external ceremonies and interior dispositions, thereby impressing on their minds a great esteem for this act. He wanted all schoolteachers and fathers of families to do the same.

Jesus Christ in the Blessed Sacrament of the altar chose

St. John Eudes to be the faithful servant and perfect adorer of His hidden majesty. Through him almighty God procured other priests who increased the glory of our Eucharistic Lord by their holiness and zeal in the midst of dreadful profanations endured by our Saviour in this Sacrament that He established to show His love for us and to win our love in return.

NOTES

[1] The book, entitled *The Admirable Sacrifice of Holy Mass,* was among the unpublished manuscripts lost during the French Revolution. See *Oeuvres Complètes,* vol. 1, p. XII. Also *The Priest,* p. v, footnote 2.

[2] This is quoted by all biographers of St. John Eudes. See Henri Joly, *A Life of Saint John Eudes,* p. 28.

[3] See Eudes, *The Kingdom of Jesus,* p. 166.

[4] *Ibid., loc. cit.*

[5] Exod. 3:3.

[6] *Ibid.,* p. 169.

[7] Eudes, *Letters and Shorter Works,* p. 276.

[8] Jer. 48:10.

[9] See Eudes, *The Sacred Heart of Jesus,* p. 173.

[10] See Eudes, *The Admirable Heart of Mary,* p. 27. Also *Oeuvres Complètes,* vol. 6, p. 109.

[11] Ps. 102:1.

[12] Anne Le Haguais, who married James Blouet, Lord of Camilly, was an intimate friend and benefactress of St. John Eudes. For many years Madame de Camilly was under the Saint's spiritual guidance. She frequently assisted him in his projects with her wealth and influence, especially when the Saint undertook the founding of his two religious societies. See Eudes, *Letters and Shorter Works,* p. 29, footnote 2.

[13] *Ibid.,* p. 33. It is obvious from the advice given in this letter that St. John Eudes encouraged frequent and daily Communion at a time when the Jansenists were keeping Catholics away from it by exacting too rigid a preparation and a purity of conscience and perfection of life unattainable by many Christians. It was about this time, 1643, that the Jansenist Antoine Arnauld published his book on "Frequent Communion."

[14] See Eudes, *The Priest,* p. 48.

[15] Mt. 22:11–12.

[16] Eph. 4:24.

Chapter 20. Prayer

PRAYER IS A participation in the lives of the angels and the saints. It is the unending pursuit of Jesus Christ, the Son of God made man, who does nothing else throughout eternity except contemplate and love the Blessed Trinity.[1] Prayer is compared to the burning bush in which Moses discovered the secrets of divine love.[2] It is Mount Sinai where the Prophet conversed intimately with God.[3] It is that mysterious night when the patriarch Jacob learned of the angelic ladder that unites heaven and earth.[4]

For St. John Eudes prayer was considered the supreme happiness of the Christian life. "A thousand years of worldly pleasure," he declared, "are not worth a moment of the delights that God communicates to a soul who seeks happiness in conversation with Him in prayer. Through this holy practice the soul possesses God and is possessed by Him; it renders Him homage, adoration and love, and from Him it receives enlightenment, blessings and a thousand proofs of His bounty. God is pleased by such a soul, just as the soul finds happiness in Him."[5]

St. John Eudes used to exhort everyone most diligently to pray, quoting the invitation that Sacred Scripture applies to wisdom: "Her conversation hath no bitterness, nor her company any tediousness, but joy and gladness."[6] The Saint considered prayer to be more necessary for the soul than the air that we breathe, the food that we eat and the heart that beats in our breast are for our bodily life.[7] What he said one day to a group of priests might well be applied to Christians in general: "If you seek to know the meaning of piety and to possess it, practice mental prayer; then you will soon understand it well and acquire it. But as long as you do not know from experience what mental prayer is, you will not understand true piety and you will never be fitted to perform priestly functions, the aim of which is to destroy sin and establish virtue in souls."[8]

The Saint regarded prayer as the first, the principal, the most necessary, the most urgent and important of all his affairs. He would set aside other occupations as much as duty and prudence permitted, in order to give more time to prayer; he made it the one necessary thing, thereby choosing the better part. Rarely has a priest been able to accomplish so much active ministry, and yet spend so much time in prayer, thus effectively linking action with contemplation. Rarely has an apostolic preacher had so much intercourse with God and men. The moment he finished the day's work of service toward his fellow men, he would take his place before his crucifix to study that all-divine book, to learn the laws of truth and educate himself in the maxims of true wisdom. He never made any resolution before discussing the problem at length with our Lord and His most Holy Mother. He always hoped to obtain through prayer what his unworthiness might otherwise have denied him. He knew that our Saviour's word is pledged: "Ask and it shall be given you."[9] In St. Mark our Lord assures us of the divine promise that "all things whatsoever you ask when ye pray, believe that you shall receive: and they shall come unto you."[10]

If divine bounty was sometimes slow to grant a request, St. John Eudes would say that the delay was meant to keep him a little longer in humiliation and self-contempt, as well as in high esteem of the graces that God wished to grant him. His life includes countless instances to show how God favored him with enlightenment in the exercise of prayer, especially when it was devoted to the good of his neighbor. Among other examples was that of a young woman who contemplated embracing the religious life, but spent more than two years without being able to make up her mind because of the repugnance she felt toward such an isolated and dependent existence. Finally she appealed to St. John Eudes in an effort to determine, through him, the will of God concerning her vocation. He promised to pray for her, and when she returned for a reply, he told her with firmness and confidence that she was to become a religious of Our Lady of Charity, that our Lord wished to see her in this state, and that she should no longer delay in carrying out His plans. This assurance strengthened her resolution, and she never again felt a distaste for the religious life.

The Saint emphasized repeatedly that the members of his Congregation should devote themselves attentively to meditation, a practice to which he remained faithful despite his activities. The clerics who entered his seminaries were advised to be most diligent in the practice of prayer, allotting a reasonable amount of time to it each day. It once happened that the Bishop of a diocese[11] where one of his seminaries was located ruled absolutely that the candidates for ordination should spend only half an hour a day in prayer. This mandate caused great concern to the Saint and prompted him to write to the superior of that seminary: "Without prayer, my dearest brother, it is impossible for a Congregation to subsist in the spirit of piety and virtue so necessary for it to be pleasing to God and useful to the Church. To make only a half hour of mental prayer is practically like making none at all. Yet there is nothing of greater importance to priests than prayer. But if the authorities are absolutely set on limiting the seminarians to half an hour, please arrange so that the community can always make a full hour of prayer. Otherwise it would be better for us to give up the seminary."[12] That is how he wrote to avoid cutting short a time which he believed to be the most usefully spent of the whole day; eventually he had to give in to the regulations that were made. The candidates for ordination were allowed to apply themselves to meditation only a half hour each day, while the priests of the seminary continued their laudable custom of devoting an hour every morning to this holy exercise.

St. John Eudes opened his meditation with an act of self-annihilation at the feet of the divine majesty, acknowledging himself to be unworthy of appearing in the presence of God. He would renounce all intellectual curiosity and self-satisfaction in order to seek only the establishment of the reign of God in his soul. He would abandon himself to God that He might possess him and guide him along the paths of prayer according to His most holy will. He would try to enter into the dispositions of Jesus Christ who is perpetually absorbed in the eternal Father. Since Jesus alone is worthy to appear before the eternal Father, the Saint would beg Jesus with humility to establish Himself within him and pray there in his stead. To obtain this grace he would also appeal to the most Blessed Virgin, the angels and the saints.

His surrender to God in union with Jesus Christ sometimes occupied his mind during the whole time that he prayed.

The usual topics of his meditations were the divine perfections and the mysteries, virtues, words and actions of our Saviour. It is evident, from the books[13] that he published on this subject, how much the divine Majesty delighted to reveal His secrets to the apostle of the Sacred Heart. From these experiences the Saint emerged like Moses from the mountain, not with horns of light on his head, but with his mind enlightened and his heart inflamed after his sacred and intimate intercourse with God. These pleasant conversations with the Almighty rendered the Saint not prouder but humbler, not slower in the discharge of his priestly functions but more faithful and more courageous in serving the Most High who treated him so kindly, when he felt that he deserved to be deprived of grace and to be totally abandoned by Him. He would return his inspiration, joys and sentiments to God from whom he had received them, praying Him to make whatever use of them He wished for the sake of His glory.

Possessing the gift of contemplative prayer, St. John Eudes enjoyed it without strong attachment, being always ready to receive from the hand of God the bitter with the sweet, scarcity with abundance, barrenness with consolation. God, who in the realm of nature makes night succeed day, frequently allows His servants to lapse into fearful darkness. St. John Eudes experienced his share of spiritual aridity when he felt incapable of concentration. The pain he suffered upon seeing himself reduced to such a state, and the fear that it might be due to his own fault, obliged him to have recourse to a person extraordinarily favored by God.[14] When the Saint revealed his dryness to her, she assured him that he was in no way responsible for it; that the road along which he had to travel was the way of the Cross, a continual martyrdom, a participation in the sufferings of Jesus Christ. She also told him that divine providence had destined him for this state of spiritual aridity from all eternity, and that he should guard well against desiring any other.

During these periods of interior darkness the Saint acknowledged himself unworthy of any consolation. He believed that our Lord was still granting him too much grace in allowing the earth to support him. He would humble himself at the sight of his accumulated sins without examining them individually. He would adore divine justice, offering himself to God in order to suffer whatever pleased Him, deeming that he was not even worth the trouble of being treated with severity. The Saint used to say that God's purpose toward a soul in those forlorn moments of spiritual abandonment was to humble it and to destroy all pride in it, that He might afterwards shower still more graces on it. St. John Eudes also declared time and time again that without this humility, the human mind, so prone to conceit, might attribute to its own efforts and cooperation the feelings of spiritual elation that it received from God's bounty, that were purely an effect of His mercy.

Even at times when the mystical banquet of prayer gave him delight, St. John Eudes never ended without offering his most humble thanks for the graces received, without asking pardon and requesting our Lord Jesus Christ to make reparation for any deficiencies and to be his perpetual prayer before the eternal Father. St. John Eudes had too holy and sound a distrust of himself to place any reliance on sensible fervor. That is why he would put his reactions in the hands of the God-Man who was given to us, as Saint Paul says, to be "all things to all men."[15] He would usually select a passage from Sacred Scripture or from the Fathers as fuel throughout the day for the fires that had burned within him during morning meditation. No matter what his personal spiritual progress, the Saint always sought to remain on the common path so that he might serve as an example to his spiritual children to follow in the holy exercise of prayer.

St. John Eudes also stressed the importance of the annual retreat, which he regarded as a small portion of eternity.[16] The solitude of the retreat was for him a foretaste of paradise; yet he sought no consolation for himself but only the satisfaction of God. By this practice he desired, first, to perpetuate and honor the periods of prayer in the life of Jesus Christ and of the Blessed Virgin Mary, always keeping in mind some particular one of them; secondly, to atone for the sins he had committed during the year in the service of the Son and the Mother; thirdly, to gain new strength to travel more courageously along the paths of divine love, and to prepare himself to receive new graces, as he once wrote to one of his spiritual children at New Year's: "May God grant us the grace," he said, "to make perfect use of this new year in His service and in that of His most holy Mother, and with as much care and fidelity as if this year were to be our last. That is what I desire to do with all my heart, and for that reason I have withdrawn into solitude, that I may make a good retreat, with the grace of God, for as long a time as I can arrange. Help me to do so, my dearest brother, by your holy Masses."[17]

At retreat time St. John Eudes always renewed the promises he made in Baptism and in Holy Orders. He would find, like the symbolic phoenix, a whole new life in his ashes, that is, in the realization and study of his shortcomings in the ways of God. He adored Jesus Christ and thanked Him for the honor that He rendered to His eternal Father by the fulfillment of the vows made by Him, and of course he solicited special aid from the Blessed Virgin, the angels and the saints.

St. John Eudes constantly taught the value of these days of separation from the world. During the whole retreat he was completely oblivious of all creatures and used to occupy himself solely with the Creator, with the things pertaining to the service of God and to the establishment of the reign of Jesus in the hearts of men. With recollection similar to Moses during the forty days of retreat on Mount Sinai, he spoke to no one, leaving to his colleagues the task of settling house matters and outside business that might arise. When he came out of retreat, his mind would be filled with the divine light and the law of the Lord would be more deeply engraved in his heart through the ministry of the Holy Spirit, who had taught him new understanding of truth in the guest chamber of retreat, as Jesus Christ promised to the Apostles.[18]

The Saint compiled a retreat directory[19] especially for priests and candidates for the priesthood, listing the intentions they should propose for themselves, the dispositions they should have, the best way to use their time and the exercises to perform, the subjects for prayer and the books they should read. He also explained how to make these readings profitable and how to select the subject matter for the special examination of conscience.

St. John Eudes found the retreat so beneficial that he strongly recommended it also to laymen and laywomen,[20] maintaining that it was just as fitting for them to give an extra measure of their time to the service of God, in addition to required devotions, as to have banquets at which they served much more elaborate food than at the regular daily meals. The retreat he described as a powerful means of purifying and enlightening the soul, of progressing along the paths of grace and of preparing for a happy death.

Aside from the annual retreat the Saint recommended individual days of recollection and prayer, like those which the Psalmist calls "full days."[21]

NOTES

[1] Eudes, *The Kingdom of Jesus,* p. 25.

[2] Exod. 3:5–20.

[3] Exod. 25:15 ff.

[4] Gen. 28:12.

[5] Eudes, *ibid., loc. cit.*

[6] Wisd. 8:16.

[7] Eudes, *ibid., loc. cit.*

[8] Eudes, *The Priest,* p. 154.

[9] Lk. 11:9.

[10] Mk. 11:24.

[11] His Excellency Francis de Harlay de Champvallon, Archbishop of Rouen (1651–1671).

[12] Eudes, *Letters and Shorter Works,* p. 278.

[13] See *The Kingdom of Jesus,* pp. 24–32. Also *Meditations on Various Subjects* (New York, P. J. Kenedy, 1947).

[14] Marie des Vallees, a saintly woman of Coutances in Normandy. St. John Eudes met her during a mission at Coutances in August, 1641. See *Letters and Shorter Works,* p. 295, footnote 27, and Sargent, *op. cit.,* p. 59.

[15] 1 Cor. 9:22.

[16] Eudes, *The Kingdom of Jesus,* p. 281.

[17] Eudes, *Letters and Shorter Works,* p. 281.

[18] Jn. 15:26.

[19] Eudes, *The Priest,* p. 65. This was called "Directory of Retreats" in the original edition.

[20] Eudes, *The Kingdom of Jesus,* p. 280.

[21] Ps. 72:10.

Chapter 21. His Interior Life

ST. PAUL REVEALED that by his suffering he completed what was lacking in the passion of the Saviour for His Mystical Body, which is the Church.[1] All the faithful are members of Jesus Christ and are united with Him through His grace; thus by the actions they perform in virtue of His spirit, they complete the work that He Himself began on earth. Their prayer life is the continuation of the prayer life of our Lord; and their work, the extension of His life of labor. By their charitable conversation they continue the social life of our Blessed Lord, and by their eating and sleeping, they share with Him their subjection to all such necessities.

If anyone ever contributed outstandingly to the perfection of the Word Incarnate and to the "age of the fulness of Christ,"[2] it was surely St. John Eudes. His outward and inward life was the lively expression of the exterior and interior life of God made man. Few have lived more closely united with Him. Few members of the Mystical Body have been more animated by the spirit and life of the Head. The holy dispositions with which he performed all his actions furnish us with indisputable proof of these assertions.

St. John Eudes began and ended the day with fervent acts

of love for God.[3] On awakening he would utter the words of the Canticle of Canticles: "I will rise . . . I will seek him whom my soul loveth."[4] "O Jesus, I give Thee my heart." This act he united with the love of all creatures in heaven and on earth for their Creator. The act of dressing[5] he offered in honor of the mystery of the Incarnation which clothed the divinity of the Son with our humanity, even to the extent of needing garments. He admired and blessed God's mercy for providing him with clothes at a time when so many poor people went about insufficiently clad. Yet in his estimation they had not offended God as much as he had.

The interior conduct of St. John Eudes in prayer, as we have already said, was to submerge himself into the innermost depths of his nothingness, to lose himself in the immensity of the mind of God and in all the virtues of our Lord, uniting himself with the love, humility, purity and perfect attention of His prayer, and beseeching Him to instill in him His own holy dispositions and those of the Blessed Virgin Mary, the angels and the saints. He would follow the same procedure in all his other exercises. This practice transformed him into the image of Jesus Christ, according to the words of St. Paul to the Corinthians, "we . . . are transformed into the same image,"[6] making our Blessed Lord live and reign in him. It also implemented the words of our Lord recorded by St. John the Evangelist: "I in them and thou in me; that they may be made perfect in one."[7] St. John Eudes advised complete surrender of self as the most important of all things for those who wish to advance in grace. He taught that the secret of secrets in the spiritual life is to abandon oneself completely to the spirit of our Saviour and to respond fully to the movements of grace that He stirs up in our souls. He pointed out repeatedly that we must never hinder His operations by the thoughts, inventions and activities of our own mind, but must give Christ full liberty to act in us and to guide us along His paths in accordance with His divine plans.

The Saint believed himself obliged by baptism to die to every created being in order to live the divine life of grace. He considered himself as a person no longer belonging to earth but rather to heaven, and therefore bound to direct his thoughts perpetually heavenward in one continuous exercise of adoration, praise and love. This was his usual practice, as he revealed a number of times to a colleague in whom he confided. He assured his confrere that he never lost the presence of God, and that by a special grace, he directed to our Blessed Lord everything, even the most lowly actions of his daily existence. The Saint was often heard exclaiming, "O good Jesus, nothing for myself, nothing for self-love, nothing for the world, but all for Thee, all for Thine honor and glory."[8]

Fearing that mundane activities or necessary business might alienate him from his Beloved, either by the length of their duration or by the mental concentration that they required, before beginning these tasks he would appeal to the angels and saints, asking them to love and glorify Jesus in his name while he was otherwise occupied. He never did anything without first uniting himself with the sum total of love in heaven and on earth; he would have preferred to devote himself to glorifying God at every moment of his life.

Whenever the Saint took some necessary nourishment, he would keep in mind our Lord's charity toward him.[9] He always took care of his health in the interests of the Sacred Heart, allowing himself what was necessary for his strenuous ministerial work. His devotional practice during mealtimes was to acknowledge in a spirit of humility, that he did not deserve to have bread to eat; that there were many poor hungry people who were not so blameworthy as he. Renouncing natural sensible satisfaction, he used to give himself to Jesus Christ to partake of food and drink, even as our Lord and His Blessed Mother had done. He offered every bite that he ate and every drop that he drank as so many acts of praise to the most Blessed Trinity who gave us God made man and His Mother to eat and drink with us here on earth.

Whenever St. John Eudes was called into conversation,[10] either with an individual or a group, he would recollect himself for a moment, and consider our Lord walking and talking with men and women. Then he would adore Christ in His sentiments of love toward His Father, His charity toward men and His humility, forbearance, affability and modesty in His association with all kinds of people. With complete self-renunciation the Saint would ask for a share in the virtues of our Lord, humbling himself in constant awareness of the fact that he deserved to be banished forever from the society of the children of God and to be relegated to the wretched company of the damned. He usually saluted the guardian angels of the persons with whom he was to talk, imploring these powerful protectors to influence his hearers favorably toward the things he had to tell them. During a conversation it was his practice to contemplate and adore the life of Jesus in the soul of those present.

In public or private conferences with his neighbor, St. John Eudes always followed the rule laid down by St. Paul to speak "from God, before God, and in Christ."[11] The Saint always spoke as an instrument of God, drawing upon Him who is the source of all enlightenment for his thoughts and words, giving himself to our Lord at the opening of every spiritual discourse so that Christ might place in his mind and on his lips the things He wished to proclaim through him.

Thus he could say what Christ testified to the Eternal Father: ". . . the words which thou gavest me, I have given to them. . . ."[12] He always conversed in the presence of God, with recollection and modesty, surrendering himself to Jesus to convey the effects of what he was saying or hearing. He always spoke in Jesus Christ, that is, with the divine dispositions that our Blessed Saviour had when He spoke while on earth, or He would have had if He had been in his place. These sentiments which the Saint never ceased to beg of our divine Lord were deep humility toward himself, great meekness and truly cordial charity toward his neighbor, and ardent love and complete attentiveness toward God the Creator.

Whenever the Saint paid tribute to the person or generosity of anyone, it was his custom to regard that person as the image of God and a member of Jesus Christ. Before making these acts of humility, he used to adore our Lord in His divine role as servant of mankind, as attested by His own words: ". . . the Son of man is not come to be ministered unto but to minister."[13] He would humble himself then, admitting that he was unworthy of doing anything that had been done by so many saints, and especially by the Saint of all saints who had lived in the midst of His Apostles not as one who is waited upon but as one who serves.

Before going to Paris or any other city, and before traveling through the country, the Saint never failed to kneel before the Blessed Sacrament to consecrate his journey to the glory of the most Blessed Trinity and the honor of our Lord Jesus Christ, to place himself under the protection of the Blessed Virgin Mary, and to implore the aid of the guardian angels and patron saints of the places and persons that he was about to visit.

During the time he spent journeying St. John Eudes would

meditate on the perfections of God or on one of the mysteries of our Saviour. The hymns of the offices[14] that he wrote were composed while walking through the streets of Paris on business for his Congregation. Every trip, long or short, he dedicated to one of the journeys made by our divine Saviour. En route he was accustomed to recite various prayers. He would adore the Blessed Sacrament dwelling in the churches that he passed and would greet the Blessed Virgin, the angels and holy protectors of such places. He would ask his guardian angel to greet them in his name and obtain their permission, as angelic guardians of those places, to pass through or remain there, believing that they could very justly forbid him to enter because of his sins. He asked them to glorify and love Jesus for him and to atone for any lack of love during his sojourn there. When he arrived in his room at the rectory or the inn where he was to stay, he would kneel down and pay his respects to God, and he would never leave without doing the same thing. He also used to give spiritual counsel to the persons who took care of his requirements, and often addressed the host and hostess as well, leaving everywhere the inspiration of his holy life.

St. John Eudes was never satisfied merely to offer himself to our Lord when beginning an action; from time to time, during the course of the work, he would raise his soul to Christ. He was often heard to offer this prayer: "Come, Lord Jesus, come in the fulness of Thy virtue, in the holiness of Thy spirit, in the perfection of Thy mysteries and in the purity of Thy ways. Come, Lord Jesus."[15] He also exclaimed frequently: "O Jesus and Mary, salvation and joy of my soul!" He recommended these aspirations to all his spiritual sons and daughters as the best means of living the interior life in the midst of the exterior occupations demanded by their vocation in the ministry.

The Saint spent his nights as well as his days in praise and love for God. He never went to bed except in the state in which he hoped to die, giving himself to our Lord to share more fully the dispositions with which Christ, His Blessed Mother and His saints had died. Before going to sleep he pronounced these words of the dying Saviour: "Father, into Thy hands I commend my spirit,"[16] with the desire to share, from that moment until the hour of death, in the dispositions of the Son of God dying for love of mankind.[17]

St. John Eudes always regarded as a serious obstacle to spiritual progress and to the presence of God any secret attachment of the soul even to things considered holy or any undue haste in attaining them, a matter that St. Francis de Sales[18] called the greatest traitor to devotion.[19] This complete detachment from creatures made St. John Eudes always strive to avoid embarking upon any undertaking with too much ardor. Although he spared no effort to bring about the success of his projects for the glory of the Sacred Heart, it never upset his peace and tranquility when something unforeseen obliged him to interrupt or abandon his plans. He loved the divine will equally in good or bad fortune.

The Saint endeavored without worry to destroy his imperfections, remaining at peace in his humility. Loving his own abasement, he was happy with whatever God was pleased to grant him, whether frustration or success. He always persevered in his desire to overcome himself and advance spiritually, trusting in the goodness of his Saviour who would not refuse him the graces necessary to that end. Although he ardently desired, like Saint Paul, to die and to be with Christ,[20] he was, nevertheless, prepared to be deprived of the happiness of heaven until the Day of Judgment if such was the holy will of God. He applied himself assiduously to acquiring the habit of absolute detachment. Glimpsing the wondrous beauty of the Almighty, he sometimes cried out: "Ah, my God, what marvellous things dost Thou accomplish in a soul which is detached from all things, that it may belong wholly and more perfectly to Thee! How strongly dost Thou unite it with Thyself! Take it wholly unto Thyself, plunge it into the abyss of Thy holy love! How admirably dost Thou transform it to Thyself, clothing it with Thy qualities, Thy spirit and Thy love."[21]

St. John Eudes worked to inspire similar detachment in souls whom he believed capable of it, assisting them to enter into the holy liberty of the children of God and to enjoy all the sweetness of an anticipated paradise. This is what he wrote to a stricken Benedictine nun:[22] "What shall I say to you, dear Sister, to comfort you? Shall I say what the world says to those who are ill—that this is nothing and you will soon be well again? But that is not what you seek. Shall I tell you then that there is reason to hope that you will soon be free from the troubles of earth and the exile you are suffering? But that is still not what you are seeking, since you want to avoid any consideration of your own self-interest. What shall I tell you, therefore, to console you? I shall speak only of Jesus, who alone should be the subject of our thoughts, our words and our comfort. And what shall I say to you about this estimable and infinitely lovable Jesus? I shall tell you that He is all yours and you are all His, my dear Sister. What a consolation! What more could you wish? Live henceforth in peace, then, and fear nothing, for Jesus is wholly yours and you belong wholly to Jesus who loves you infinitely, and who has no thoughts or plans for you except those of love and goodness.

"Do not be troubled because you cannot recite the Office. Say the prayers and perform your exercises in whatever way you are able, for there are several persons who are doing these things on your behalf. And what infinitely surpasses them is that Jesus Himself, your all, is unendingly absorbed in contemplation, praise and love of His eternal Father in your name. Finally, all things are yours in heaven and on earth. Dwell in peace, therefore, and in complete and total abandonment of yourself, your health, life, soul and salvation into the hands of your most amiable Father who is Jesus."[23]

This behavior, to which the Saint adhered in all his actions, perfected him in interior recollection, and made of him a quiet and meek spirit, to use the expression of St. Peter.[24] It also helped him to acquire numberless spiritual riches in the sight of God. Living in the presence of our Lord through this practice, as our Lord lived reciprocally in him, he advanced far along the paths of holiness and wrought marvellous changes in the souls of thousands upon thousands of persons whom he met in his missions and spiritual retreats.

NOTES

1 Col. 1:24.
2 Eph. 4:13.
3 *The Kingdom of Jesus,* p. 105.
4 Cant. 3:2.
5 *The Kingdom of Jesus,* p. 106.
6 2 Cor. 3:18.
7 Jn. 17:23.
8 These aspirations of St. John Eudes are found in *The Kingdom of Jesus,* pp. 223–237, and in *The Sacred Heart of Jesus,* p. 79.
9 *Manual of Piety,* p. 48. "Christian dispositions with which we should eat our meals." Also *The Kingdom of Jesus,* p. 154.
10 *Ibid., loc. cit.*
11 2 Cor. 2:17.
12 Jn. 17:8.

[13] Mt. 20:28.

[14] See *Oeuvres Complètes,* vol. 11, p. 217.

[15] *The Kingdom of Jesus,* p. 209. St. John Eudes learned this prayer from Father de Condren, his spiritual director at the Oratory in Paris. Father Olier in the course of a retreat made under de Condren also used this prayer. In a slightly modified form he incorporated it into his beautiful Sulpician prayer: *O Jesus vivens in Maria.* See *Oeuvres Complètes,* vol. 1, p. 440, footnote.

[16] Lk. 23:46.

[17] *The Kingdom of Jesus,* p. 123.

[18] Father Herambourg refers to St. Francis de Sales as "the Blessed Bishop of Geneva," a name by which the Saint was popularly known in the seventeenth century. St. Francis de Sales was beatified in 1662 and canonized three years later.

[19] See *Treatise on the Love of God* (Westminster, Md., Newman Press, 1945), translated by Reverend Henry Mackay, O.S.B., Book 4, chapter 9, p. 288, "How the purity of indifference is to be practiced in the actions of sacred love."

[20] Phil. 1:23.

[21] Eudes, *The Kingdom of Jesus,* p. 23.

[22] Eudes, *Letters and Shorter Works,* p. 13, footnote.

[23] *Ibid.,* p. 17.

[24] 1 Pet. 3:4.

Chapter 22. Love of Neighbor

LOVE OF GOD and love of neighbor are inseparable. They are not two loves but a single one. It is in God and for God that we are commanded to love all men, our brethren, as Jesus loves us in His Father and for His Father's sake. It is God whom we should love in other persons, as our Lord loves His heavenly Father in us. His charity is the standard set for our love towards others.

St. John Eudes studied this commandment of brotherly love in all its aspects, particularly while praying, so that he might conform perfectly to it. He used to contemplate the divine Saviour giving Himself to all men, employing all the means in His power, the secrets of His wisdom and the manifestations of His goodness in order to benefit mankind. Jesus bears our shortcomings with patience, takes the initiative in seeking us out when we have offended Him and seems to prefer our interests to His own. During the course of His life, the Master subjected Himself to all sorts of trials and sufferings in order to deliver us from them; He was all love toward us in His thoughts, words and actions. St. John Eudes would thank our Lord for the glory rendered to the eternal Father through the continual exercise of His divine charity, which he would offer God in reparation for the sins committed against it, asking for the entire destruction of anything in him that could hinder the establishment of charity in his soul.

St. John Eudes considered his neighbor from various points of view in order to stimulate fraternal charity. Sometimes he considered his neighbor as having sprung from the heart of God, where he was to return so that he might glorify and enjoy God for all eternity. At other times he envisaged individuals as children of the same Father, created for the same end, redeemed by the same precious blood of the Son of God, members of the same Mystical Body, nourished with the same heavenly food as he. Then again, he reflected that his fellow Christians were temples of God, members of Jesus Christ,[1] His lieutenants on earth to whom were transferred the rights that He has over our hearts. All these incentives inspired St. John Eudes to love his neighbor. He was constantly on guard against doing or saying anything that might cause offense. He undertook and endured everything for his neighbor's welfare, offering excuses for imperfections, using a gentle reproach that might help to inspire and move his hearer.

The Saint frequently read and pondered the words of St. Paul to the Corinthians: "Charity is patient, is kind: charity envieth not, dealeth not perversely, is not puffed up, is not ambitious, seeketh not her own, is not provoked to anger, thinketh no evil: rejoiceth not in iniquity, but rejoiceth with the truth: beareth all things, believeth all things, hopeth all things, endureth all things."[2] The behavior of St. John Eudes was a lively expression of charity, as St. Paul would have it be. "Wherefore show ye to them . . . the evidence of your charity."[3] Whenever he felt a slight dislike or aversion for a person, he would annihilate himself at the feet of our Lord, asking Him to fill his soul with His divine attraction. He would act contrary to his innermost feelings, going out of his way to converse with such a person and to serve him. He would offer himself to God, to do and suffer whatever was pleasing to the divine majesty on behalf of such an individual, and he never discontinued these practices until he had gained complete mastery over his feelings. When a conversation was being carried on in his presence that was derogatory to anyone, he would gently but firmly change the subject.

Since St. John Eudes had professed his willingness to serve all men in imitation of the Saviour, he believed that like a slave, he possessed nothing which he had the right to use any longer for himself. He also believed that his body and soul, his goods, his time and his life were for the exclusive use of Jesus Christ and the members of His Mystical Body. He always gave a most cordial reception to all persons who came to consult him or wished to speak to him, particularly the poor, and each one would leave completely edified by the interview with him. Whenever he was asked to hear confessions or to give an instruction or spiritual advice, he would hasten to the task with joy. If he encountered anyone harassed with difficulties, he would immediately recall the immense charity of our Blessed Lord who came on earth to console the afflicted, fulfilling the prophecy of Isaias: "[He sent me] to comfort all that mourn."[4]

St. John Eudes always treated a distressed neighbor as a child of God and a member of the Saviour. After he had united his heart with the charity of the divine heart of Jesus, he would approach the afflicted person and would speak to him with cordiality, gentleness and compassion, expressing a sympathetic share in his sorrow and the desire to ease it as much as possible. Then, counseling him, he would suggest the most effective reasons to persuade his neighbor to make good use of his affliction. He would exhort the person to become reconciled with God, if he was not in the state of grace, or at least to humble himself profoundly in view of his sins which were the cause of the affliction he was suffering. He would further counsel him to submit himself to the most holy will and to all its intentions in his regard, to express his gratitude to God, to adore our Lord crucified, covered with wounds from head to foot for love of us, to consider the saints who suffered so courageously, and to have recourse to the Blessed Virgin Mary, the comforter of the afflicted and refuge of sinners.

The Saint tempered his advice to the capacity of the person addressed and to the extent of the difficulties. If the time and place were suitable, he would invite sinner or sufferer to kneel and join him in acts of resignation and love. Orphans, widows and strangers were his special concern. He knew that God, in Holy Scripture, proclaimed Himself their protector and defender,[5] and so he never allowed an occasion to pass without serving them. Moreover, he sought out opportunities to help them give thanks to divine Bounty who had presented these occasions to him. He was always especially kind to manual laborers who worked for him, and never sent them away without giving them advice and encouragement concerning the salvation of their immortal souls.

If the charity of St. John Eudes extended to the whole Mystical Body of the Son of God, it was particularly resplendent toward priests and religious who constitute the noblest part of Christ's Church, and are called by vocation to devote themselves to the service of God and to contribute by their ministry to the fulfillment and perfection of the Mystical Body. He advised them to shun like the plague the spirit of rivalry, coldness and disunity that blights some communities, clerical as well as religious. He urged them to preserve peace and harmony with everyone. When drawing up the Constitutions of his Congregation of priests, he commanded that the superior of each house visit the superior of every other religious community in the city or town two or three times a year in a spirit of true and sincere charity, and he himself would go to celebrate Holy Mass in the churches of the religious orders on their patronal feasts.

St. John Eudes had a particular veneration for the Society of Jesus and the sons of St. Ignatius. The outstanding services rendered to God by the Jesuits, their wonderful usefulness to the Church and the many marks of kindness extended by them to the infant Congregation of Jesus and Mary were the reasons for this special love. He instilled similar appreciation in the hearts of his brethren, ordering them to follow his own example and to show the Jesuit Fathers every possible mark of honor and respect. He looked upon their interests as his own. Whenever God granted them some favor, he would manifest his joy over it, and in gratitude to God he would have the Holy Sacrifice of the Mass celebrated in the houses of his Congregation. This esteem and love was indeed mutual, since the Father General of the Society of Jesus associated the Congregation of Jesus and Mary with all the good that was done by the members of the body of which he was the head.[6] This same favor was granted to the Congregation by the Minister General of the Order of Our Lady of Ransom.[7]

There was also a close union between the new Congregation of St. John Eudes and the nuns of the great Benedictine Abbey of Montmartre, as is revealed by correspondence.[8] When the Abbess, Mother Frances Renée de Lorraine,[9] learned the aim of the new institute of St. John Eudes, the training of candidates for the priesthood, and the special object of its devotion, love of the Hearts of Jesus and Mary, she determined to associate all her daughters with it and to share in the good it was accomplishing. A mutual agreement in the name of the sisters and brethren of the two religious societies was enacted and signed on March 25, 1661.[10]

St. John Eudes wished, moreover, that great honor be shown all religious orders, consecrated to God by the sanctity of their vows. He used to say that the members of his little Congregation should have all the more respect for the religious profession made in these orders since their Constitutions[11] do not empower them to make such a profession themselves.

The charity of St. John Eudes was truly catholic, universal, extending everywhere and to all sorts of persons. One of his special devotions was to the poor souls in purgatory. The pain they suffered from the cleansing fire and, still more, from their enforced separation from the God whom they loved caused him to suffer with them. Filled with pity for their misery, he spared no effort to help them. It was his wish that prayers should be offered frequently for the holy souls, especially after Holy Communion, and he even commanded that a daily Mass should be said in each of his houses for their intention. Through such acts of devotion his charity attained the universality that the charity of a Catholic priest should always have. Everyone found a place in his heart. Like the sun which penetrates the earth with its warmth and illumines it with its rays, he did good to those who came in contact with him, or if they refused to let him, he would at least show friendliness to them. Thus can it truly be said of him that no one who realized his charity shunned it, according to the words of the Psalmist: "No one . . . can hide himself from his heat."[12]

NOTES

[1] 2 Cor. 6:16; 1 Cor. 6:15.

[2] 1 Cor. 13:4–7.

[3] 2 Cor. 8:24.

[4] Isa. 61:2.

[5] Ps. 145:9; Mt. 23:14; Lk. 20:47.

[6] From 1643 to 1680 six superiors general governed the Society of Jesus. It is impossible to ascertain with what particular general this union of prayers and good works was concluded.

[7] It is impossible to identify this superior general of the Mercedarians.

[8] Out of the 253 letters of St. John Eudes that are now extant, 20 were written to the Benedictine nuns of the Abbey of Our Lady of Montmartre. See *Saint Jean Eudes, Letters choisies et inédites* (Namur, Editions du Soleil Levant, 1958), p. 177. This recent critical edition of some letters of the Saint was prepared by Reverend Charles Berthelot du Chesnay, C.J.M.

[9] See chapter IV, note 7.

[10] See chapter IV, note 5.

[11] The Eudist Fathers do not make the three vows of the religious state. They bind themselves to the Congregation of Jesus and Mary by a perpetual promise of obedience to their superiors and to the Constitutions.

[12] Ps. 18:7.

Chapter 23. Love for the Poor

CHARITY IS A catholic virtue which embraces all men. Yet it is nevertheless true that charity does not manifest itself impartially. The Word Incarnate gave special marks of His affection for the poor while preaching here on earth,[1] and He made it clearly understood that He had come on earth principally to announce the kingdom of God to them.[2] So it was, then, that St. John Eudes, in imitation of his divine Master, conversed more gladly with the poor than with the rich. He was more prompt to visit them in their illnesses and to comfort them in their afflictions. He would hasten with joy to the confessional whenever they asked for him there. He had nothing but love and respect for them, frequently calling to mind the words of our Lord in the Gospel: ". . . as long as you did it to one of these my least brethren, you did it to me."[3]

The Saint used to say that God brought the Congregation of Jesus and Mary into existence for the purpose of instructing, comforting and helping the poor. He made it a rule that in all communities of his Institute, dinner would be given several times a year to twelve poor persons, and that on Sunday and Thursday of each week one of them would eat in the refectory with the members of the community.[4] He even had public alms distributed to them twice a week at the door of the Caen Seminary, where he ordinarily resided, and it was his wish that they be taught catechism either before or afterwards, because, he used to say, the soul being superior to the body, spiritual nourishment as well as bodily food must be given. He inspired his confreres with a special tenderness towards the poor and encouraged them to show themselves, everywhere and at all times, as much as they could, their protectors, advocates, mediators and fathers; to be always ready to help, instruct, visit and comfort them, both in hospitals and their homes. Every Friday he used to send two of the priests or clerics of his Community to the hospital or the prison to discharge these good offices in their behalf; he also desired to have this holy custom observed in his entire Congregation.[5]

The Saint preferred that his priests hear the confessions of the poor rather than the rich, because, he used to say, the wealthy find directors easily enough; there is even competition in determining who shall have the post. The poor, on the contrary, are sometimes abandoned in soul as well as in body. On a feast day, during recreation, he once asked a priest of the house if he had administered the Sacrament of Penance to many people that day. He received the answer that the priest had not left the confessional from six o'clock until eleven. "Did you hear well the confessions of the poor?" continued the Saint. "Father," replied the confessor, "I heard no others. Since my confessional is very close to the door, the poor are the only ones who stop there." "You are indeed blessed, my dearest brother," St. John Eudes said to him. "God will be your reward."[6]

While living in Caen the Saint brought together several persons of rank[7] for the purpose of undertaking all works of charity that might present themselves, particularly those of caring for the sick poor and visiting hospitals. He sometimes gave talks to these charitable groups in order to encourage and sustain them in their undertakings, and he himself joined them so that he might help them in every way possible.

When in 1651 Paris was caught in the throes of a great famine,[8] the Ladies of Charity[9] had recourse to the Saint because they had often heard of his zeal for the relief of the unfortunate, and had witnessed on several occasions the great blessings with which God had crowned his sermons. They therefore begged him to exhort the people, from the pulpit, to give alms. He did so with such great fervor and success that in a short time the purses were filled and the poor received considerable aid through this means.

The same thing happened several years later[10] in the city of Caen, when a large hospital was being built. Several patients had been received into this building before its completion, but the poverty became so great there that the things necessary for the maintenance and the continuation of the building were lacking; in consequence it remained unfinished. M. John de Bernières de Gavrus,[11] who was in charge of the construction and administration of this hospital, and who had defrayed the greater part of the expenses that had been incurred up to that time, went to the seminary to beg the Saint to deliver several sermons on almsgiving in St. Peter's Church in Caen. St. John Eudes, who might well be called the father of the poor, accepted the proposal with manifest joy, although he was then frail and broken with age.[12] During the month of August he preached five times with all the zeal and forcefulness of a young man on Psalm 40: "Blessed is he that understandeth concerning the needy and the poor."[13] Afterwards the faithful treasurer of France came to him and said: "Father, you have preached enough.

We now have means in abundance." As a matter of fact, there was no one, rich or poor, who did not wish to contribute to the construction and furnishing of the hospital. Some brought money or grain; others supplied linen, beds and furniture. There was actually difficulty in finding room for everything that was offered. It reminded one of the charity of the first Christians, who cast at the feet of the Apostles the goods they possessed,[14] or of the devotion of the ancient Israelites who brought riches to Moses from all sides for the construction of the Tabernacle.[15]

The same charity was manifested several times during the lifetime of St. John Eudes, particularly when he was giving missions in the large cities in which he founded houses of refuge for the poor and the sick, or restored old ones which had fallen into a dilapidated condition. He induced everyone to contribute to these establishments. A number of persons who had heard him speak offered two or three hundred pounds for one or another of these praiseworthy causes; others, five hundred; still others, as high as a thousand; and one individual, during a mission at Autun, pledged in writing to give five thousand francs to begin the building of a hospital. So great was the power of the Saint over hearts that he could influence them as he wished.

St. John Eudes also had a rare sympathy for prisoners; the unfortunate condition of some of them touched him deeply. In their imprisonment he honored the captivity of Jesus Christ; he did all he could to have them freed, striving on every occasion to further their spiritual welfare by having Masses said in prisons on Sundays, feast days and certain week days, as well as by many other devotional exercises.

The poor who were ashamed to beg were not forgotten by the Saint; they also felt the effects of his charity. He did good to them all the more willingly because he was less exposed to the dangers of vanity in doing so. While he was conducting missions, he wanted catechism to be taught to the beggars of the locality, who sometimes numbered close to two thousand. At his request alms would afterwards be given to them. He overlooked no means to establish schools for poor children in places where he happened to be, so that they might have a place to learn the things necessary for their salvation.

Besides all these concerns, St. John Eudes did not forget the sick, whom he made one of the principal objects of his charity, in imitation of our Lord who had come upon earth for that purpose, as Isaias tells us.[16] Two years after his ordination[17] to the priesthood, his father wrote him that the plague had broken out in several parishes in the Diocese of Séez. The stricken people there were entirely forsaken and were dying without aid, either spiritual or corporal. God alone knows what grief the Saint felt upon hearing this, and how deeply his sympathetic heart was wounded by such sad news. After he had seriously considered how he might remedy this great misfortune, he offered himself to God as a sacrifice in behalf of the poor abandoned people. The charity of Jesus Christ, which consumed St. John Eudes as it did St. Paul,[18] made him resolve to stint nothing of himself for the relief of those unfortunate victims of the plague, even though it might cost him his life. In these sentiments he went to see his Superior, Cardinal de Bérulle,[19] disclosing to him his feelings and plans about undertaking this noble ministry. The worthy Cardinal, so enlightened in the workings of grace, had a particularly keen insight into the minds of persons, and he understood at once that his disciple's inclination was heaven-inspired. Glorying in the thought of immolating one of his spiritual sons for an entire people, he granted Eudes the desired permission, along with his blessing. The Saint, more overjoyed to have obtained it than if he had conquered a whole kingdom, left Paris, taking with him a portable altar and the things necessary to celebrate Holy Mass, which he desired to do along the way. He was another Isaac who was not content to offer himself in death but brought with him the instruments which were to be used in the sacrifice.[20]

When he arrived at the plague-stricken area, St. John Eudes was unable to find lodgings with any parish priests or prominent laymen. In this respect he shared the plight of his Master, who, having come down from a throne of glory in order to take care of men and to deliver them from their physical and spiritual ills, was shamefully rejected: "He came unto His own, and His own received Him not."[21] He finally stayed with an impoverished priest[22] in the parish of St. Christopher, who very charitably received him into his house. Every day these two devoted priests would say Holy Mass in the chapel of St. Euron,[23] not far distant, and the Saint, putting some consecrated hosts in a tin box which he wore around his neck, would go, accompanied by this good priest, in search of those who were sick, sometimes in one parish and sometimes in another. There he worked in the midst of these poor people, comforting and giving them all possible aid. He would hear the confessions of some and administer Holy Communion to them; he would give Extreme Unction to others and exhort them to die well. He encouraged them all, and never did he abandon a single one of them through fear or cowardice. He worked in this manner from the end of August until All Saints' Day, when the contagion disappeared completely, and God, who always renders Himself the protector of charitable persons, preserved the Saint so well that he never felt any ill effects from his experience.

This was not the only time that St. John Eudes devoted himself courageously to the service of the victims of the plague. In 1631 the city of Caen was attacked by this dangerous pestilence which was so widespread that it penetrated even the religious communities. The house of the Oratory[24] was particularly hard hit and lost a number of its most outstanding subjects, among them Father Gaspard de Répichon, who was its superior and a man of great virtue. St. John Eudes had the happiness of assisting them all, administering the sacraments to them and preparing them for a happy death.

The plague raged so furiously and stubbornly that the city of Caen was desolated by it. General consternation reigned in the streets and nothing but groans and sobs were heard everywhere. Parents deserted their children and children their parents; wives were separated from their husbands and husbands from their wives. Even in the case of priests, some left the city, others hid in their houses, frightened by the image of death which they saw stalking by. They had forgotten that their vocation obliged them to take censer in hand in order to appease the wrath of God, as Aaron once did for the people of Israel; that they ought to cast themselves, as the Prophet had done, in the midst of the flames and risk their lives to care for those of their brethren whom the hand of the Lord had smitten.[25] St. John Eudes, animated by the same zeal as Aaron, the Pontiff of old, passed unhesitatingly among the corpses; he hastened from the house of a man who had just died to that of another who had just been stricken, and all the time that death was taking its toll he comforted, exhorted and strengthened with the sacraments those who were attacked by this contagion.

Whenever the Saint visited a sick person, it was always in union with the great charity of our Lord toward mankind.

Entering the room, he would look upon the suffering person as a member of the Saviour. Speaking gently and compassionately to him, St. John Eudes would tell him that there were two principal causes for our afflictions: first, the will of God who disposes all things in the best possible way for our greatest good; second, our sins which bring down the divine wrath upon us. Then he would exhort the sick man to humble himself in view of the offenses which he had committed and for which he had deserved to be punished severely. The Saint would then suggest acts of submission, urging him to suffer patiently for love of Christ who suffered for his sake. He would prepare the sick man to receive the Sacraments of Penance and Holy Communion and instruct him how to make his thanksgiving afterwards. He would urge him to raise his mind and heart frequently to God, suggesting acts of faith, hope, trust, contrition and love. He would propose to him various points of the sacred passion of our Blessed Lord to honor at different times in the course of his painful illness. If the Saint believed that the patient was going to die, he would have him offer his life in sacrifice to our Lord who had sacrificed His own life on the Cross—a life of which a single instant was worth infinitely more than all the lives of angels and of men. For that purpose, St. John Eudes used to propose various intentions which he believed most in accord with the dispositions of the sick person. He would remind anyone in danger of death of his duties to God, Jesus Christ, the Blessed Virgin Mary, the angels, the saints and his neighbor before leaving this world. He always tried to have him gain some indulgence, preparing him for the Sacrament of Extreme Unction and persuading him, last of all, to renew his baptismal promises.

Such were the various charitable practices of the Saint

with respect to the sick—practices that might well be followed by priests in caring for the suffering members of their flocks. In a word, St. John Eudes spared no effort to contribute in every possible way to the cure of their bodies and to the sanctification of their souls. This is what we have noted on various occasions; among others, when the plague was raging in Rouen in 1668. During these terrible days the Saint had Masses said, together with special prayers, in all the houses of his Congregation for the intention of his confreres who were living in the Rouen Seminary, as well as for all the poor people of that city.

St. John Eudes wrote about this matter to the Superior of his seminary at Rouen: "I beseech you," he said, "to make a novena of Masses in honor of the Maternal Heart of the most Blessed Virgin Mary, and another in honor of St. Charles[26] to implore him to intercede for us with this most charitable Heart, not only to place you under its protection but first and foremost for the intention of all those who are victims of the plague or in danger of it.

"I likewise entreat all our dear brethren to render to God all the honor we owe Him on this occasion and to use these circumstances as He would have us do. To that end we should do a number of things, the first of which is to adore His divine justice and humble ourselves for our sins in the name of all the people. The second is to remember that we ought to be more grateful for afflictions than consolations, and then thank Him for this scourge, seeing in it a manifestation not only of His justice but even more of His mercy, which chastises us that we may be reformed and saved. The third is to adore the divine will in its plans for us, and to offer, abandon and sacrifice ourselves wholly to it in order that it may do with us what is most pleasing to it. The fourth thing we should do is to adore our Lord Jesus Christ on the Cross and in the infinite love with which He bore so many sufferings for our sake, and to offer ourselves to Him to suffer all the crosses it may please Him to send us, in thanksgiving for His. The fifth is to offer Him all the stricken people and to implore Him to grant them the grace to use their affliction to good advantage. The sixth thing is to recommend them to her whom we call the consoler of the afflicted. The seventh is to give ourselves to the immense love through which our most lovable Saviour took upon Himself all the sins of the world and offered Himself to His Father to atone for them; and in union with this same love, to offer ourselves to Him as victims in order to be immolated to His divine justice for the sins of our brethren and sisters, as well as for our own. We should also offer ourselves to Him, in union with the same charity which brought Him into the world that He might assist and succor the victims of the spiritual plague, that is, sinners, and we should offer ourselves to Him, I repeat, in order to help the afflicted, if such be His holy will. The eighth and last thing of all is to beg our holy Mother, our guardian angels and our patron saints to do all of the above mentioned things for us."[27]

St. John Eudes knew only too well how to draw good from public calamities. Indifferent alike to both prosperity and adversity, he always blessed God in either circumstance, being happy if only he could help his neighbor, humble himself and render to our Blessed Lord all the duties of a Christian and a priest. One had only to be unfortunate to find a place in his heart and win his love. Thus did each one come to him, as to a public refuge, with the hope of finding a cure for his ills or relief from them. This heroic love for the sick and the poor is the glory that will remain his own and will endure until the end of time.

NOTES

[1] Mt. 5:3; 11:5.

[2] Lk. 4:18.

[3] Mt. 25:40.

[4] See *Oeuvres Complètes,* Vol. 9, pp. 162, 169.

[5] *Ibid.,* Vol. 3, p. 163.

[6] This incident was probably related to Father Herambourg by the Eudist father actually involved or by an eyewitness.

[7] The "persons of rank" referred to here are M. John de Bernières and the members of "The Hermitage," a house built by de Berniéres in Caen as a residence for a group of devout laymen. These "solitaires," as they were called, were in all probability affiliated with the Company of the Blessed Sacrament. They practiced the corporal works of mercy in the city of Caen, caring for the poor and visiting the sick in their homes. See Joly, *A Life of Saint John Eudes,* p. 134, and Sargent, *Their Hearts Be Praised,* p. 178. Also *Letters and Shorter Works,* p. 35, footnote 12.

[8] The famine with an epidemic called "fire of St. Anthony," which was raging in Paris in 1651. See Boulay, *Vie du Vénérable Jean Eudes,* Vol. 2, p. 451.

[9] The Ladies of Charity of Paris were a pious association of Catholic laywomen who devoted their time and money to corporal works of mercy. This organization was founded in 1617 by St. Vincent de Paul. Later, in 1633, a group of these ladies became the Daughters of Charity of St. Vincent de Paul, whose first superior was St. Louise de Marillac. See Pierre Coste, *Saint Vincent de Paul et les Dames de la Charité* (Paris, 1917).

[10] This was in 1678.

[11] M. John de Bernières de Gavrus (1632–1691) was the son of Peter de Bernières, d'Acqueville and the nephew of John de Bernières, founder of "The Hermitage" of Caen. Royal Treasurer at Caen, John de Bernières de Gavrus spent most of his personal fortune for works of charity. When he died on June 26, 1691, he was buried in the General Hospital at Caen. It was for this hospital that St. Eudes gave several charity sermons at the request of de Bernières. In 1914 the remains of de Bernières were transferred to the Church of St. John in Caen.

[12] St. John Eudes was then 77 years of age.

[13] Ps. 40:1.

[14] Acts 4:35.

[15] Exod. 30:16.

[16] Isa. 61:1; Lk. 4:18.

[17] In 1627. See Sargent, *op. cit.,* p. 33.

[18] 2 Cor. 5:14.

[19] See chapter I. note 11.

[20] Gen. 22:6.

[21] Jn. 1:11.

[22] The name of this priest was Father Laurens. See Eudes, *Letters and Shorter Works*, p. 291.

[23] St. Euron is a misspelling of St. Evrou or St. Evroult, as it is usually written today. St. Evroult's name is in the Roman Martyrology for December 29. See *Ecclesia* (Paris, Bloud et Gay, 1941), p. 783.

[24] The Oratory of Jesus, a Congregation of priests living in community without the three regular vows of the religious life. See chapter I, note 11 of this work.

[25] Num. 16:46–48.

[26] See chapter 1, note 11.

[27] Eudes, *Letters and Shorter Works*, p. 208.

Chapter 24. Meekness

MEEKNESS WAS THE characteristic trait of the Saviour of the world. To be convinced of this fact one need only read the testimony given by the prophets and by His Apostles and Evangelists, the irrefutable witnesses of His actions. Christ is shown to us in Sacred Scripture as a sheep that allows itself to be led to slaughter without resistance, as a lamb that permits itself to be shorn and even flayed without making the slightest complaint.[1] St. Peter tells us that, no matter how shamefully our Blessed Lord was treated, He remained silent,[2] showing no sign of anger when threatened and abused. This virtue of meekness Jesus wants all Christians to imitate. "Learn of me, because I am meek and humble of heart."[3]

It was this same beautiful lesson of meekness that St. John Eudes retained and practiced with great fidelity. He adored the thoughts, intentions and love of our Lord uttering these words: "Learn of me, because I am meek and humble of heart." Then the Saint gave himself wholly to Jesus Christ for their realization in his soul, beseeching Him to destroy all the obstacles that He might encounter in doing so. Although the manner and conversation of the Saint were deeply serious, his attitude was most affable to all. He treated his neighbor kindly, regarding him with a serene countenance, speaking civilly and being patient with human moods even when they were harsh and disagreeable.

His zeal for the glory of God and the interests of the Church, His spouse, evoked an astonishing intensity of spite against St. John Eudes. Imbued with a spirit similar to that of the prophets of old, called to war against vice, hypocrisy and corruption, the Saint would not compromise the truth in private or in public. Although he was careful never to mention names when he inveighed against sinful abuses, those who were guilty openly worked to discredit him in the public mind, writing libels against him and opposing his plans. But as he had found the secret of remaining patient and meek of heart, John Eudes was never heard, in the face of much annoyance, to become angry or lose his temper, nor even to complain of or resent their interference. On the contrary, he always spoke well of his enemies, putting into literal practice these words of the Son of God: "Who when he was reviled, did not revile; when he suffered, he threatened not; but delivered himself to him that judged him unjustly."[4]

On several occasions St. John Eudes sought out his calumniators, in obedience to the words of the Saviour who commands us in the Gospel to go and reconcile ourselves with our brother whenever he has something against us,[5] and to imitate the behavior of God who always comes to us first. He used to pray for his opponents with special fervor, exhorting his spiritual children and friends to use their influence with the divine majesty of God in obtaining the conversion and salvation of those who opposed him. For example, there was a priest, highly distinguished for his learning, while shockingly lax in his morals, who persecuted the Saint for a number of years by acting, speaking and writing against him. Once when this priest was devising every possible means of making trouble, St. John Eudes worked equally to win him over. He sought to overcome the hardness of that heart by the tenderness of his own, and he stormed heaven for this intention, enlisting the help of everybody to ask for this grace. He even went to call on him, talked with him, humbled himself, pleaded, and after months of prayer, fasting and mortification, he finally converted the man and bound him to a life utterly different from his previous one. Finally the Saint had the consolation of seeing his former enemy die a holy death in his arms.

If St. John Eudes had so much kindness toward those who persecuted him, we can well imagine how much more he had for his spiritual sons and daughters and all individuals with whom grace had united him closely. This beautiful virtue of meekness constituted the soul of his government; it presided over all the commands that he was obliged to issue. If he gave an order, it was really an entreaty. He adhered strictly to the advice of Sacred Scripture, which counsels us not to glory in our own eminence but to conform in every respect to those who have enough humility to set us up as their superiors and to acknowledge us as such.[6]

This revealed itself in countless incidents during his lifetime; one is chosen as an illustration. The superior of one of his houses was creating a difficulty about sending the Saint a priest whose services he had requested; whereupon St. John Eudes wrote: "If you persist in your obstinacy and disobedience, I shall complain about it to our Lord and His Holy Mother! I am wholly confident that they will take the matter in hand and not allow you to ruin and destroy their Congregation in this manner. It is charity alone which constrains me to write you these things. I urge you, my dearest brother, by the loving Heart of our Blessed Lord and of His holy Mother, to make good use of them and to accept them in a spirit of humility, obedience and charity."[7] Such was his custom of complaining to our Lord rather than to other colleagues and friends; and he firmly but gently won the recalcitrant ones back to the path of duty and the acknowledgement of their faults. If all superiors acted in this manner, they would spare themselves many of the crosses that result from an attitude of domination rather than from a sense of responsibility, which causes their subordinates to find pleasure in submission and obedience.

It was this spirit of meekness that St. John Eudes tried to instill in those who depended on him or who exercised authority over others. He once wrote the following advice to his niece[8] during her term as Mother Superior of the Convent of Our Lady of Charity of Bayeux, for which post she had been chosen by the Bishop himself.

"Enclosed, my dearest and beloved daughter, are two books for you, which have been most useful to me. Please study them carefully and put them diligently into practice, particularly their teachings concerning meekness, for a hard, harsh, haughty and domineering disposition serves only to spoil everything, ruining the filial affection, confidence and tenderness which should be present in the hearts of those in our charge, and tends to fill them instead with fear, terror, contempt, aversion and hatred. In a word, harshness is good only to destroy a community and put the head of the superior on the block. I do not think, my dearest daughter, that you are behaving in this way, nor has anyone said so to me, but since I know from experience that being a superior ruins many individuals by giving them a haughty, domineering, hard, bitter and harsh spirit, I am always afraid. Strive, therefore, I entreat you, to guide your daughters with all possible gentleness, kindness, cordiality and tenderness. It is the spirit of our Lord and His most holy Mother; pray to them frequently to grant it to you and me, and ask one of the Sisters to tell you of your shortcomings in this respect."[9]

These words, which show how highly the Saint esteemed meekness and the obligation of all superiors to practice it, are at the same time proof of how he himself made a habit of practicing it, since he studied the problem daily at the foot of the Cross, and never preached what he himself did not first practice in imitation of his divine Master.

Neither did the Saint refuse anything that was asked of him. One of his most common maxims was that we must readily grant and willingly do whatever is not prejudicial to anyone and can result in some benefit. He looked upon litigation as the sworn enemy of charity. Whenever a lawsuit came up in his community he would humble himself before God, acknowledging that this was a punishment sent by heaven for the castigation of sin as St. Paul seems to mean by the words addressed to the Corinthians: "Already indeed there is plainly a fault among you, that you have lawsuits one with another."[10]

At a time when pride insisted on pressing for court victories, the Saint always sought to reach a settlement through the mediation of men of integrity. Before he had recourse to legal action, he would even employ negotiators lacking in worldly qualifications, if they could be useful in effecting a reconciliation, in conformity with this divine teaching of the Holy Spirit through the pen of St. Paul: "If therefore you have judgments of things pertaining to this world, set them to judge, who are the most despised in the church."[11] But whenever the matter could not be settled by arbitration, he used to have his council convene in order to determine if it was more Christian to sustain the damages rather than go to court, judging that it was much better to suffer losses than to offend against charity, and even to part with his coat as our Lord counsels rather than have a lawsuit over the garment.[12] He would have novenas made in honor of the charitable Heart of Mary, Queen of Peace, seeking her intercession to pacify the minds of agitators, to check and ward off the dispute, or to guide the matter in whatever way was most pleasing to her Divine Son. This was his counsel to a Superior of his Congregation: "I am asking you," he wrote, "to have a novena of Masses and rosaries offered for all those who are involved in lawsuits, particularly for those who are poor and defenseless, in order to ask our Lord Himself to be their judge, the Blessed Virgin their counsel, St. Joseph their attorney and St. Gabriel their petitioner."[13]

Such was the conduct of this heroically tolerant man in affairs where he feared that the laws of meekness might in some way be violated. His concept of this virtue was so high that he would have given everything for its preservation, retaining nothing for himself except on occasions when the interests of God were at stake. He had studied too long the forbearance of Jesus Christ not to profit from it, and he allowed even his poorest garments to be taken from him without a word of reproach. Of all the virtues it was particularly meekness that he contemplated as having as source the benign Saviour. Although he had learned all the other virtues from our Lord, he had nevertheless received special instruction in meekness from the divine lesson in the Gospel: "Learn of me, because I am meek and humble of heart."[14]

NOTES

1 Isa. 53:7.
2 1 Pet. 2:23.
3 Mt. 11:29.
4 1 Pet. 2:23.
5 Mt. 5:24.
6 Ecclus. 3:17–19.

[7] *Letters and Shorter Works,* p. 279.
[8] Mother Mary of the Nativity Herson. See chapter III, note 17.
[9] *Letters and Shorter Works,* p. 237.
[10] 1 Cor. 6:7.
[11] 1 Cor. 6:4.
[12] Mt. 5:40.
[13] *Ibid.*, p. 278.
[14] Mt. 11:29.

Chapter 25. Zeal for Souls

TO LABOR WITH JESUS Christ for the salvation of souls is the most divine work on earth. Souls are so dear to our Blessed Lord that He shed His Precious Blood and sacrificed His life for them. One of the greatest offices of His providence in the Church was to give her apostles, whom He sent into the world to convert it. Since he wished to continue the functions of those first ministers of the Gospel to the end of time, Jesus Christ raised up a succession of men endowed with the zeal of the first apostles. St. John Eudes was of this number. To become convinced of this fact, it is necessary merely to reflect on the abundant blessings which God shed on his labors. From his earliest years as a priest he cherished a high ideal of this office. He considered the salvation of souls to be the chief occupation of God, the angels and the saints. He had learned through his reading of the Fathers[1] that the care of the sick, fasting, the gift of miracles, even martyrdom itself, are secondary in comparison with works of zeal undertaken to cooperate with our Lord in the salvation of souls. That is why the Saint gave himself to the works of zeal perseveringly and without stint.

Apostolic zeal must possess many qualities in order to be

perfect; that of St. John Eudes had them all. He was fervent in his desires; he frequently begged the Incarnate Word to fill his heart and those of all Christians with burning charity for souls. The Saint considered it a blessing for him to expend his health, his life, his time, his all to save a single soul. His strongest desire was to die in the battle for souls, while still carrying out the functions of preaching, hearing confessions and actively working in the service of those same souls. He was deeply grieved to behold so many souls perishing day by day because of the dearth of apostolic men to stretch forth a hand to sustain and prevent them from falling into hell. He used to say that a whole lifetime of blood and tears would not be sufficient to lament this great evil.

St. John Eudes would frequently offer himself to God to be sacrificed and reduced to ashes, in order to obtain from His divine bounty that all hearts be enkindled with the celestial fire of their salvation. It was his desire that all particles of his ashes be transformed into so many apostolic workers who might labor with all their hearts to save their brethren. He longed for the complete destruction of himself, provided he would be granted the power to destroy sin in turn, especially sins of impurity which cause such a great number of souls to be cast into hell. But because he knew that his being was as nothing in the eyes of God, he used to declare to our loving Saviour that, if all created beings were his, he would offer them to the divine majesty for the salvation of souls, reserving for himself a single favor, namely, that his desire to love God might endure for all eternity.

Appealing to our Lord, St. John Eudes was often heard to say: "O my Saviour, when shall we see the fulfillment of these divine words spoken by Thy holy Mother: 'He hath filled the hungry with good things; and the rich he hath sent empty away'?[2] When will the demons be despoiled of the immense wealth that they seem to possess on earth and which they have stolen from Thee? When will the extreme hunger of Thy children for the salvation of souls be satisfied? Oh, let all creatures of heaven and earth prostrate themselves, together with Thy holy Mother, before the throne of Thy mercy, that they may obtain from Thee this great favor!"[3] Such were the ardent desires of this great Saint.

His deep supernatural zeal made him very gentle and understanding in his dealings with souls. He resorted to every means to convert sinners, looking upon them as sick persons covered with sores. He would urge them gently to lay bare their souls; he would excuse them, pity them and at times he seemed even to justify them. He would speak tenderly and affectionately, telling them that he loved them with his whole heart and that he was seeking only their salvation. He would remind them of the great mercy of God who had pardoned so many others and was always ready to grant them the same grace if they would correspond with it ever so little. He would quote passages of Sacred Scripture to convince them and to make them realize how easy it was to save themselves.

In the difficulties that the Saint encountered in this task of saving souls, he always put before sinners the example of our Lord and the saints. Injuries and outrages were often the reward of his charitable pursuits, but never was he known to overstep the bounds of meekness or to become disheartened by the harsh treatment that he received now and then. When he could make no headway despite all these persuasive methods, he would exhort sinners to pray and to ask the light and grace of God that they might realize and repent of their sins or at least consent to let him and other persons pray for them. He would always urge them to cultivate devotion to the Mother of God, since experience had taught him that this is one of the most efficacious means of converting even the most hardened hearts. He resorted to it to obtain the salvation of a number of persons, among others, a man of very wicked life, who was one of his bitterest enemies. This individual died with all the marks of true repentance.

St. John Eudes' gentleness conquered everyone, and during his lifetime many persons acknowledged their great indebtedness to him for his charitable actions performed in their behalf in order to win them over to our Lord and put them in a state in which they could work out their salvation. A nobleman, distinguished for merit as well as rank,[4] wrote our Saint one day: "You are, dearest Father, the most effective of priests whom divine Bounty has deigned to use to withdraw me from that broad road which leads to perdition and place me mercifully on the path of salvation, that I may know and adore His divine and eternal designs. I ask God with all my strength, and with as much fervor as possible, that this charity which you are still continuing to use may not be without its reward, and that His blessings may accompany you everywhere. May He favor those who love you and may He grant confusion and repentance to those who commit outrages against you."

Our Saint's zeal was single-minded in intention. Forgetful of his own interests in the labors he undertook, he sought only the interests of God and of the souls that he wished to convert. He was just as fervent in preaching to the poor and rough villagers as to the King and Queen[5] and their impressive royal court. All were equal in his sight, because he saw in them souls to be saved. He thought just as highly of preaching the Gospel in any country parish as in the elaborate circles of St. Germain,[6] Versailles or Paris. The purity of his zeal made him scorn high offices and advantages which his talents could have obtained. He was satisfied to live as a simple priest in order to have more freedom to work for the conversion of sinners.

His zeal was all-embracing in its inspirations and daring in its accomplishments. Every opportunity to work for the salvation of souls was infinitely precious to him. He would have considered himself guilty of a great sin if he had allowed a single opportunity to escape. Whenever such an occasion arose, he would first cast himself at our Lord's feet in order to beg His grace, then he would surrender himself completely to Christ with all possible love and diligence. He considered this ministry for souls the most important business of all. If he had been given all the wealth in the world, it would have meant nothing to him compared with the winning of a single soul. Instruction, example and prayer were the means he used to attract them. Those souls whom divine providence had directed to his guidance were dearer in his sight than himself, and he experienced profound sorrow whenever he was unable to help them in their troubles.

Like the incomparable Francis Xavier, Apostle of the Indies, St. John Eudes was aflame with zeal for the glory of God and the salvation of souls. "The sun," says Philo,[7] "needs no interpreter to demonstrate that it gives light and heat, since this is quite evident through the beauty of daytime and the brilliance of the rays which shine upon all who behold it." St. John Eudes was the sun bursting forth in the temple of God to which reference is made in Ecclesiasticus.[8] Because of his outstanding success as a missionary, he was known throughout France as a man full of the grace, spirit and zeal of the first disciples of our Saviour. Love, which possesses both fetters and wings, sometimes halts apostolic men and then causes them to fly. At first, it kept the Saint in his study and his oratory, that he might become imbued with the spirit of God, but afterwards it transported him from his solitude to large areas of France, there to sow the seeds of the Gospel. In hundreds of parishes this illustrious conqueror selected battlefields where he won an extraordinary number of victories over sin, the devil and hell. He was an angel who hastened and gained access to any place where he might labor for the salvation of souls of all sorts of persons without distinction. He had learned from St. Paul that no difference should be made between Hebrews and Greeks, since both have the same Lord who is rich and liberal toward all who invoke Him;[9] that Jesus Christ died for all mankind; that He gave His blood and life for each soul in particular; and that He would be ready to do so again if it were necessary.

We must confess, however, that St. John Eudes felt special affectionate preference for hardened sinners who had the greatest need of his help and of the mercy of heaven. In this he followed the example of our Saviour, who says of Himself in the Gospel that He came on earth particularly for sinners.[10] God alone, from whom nothing is hidden, knows what tenderness the Saint felt for sinful souls. Many a journey he made, many an action he performed, many a night he spent, many a labor he endured, that he might snatch these precious souls from sin and win them back to the divine majesty of God. A number of heretics and atheists were among his fortunate conquests.

One of the magnificent, unusual and difficult efforts of his life was the reclaiming of wayward girls and women. His first idea was to open rescue-shelters supported by charitable donations, but he made little headway with these weak souls, who would often return to their evil ways. He then found that the most powerful remedy for this situation was the establishing of the Order of Our Lady of Charity,[11] composed of dedicated women who found glory and merit in the eyes of God by bringing these souls to repentance, contrition and amendment.

Although sinners never loved the Saint as much as he loved them, he was nonetheless ready, in imitation of St. Paul, to give everything freely for the sake of souls,[12] even his own person and the persons of his brethren, dear to him as they were. This was made clear on countless occasions, particularly when he was asked to give a mission from which great good might result, but where there was every reason to expect that the workers would encounter great difficulties and hardships. In this connection he wrote one day: "Since death is inevitable, what happier death could there be for us than to die for the same cause for which the most lovable Saviour sacrificed His life? 'Greater love than this no man hath, that a man lay down his life for his friends.' "[13] The Saint's love for souls obliged him quite often to risk death in order to save them. Since zeal for their salvation, according to the Fathers of the Church,[14] is the most pleasing sacrifice that one can offer to God, St. John Eudes, who in all things sought nothing save the glory of God, had only the good of souls at heart. He was thoroughly happy provided he found souls to save, no matter what unpleasantness or risk the work involved.

NOTES

[1] St. Dionysius, *De Caelesti Hierarchia,* cap. 3; St. Augustine, *Lib. 50 Homiliarum,* Hom. 7; St. John Chrysostom, In cap. IX, *Epist. ad Rom.;* Cassianus, *Collat.* 32, cap. 6; St. Greg. apud S. Bonaventura, *Pharetra,* 1, 1, cap. 4; St. Thomas Aquinas, *Expositio aurea in Joannem,* 10, 15. See *The Priest,* pp. 140–142 for these references to the Fathers.

[2] Lk. 1:53.

[3] This quotation is substantially the same as a paragraph in *The Priest,* p. 137.

[4] The nobleman in question is probably Augustine le Haguais. See *Letters and Shorter Works*, p. 109.

[5] King Louis XIV and Queen Mary Teresa.

[6] This is in the district of Versailles. The royal palace at St. Germain was the official residence of the King and the court.

[7] Philo Judaeus, born about 25 B. C. He received a Jewish education, studying the laws and national traditions, but also followed the Greek plan of studies, which he regarded as a preparation for philosophy. His writings belong for the most part to the literature of commentaries on the Jewish Law. The quotation is from *De Septenario, Omnia opera* (Paris, 1640), p. 1189.

[8] Ecclus. 50:7.

[9] Rom. 10:12.

[10] Mt. 9:13.

[11] In their modern progressive institutions the Religious of our Lady of Charity of Refuge and of the Good Shepherd continue this apostolic work of educating and rehabilitating wayward girls and women.

[12] 2 Cor. 12:15.

[13] Jn. 15:13.

[14] See Eudes, *The Priest*, pp. 136, 138, 140.

Chapter 26. Hatred of Sin

SIN IS THE GREATEST enemy of God. It is infinitely opposed to His divine perfections and attempts insofar as it can to annihilate His essence. Thus have the Fathers of the Church described it. All saintly souls have spared nothing to combat and destroy sin in their battle for the triumph of divine glory. Love for the establishment of Christ's kingdom has put speech in their mouths, pens in their hands and ardent blood in their veins for the avowed purpose of crushing the monster of sin that, through sheer malice, prevents the progress of the kingdom of God. Detestation of sin inspired the Prophets to speak with zeal, incited the Apostles and Martyrs to appear with firmness before the tribunals, compelled the Fathers and Doctors of the church to write with force and eloquence, prompted the Confessors and Virgins, and all the just in general, to pray earnestly and devoutly. Victory over sin was the goal of all their holy undertakings; they had sworn to work for its destruction and they conspired to overthrow it with the resolution never to compromise.

St. John Eudes was one of the most determined foes that the hellish monster of sin has ever encountered. Enlightened with supernatural knowledge that revealed its ugliness to him, animated with something of the same hatred that God holds towards the breaking of His all-holy laws, the Saint overlooked no means of destroying sin in himself and in others. His mind was frequently occupied with incentives to increase his aversion. Sometimes he considered sin in the light of its opposition to the divine majesty and to the holiness of Jesus Christ, who came down from heaven and for thirty-three years endured toil, contempt and pain, shed His blood and suffered the cruelest of deaths to crush the power of evil. St. John Eudes was always deeply moved by meditation on the justice of the eternal Father, overflowing in the person of His only-begotten Son, spotless, yet burdened with the sins of mankind. He often pronounced the words, which he later wrote in one of his books: "O sin, how hateful thou art! O sin, if men knew thee! O sin, truly it must be said that there is something in thee infinitely more horrible than anything within the power of speech or thought to express, since a soul soiled with thy corruption cannot be washed and purged except in the blood of the Incarnate Word Himself, and thou canst not be destroyed and annihilated save only by the death of the God made man!"[1] Sometimes he looked upon sin in the light of the great evil that it inflicts upon man, making him, the servant and child of God, a slave of the devil, even as our Lord spoke of Judas: ". . . one of you is a devil."[2] Sin fills man with dreadful qualities, even as divine grace, uplifting man, renders human beings participants in the perfections of God.

These thoughts aroused in John Eudes an aversion to sin so great that the slightest appearance of it caused him pain. He hated sin more than death and hell; he hated nothing but sin, deeming it the only thing in the world that deserved our hatred. He was never troubled by anything except the offenses committed against the divine majesty of the Most High. He experienced the same feelings that our Lord communicated to other great souls whose lives inspire us with faith. The reader will better understand his attitude toward sin after reading two prayers[3] written and signed by his own hand, which were discovered after his death. In them he implores God for the annihilation of sin. Here is the first, written in his own blood, when he was sixty years old:

"Live Jesus and Mary!"

"O my Lord Jesus Christ, I adore that infinite love with which Thou didst sacrifice and empty Thyself in order to destroy sin, save all souls and bring about the reign of Thy Father in all hearts; I render Thee infinite thanks for it. And in union with this same love, I give myself to Thee, my Saviour, with all my great heart, that is, with all Thy Sacred Heart which is also mine, that I may be completely crushed and annihilated forever, if such be Thy pleasure, and that I may suffer whatever Thou wilt in order to cooperate with Thee in the annihilation of sin, the salvation of all souls and the establishment of Thy reign throughout the world. In witness whereof I have written and signed this in my own blood, being ready, with the help of Thy grace, to sign it with the last drop.

"O Mother of Jesus, O Holy Spouse of Jesus, O my holy guardian angel, O Blessed St. Gabriel, O Blessed St. Joseph, O Blessed St. John the Evangelist, O Blessed Apostles St. Peter and St. Paul, O all ye angels and saints of Jesus, deign to offer to my Saviour, I beseech you, this will of mine which He has given me, and beg Him to bless it and find it pleasing, for love of Himself and His Blessed Mother and for the glory of His name.

"Signed this sixth day of July in the year sixteen hundred and sixty-one. John Eudes, Priest of the Congregation of Jesus and Mary."

The second prayer was composed the same year on the

Feast of Saint Mary Magdalen; it is also written in the Saint's own hand, and is prefaced and concluded with a short note: "While I was saying Holy Mass in the Church at Ableige, six miles from Pontoise, several claps of thunder shook the whole church just after the Consecration. Thereupon I first asked our Lord to grant me the grace to be struck by one of the thunderbolts rather than ever to offend Him deliberately in any way whatsoever; then I offered myself to Him for the following intentions:

"O Jesus, I adore that infinite love which made Thee sacrifice Thyself and die on the Cross in order to destroy sin, save all souls and establish the reign of Thy heavenly Father in every heart. I give myself with my whole heart to that divine love, and in union with the holy dispositions that it inspired in Thee, particularly at the hour of death, as also in thanksgiving for Thy passion and Precious Blood, I offer and give myself to Thee to be struck at this very moment and crushed by a thunderbolt. But I ask of Thee, my Saviour, that all the particles of my ashes may be transformed through Thine all-powerful goodness into so many flashes of lightning, that Thy life and Thine infinite hatred for sin may vouchsafe to use them to strike and annihilate this monster in all souls where it resides, that they may be delivered from its tyranny and established in the reign of Thy divine love. After that is accomplished, O my Jesus, I consent most willingly to be dispatched into nothingness, both in soul and in body, for all eternity. I implore Thee to grant me only one grace, which is this, that my desire to praise and love Thee eternally may not be annihilated but that it may subsist and remain always before Thee, to render Thee undying praise and to declare unceasingly to Thee for evermore that I love Thee with all my great heart, which is none other than Thy own Sacred Heart, since Thou hast given it to me while giving Thyself to me time and time again.

"After that I offered these yearnings to my Holy Mother, to the angels and the saints whom I particularly revere, and to all the inhabitants of heaven, requesting them to present my desires to the most Blessed Trinity. I reiterated this oblation with each clap of thunder and several times more during and after Holy Mass, and it seems to me, by the grace of God, that it was and still remains deep within my heart. I even made this offering of myself with palpable joy and without the slightest fear that I might be taken at my word. What am I after all? Nothingness, sin, hell. Can anything good come from these three miserable sources? No, it is impossible! Whence, then, do these dispositions come? They come from Him who is the sole source of every good thought, word and deed, to whom alone may all honor, glory and praise be rendered for all eternity! Amen, amen, amen! Let all the angels, saints, the holy Spouse of Jesus, the holy Mother of Jesus, Jesus Himself and the most Blessed Trinity repeat 'Amen!' forevermore, and in the way most pleasing to His divine majesty, for the fulfillment of all the above mentioned things. For what is it that I seek, O my God, in this and in everything else, save to please Thee? 'O, ye lightnings and clouds, bless the Lord: praise and exalt him above all forever.' "[4]

Such were the dispositions of this great Saint that reveal to us how deeply the hatred of sin was embedded in his soul. He was so fearful of falling into it that each morning he made an act of renunciation of the temptations of the evil spirit, the sentiments of self-love and other passions that might beset him during the day. He would ask with extraordinary fervor for the grace not to succumb to them. This salutary fear also enabled him to foresee the sins he might commit and the occasions of sin he might encounter each day. He believed this practice so useful in preserving himself in the state of grace that he prescribed it for all the houses of his Congregation, where it is faithfully observed to this day. This is the sacred vigilance commanded by the Saviour to all Christians, as the thing most necessary to their salvation and perfection: "Watch ye and pray that you enter not into temptation."[5]

St. John Eudes made vows to God with reference to his desire to avoid sin of any kind. He also begged his friends and devout persons to obtain for him this grace from God through their prayers. Whenever he perceived that he had committed even the least fault, he would profoundly humble himself in spirit before God, and if the place and occasion allowed, he would cast himself on his knees to beg pardon, making acts of contrition and begging Jesus Christ our Lord to atone for his fault and to grant him new strength that he might not fall again. "Oh, who will give me," he used to cry out on those occasions, "the contrition of St. Peter, St. Mary Magdalen and all the holy penitents, that I may weep for the offenses I have committed against my God with the same feelings of remorse that they experienced in weeping for theirs! Oh, who will make me hate all my iniquities, as the angels and saints hate them! Ah, if only it were possible, my God, for me to entertain as much horror for my sins as Thou hast for them!"[6] In these sentiments the Saint would offer to the eternal Father the atonement of Jesus Christ for his personal sins, uniting himself with it and imploring the divine Saviour to allow him to participate in His expiation.

If St. John Eudes abhorred the thought of sin in himself, it was just as hard for him to put up with it in other persons. He fought evil in public and in private, speaking of it in the strongest terms of execration and anathema. He denounced it thunderingly in the pulpit. If anyone happened to say or do anything offensive to God, he would instantly take the holy and discreet liberty of warning the guilty person. He would always allow for circumstances so that the correction would not be wasted, speaking in a tone neither proud nor scornful. God alone knows how many victories he won over sin. He spared no effort to extend the reign of Jesus Christ, and he expended all his strength in the task of destroying the dragon whose head the Saviour crushed. This is the testimony of all who knew the Saint, particularly of those who attended his parish missions[7] and heard him campaigning against sin.

NOTES

[1] Eudes, *The Kingdom of Jesus,* p. 14.

[2] Jn. 6:71.

[3] These two prayers were found among the papers of the Saint after his death. The original manuscripts have been lost. See *Oeuvres Complètes,* vol. 12, p. 155.

[4] Dan. 3:73.

[5] Mk. 14:38.

[6] Eudes, *The Kingdom of Jesus,* p. 121.

[7] In the course of his priestly life St. John Eudes preached 112 missions in addition to several Advent and Lenten series and retreats. It is important to note that a parish mission in the time of St. John Eudes lasted at least six weeks. Some extended over a period of two or three months. See *Letters and Shorter Works,* p. 211; Joly, *A Life of Saint John Eudes,* p. 57; Sargent, *Their Hearts Be Praised,* p. 42.

Chapter 27. Contempt for the World

THE WORLD HAS always been abhorrent to the saints. In the sixth chapter of Isaias, the Prophet declared that his lips were impure because he was living among a people tainted with sin; thus he showed how dangerous it is even for dedicated persons to live in the midst of sinners.[1] "He that toucheth pitch," says the Holy Spirit, "shall be defiled with it; and he that hath fellowship with the proud, shall put on pride."[2] The atmosphere of the world is one of corruption, that is all too readily absorbed. If the grace of the Saviour does not especially strengthen those who are busy in the world by reason of their vocation, they are in manifest danger of becoming corrupted by the spirit of the world.

That is why true Christians have such a strong aversion to the world, deeming that what the Lord has condemned and considered undeserving of a place in His prayers,[3] is unworthy of any esteem or affection. St. John Eudes considered the world as an indefatigable enemy of his divine Master, who always disapproved of its life, fought against its laws and condemned its maxims as diametrically opposed to the saving doctrine that the Son of God came on earth to reveal. The Saint knew that divine charity is never present in a heart attached to the world; that whoever persists in loving the world makes himself the enemy of God.[4] Every day he paused to adore Jesus Christ in His great detachment from the things of the world, imploring our holy Redeemer to instill in him similar sentiments. He noted that our Lord, in His discourses to His disciples on earth, was particularly intent upon inspiring in them a profound disgust for the world, proclaiming to the eternal Father on their behalf that these chosen ones were not of the world, as He Himself was not.[5]

The Saint used to say that holy priests, following these teachings, had always held themselves aloof from the world and all things that are part of it. That is why he frequently recommended himself to all priests in heaven, asking them to use their God-given power to extinguish completely in his heart all worldly inclinations. This grace was indeed obtained for him; rarely was a man more dead than he to the world in which he actually labored. He took no voluntary satisfaction in anything material. Only when necessity or obedience to the most holy will of God commanded him to do so would he avail himself of the world's usefulness, always without esteeming material advantages or finding peace there; on the contrary, he suffered singularly in the world. In it he felt much as a Christian soul would feel in the depths of hell, and he lived in it as Jesus Christ had done, tolerating it with patience, while working to destroy its power. He constantly longed for the next world, sharing the sentiments of the Psalmist lamenting its delay: "Woe is me, that my sojourning is prolonged!"[6] Like the Prophet David he would sigh for the vision of his Creator: "When shall I come and appear before the face of God?"[7]

The Saint took no part in purely mundane affairs, even those involving his close relatives. He had read in St. Paul's

Epistle to Timothy: "No man, being a soldier to God, entangleth himself with secular businesses; that he may please him to whom he hath engaged himself."[8] This same spirit of renunciation he instilled into all the priests of his Congregation. "We must not under any circumstances," he told them, "become involved in any lawsuit. Many persons come to ask my intervention, but I always excuse myself, even in the case of my brother-in-law who traveled over thirty miles solely for that intention. I tell them all that we have a rule that strictly forbids us to support litigation, but that we shall intercede for them instead with almighty God, His holy Mother, the angels and the saints. You must say the same thing."[9]

The contempt of St. John Eudes for the world inspired in him a great aversion to its round of useless visits and conversations. He strictly avoided all places, persons and gatherings where vanities alone were the subject of conversation. It was difficult, in his opinion, for anyone to listen to people discussing worldly affairs without retaining in his mind a bad impression and in his heart a distaste for holy things. He knew only too well what a pagan[10] wisely said: "He who goes among men comes back less a man."[11] The Saint took special precaution against being curious about the news of the day and he listened to it as little as possible. It amazed him to hear Christians, who are children of God, eagerly speaking a language other than that of their Father, and to see those created for heaven perpetually intent upon the things of earth.

In his association with people of the world, St. John Eudes followed the commandment of St. Peter in his First Epistle, which would have us speak only of God.[12] By supernatural conversation the Saint strove to follow the spirit of our Lord, which is especially present in gatherings where Jesus Christ is spoken of, as He promised in the Gospel.[13] He always sought to use with holy profit the time lost in such a prodigal manner in the world. Consultation about things of this world in no way hindered the mind of Eudes in its elevation to heaven. God was his paradise, his world and his all. His heart was closed to the ideas of men but was always open to divine inspiration. After listening charitably and patiently to persons seeking advice, he would draw them gently to his way of thinking, and by expounding the eternal truths he would induce in them sincere desires to live henceforth in the fear of the Lord, and to work seriously on the important business of their salvation. No one ever came into contact with him without being better for it.

His sense of integrity toward his neighbor made St. John Eudes always speak as he thought without pretense and dissimulation. He would act wisely but without artifice, civilly but without ceremony, gently but without flattery. He never praised lay persons for their talents, wealth, rank or other things that the world esteems. He had read, in the writings of the Fathers,[14] the unforgettable sentence originated by a pagan,[15] that true nobility consists in virtue and that it alone deserves honor.

John Eudes loved the virtue of simplicity all the more because the world so despises and hates it. He had a marked aversion for everything contrary to simplicity, namely, hypocrisy, artifice, pretense, duplicity, trickery, curiosity, affectation, the wisdom of the world and the prudence of the flesh.

The Saint disliked the excessive and the unnecessary. In everything connected with prayer and worship he preferred Christian simplicity and poverty; at no time would he deviate from them in any way. Above all, he dearly loved the truth, which he knew to be the distinctive mark of the children of God. He never promised anything that he did not fully intend to carry out, nor without due consideration before making the promise. Once he had given his word, he kept it promptly and faithfully. He detested exaggeration and could not endure the language of persons who frequently indulged in hyperbole. He believed that affected refinement in speech is always very unbecoming in those who have consecrated their tongue to the Gospel, which at every turn recommends simplicity to Christians. Neither did he wish to see affectation in letters; any mannerisms expressing a worldly spirit came under his ban. He even forbade them to lay persons under his guidance, counseling the strictest integrity of expression, enforced with paternal admonitions.

One example of his gentle corrections is found in a letter to a Benedictine nun: "There was a worldly expression that escaped you in your letter. It was 'this kissing of hands' which I had forbidden you to use. I advise you, for that, to make seven or eight minutes of prayerful meditation on those words which Jesus uttered in speaking of His own: 'They are not of this world, as I am not.' Adore Jesus in His perfect separation from the world, in His manner of speech as in all other things. Adore Him pronouncing those divine words. Give yourself, as well as us, to Him, beseeching Him to separate us completely from the world, and kiss the ground as many times as there are words in this sentence: 'They are not of the world.' "[16]

He likewise reproved one of his spiritual daughters who had committed a similar fault. "I request our dearest Mother Superior to give you a penance for having written in a worldly fashion, which true daughters of the most holy Heart of the Mother of God should flee and abhor utterly, as much in this as in everything else, because all such manners are highly displeasing both to her divine Son and to her."[17]

St. John Eudes had a frightful aversion for worldliness in all its aspects. The continual change of fashion in clothing, furniture and behavior, to which the children of this generation become slaves was unbearable to him. He considered such subjugation even more reprehensible in priests, who are the salt of the earth, that is, its wisdom, who must not lose savor by going through changes like the moon in the manner of lunatics. "What disorder there would be," he remarked, "if one were to see the magistrates and officials of a city follow a madman running through the streets, if they were to dress like him and copy the gestures that rendered him contemptible in the eyes of all the people! It is just as disconcerting to see priests, who are the princes of the Church, follow a senseless world. Instead of being an example for those whom divine providence has entrusted to their care, they become, as our Lord says, spoiled salt which has lost its savor and is good only to be thrown out and trampled underfoot."[18] He therefore despised a worldly appearance and ostentation in all things, and always practiced the greatest simplicity in his clothing, furnishings, speech, preaching, and everything in general.

The Saint particularly lamented the blindness of men whom he used to call martyrs of the devil, meaning those who for the sake of a so-called point of honor, were obliged, according to their damnable code, to sacrifice their well-being, life, soul and salvation to Satan; who did not hesitate in order to satisfy their passions, to challenge to a duel anybody who contradicted them and to soak their hands in Christian blood. Eudes lived at a time when the sin of duelling was at its height in France, with quarrels to the death arising on the slightest provocation. One man even went so far as to thrust his sword through the body of another who was kneeling at the feet of his confessor, simply because the latter did not wish to allow him precedence in receiving the Sacrament of Penance. There were many young men who, being called upon to act as seconds, fought and killed in cold blood their closest friends merely to satisfy the anger or vanity of an insolent challenger who meant nothing to them. The Saint contributed greatly to the correction of this abuse by his fervent insistent preaching against the evil of duelling.

With apostolic zeal St. John Eudes opposed the world and its maxims in all things. He wrote a book vigorously attacking its vices, and gave his condemnation the title of *The Christian Man.*[19] An aristocrat of high merit, indebted to this zealous missionary for his conversion, wrote this to him: "I can well foresee that there will never be any truce between you and the world . . . We must continue to wage this holy warfare in which we have our Saviour as an example and guide."[20]

St. John Eudes considered as a very special favor the gaining of grace to withdraw from the world in order to lead a more Christian life, and he believed it was an important contribution to the salvation of a soul to help a person break the ties that bound him to the world. He had a very high esteem for the religious life. Whenever he discovered indications of a religious vocation, he made every effort to oblige the recipient to obey the promptings of God's grace. He urged parents to implant very subtly in the minds of their children the desire for such a holy life through marked antipathy for anything that would corrupt the innocence of their age, would weaken their baptismal grace or cause them to lose it. To a lady of rank, living under his spiritual guidance,[21] he wrote about her daughter,[22] who gave fair promise for the service of God: "I am of the opinion that your daughter should be wedded to a heavenly and divine Spouse who is King of heaven and earth. Try to incline her gradually to this mystical marriage. Take care that she does not see too much of her enemy, the world, and frequently counsel her to hate the vanities and fashions that arouse the anger of the Blessed Virgin. Be careful specially with whom and in what way she seeks diversion, and try to have her take her recreation with you sometimes. Have her meditate a little too; speak to her often of our Lord, striving to impress upon her a strong hatred for the world and sin, and a great love for Him who desires the exclusive possession of her heart."[23]

The advantageous results of this advice are a matter of record, for the young woman entered the Order of St. Benedict as Sister Anne of Jesus; in only two years she equalled and surpassed in fervor the devotion of the older professed nuns, and after receiving many favors from our Lord whom she had chosen as her Spouse, she died in the odor of sanctity.

The Saint viewed the grace of antipathy to the world and entrance into the religious life as one of the greatest of all blessings. Again and again he advised those who received the grace of a religious vocation to thank His divine majesty continually for this singular gift. "Oh, how happy we are!" he wrote to Mother Mary of the Nativity, his niece. "How much more advantageous is our state in life than the most fortunate positions in the world! Oh, how great is our obligation to bless, love and faithfully serve our Lord and His most holy Mother for having withdrawn us from the inferno of the world to place us in the paradise of their holy house! Ah, how willingly should we embrace all the duties of our profession!"[24]

After what has been said, we need not be astonished that St. John Eudes was so often displeased with the world, and that the world in turn inflicted such cruel persecutions on him. Human respect never deflected him from the least obligation to God, and the world never ceased to persecute him spitefully. He resembled the just man spoken of in the Book of Job, a lamp despised in thoughts of the rich;[25] he glorified in this scorn because our Lord has proclaimed as blessed those who are hated by the world,[26] whose judgments are directly opposed to those of divine wisdom.

NOTES

1 Isa. 6:5.
2 Ecclus. 13:1.
3 Jn. 17:9.
4 James 4:4.
5 Jn. 15:19.
6 Ps. 119:5.
7 Ps. 41:3.
8 2 Tim. 2:4.
9 This extract from one of the Saint's letters was overlooked by the editors of the *Oeuvres Complètes*. St. John Eudes had three brothers-in-law: Peter Herson, Azor Corbin and James Corbin. The brother referred to in this letter is probably Peter Herson, who lived at Falaise, a town nineteen miles southeast of Caen.
10 Seneca, *Epistle* 7. See *Seneca ad Lucilium Epistolae Morales* with an English translation by Richard M. Gummere, vol. 1. Epistle 7, no. 3, p. 31. This is what Seneca says: "Nothing is so damaging to good character as the habit of lounging at the games; for then it is that vice steals subtly upon man through the avenue of pleasure. What do you think I mean? I mean that I come home more greedy, more ambitious, more voluptuous, and even more cruel because I have been among human beings."
11 *Imitation of Christ,* Book I, chapter 20:2.
12 1 Pet. 2:12.
13 Mt. 18:20.
14 Ambrose, *Apologia David altera,* chapter 6; P.L. 14:900. *Et tamen inter ipsos homines major virtutis quam nobilitatis est gratia.* Augustine, *Contra Julianum Pelagum,* L. 4, no. 17; P.L. 44: 745. *Verum tu in hac causa etsi ad scholam Pythagorae provoces vel Platonis, ubi eruditissimi atque doctissimi viri multo excellentiore ceteris philosophia nobilitati veras virtutes non esse dicebant nisi quae menti quodam modo imprimuntur a forma illius*

aeternae immutabilisque substantiae quod est Deus. "You may also appeal to the school of Pythagoras, or that of Plato, where the most erudite and learned in a philosophy far excelling the others in nobility said there are no true virtues except those in some way impressed on the mind by the form of the eternal and unchangeable substance, which is God." See *Saint Augustine, Against Julian,* translated by Matthew A. Schumacher, C.S.C. ("The Fathers of the Church," XXXV [New York, Fathers of the Church, Inc., 1957]), 181.

[15] The pagan referred to here is either Pythagoras or Plato.

[16] Eudes, *Letters and Shorter Works,* p. 16.

[17] *Ibid.,* p. 106.

[18] See Eudes, *The Priest,* p. 109.

[19] *The Christian Man* is one of the Saint's works that remained in manuscript form after his death. It was lost at the time of the French Revolution. See *Letters and Shorter Works,* p. v.

[20] We are unable to say who this "aristocrat of high merit" was. It may have been John Leroux, Seigneur de Langrie, Royal Counsellor, President of the Rouen Parliament. See Eudes, *Letters and Shorter Works,* p. 70, footnote 2.

[21] Madame de Camilly. See Chapter XIX, note 12.

[22] Madame de Camilly's daughter entered the Benedictines of Holy Trinity Abbey at Caen, where she died a holy death on August 23, 1654. See Eudes, *Letters and Shorter Works,* p. 38.

[23] *Ibid. loc. cit.*

[24] *Ibid.,* p. 217.

[25] Job 12:5.

[26] Mt. 5:11.

Chapter 28. Humility

ST. PAUL, SPEAKING of humility, calls it pre-eminently the virtue of our Lord, the virtue that impresses His likeness upon us and gives us the character of true Christians.[1] It is the cornerstone of salvation, the guardian of devotion and the channel of the blessings of heaven. Sacred Scripture teaches us that God, who made all things out of nothing, continues to found His great works of grace upon nothingness.[2] The history of the patriarchs and prophets of the Old Testament, and of the Blessed Virgin Mary and the Apostles in the New Testament, proves it beyond a doubt. Their elevation under God's grace is based on their humility; they were great in His eyes only because they were small in their own estimation.

These inspired thoughts on humility prompted St. John Eudes to say: "Give me a truly humble person and I shall say that he is truly saintly; if that person be humble in great things, I shall pronounce him saintly in great things: and if he is very humble indeed, I shall avow that he is very saintly and adorned with all kinds of virtues. I shall say that God is greatly glorified in such a soul wherein Jesus Christ dwells and finds His treasure and His paradise of delights. That soul will be very great and will occupy a most exalted place in the Kingdom of God, since Eternal Truth has said: 'He that shall humble himself shall be exalted.' On the contrary, a soul without humility is a soul without virtue; it is a hell of pride, the abode of arrogant demons, an abyss of conceit and vice."[3]

According to the teaching of the Fathers, Christian humility consists particularly of two elements: first, self-knowledge; second, love of one's lowliness and nothingness. The first is called humility of mind and the second, humility of heart. How wonderfully versed in this important knowledge of self was St. John Eudes! In this chapter we shall consider his attitude toward himself, reserving for the following chapters the exercises that he practiced in cultivating this beautiful virtue of humility.

Considering himself a man, not in the presumption of the human mind but in the light and truth of God, St. John Eudes acknowledged himself to be earth, corruption and nothingness. He always kept in mind his origin, reflecting frequently on all the moments of his life when he would have been reduced to nothingness if divine bounty had not preserved his being. He was wholly convinced of his own incapacity to do good of himself. This was a common subject of his meditations, and he could say just as truly as Jeremias that he always beheld his own poverty.[4]

His realization of his own inability to think, speak or desire good obliged the Saint to raise himself to God and to cry out with David in sentiments of dependence and humility: "O God, come to my assistance; O Lord, make haste to help me."[5] He would rejoice, like St. Paul, because he was so powerless, since he, too, regarded humility as the foundation on which Jesus Christ could build.[6] He held himself to be less than dust and the most paltry things. He believed that there was no creature, no matter how despicable, who was not of greater worth than he. The corrupting influence of original sin that he felt within himself rendered him contemptible in his own eyes. Even the graces that he received from God were a source of humiliation for him, because of the inadequate use he believed that he made of them, and because of the account of them that he would have to render before the judgment seat of God. He used to say that any strength that Adam had left in our nature was but weakness, and that our feelings about it were illusions, presumption and a false opinion of ourselves. For that reason he made a daily confession at the feet of our Lord of his wretchedness as God beheld it, and renouncing the life of the senses, he would give himself wholly to Jesus in order to live in His spirit and virtue. Since the Saint lowered himself in this manner beneath all created beings, one should not be surprised that he considered himself the least of all men, and, in imitation of his divine Master, thought of himself as a worm and no man.[7]

The knowledge of his own unworthiness went even further. As a son of Adam, St. John Eudes beheld himself conceived and born in original sin, an enemy of God, in some sense, a subject of the devil. He knew that he was a person incapable of doing good or avoiding evil through his own virtue, subjected as he was to the slavery of sin from which he would have been unable to deliver himself if the grace of God had not been powerfully active in him. He expressed these feelings in this manner. "The being that we have received from Adam and have acquired by our sins is a sinful and evil being. According to that being, we are nothing but sin, malediction and abomination. Just as a little leaven completely ferments the lump of dough with which it is mixed and changes it into leaven, and just as a little gall or poison poured into a glass of wine changes it completely into gall or poison, so also has sin depraved, corrupted and poisoned all parts of our bodies and souls so that we are nothing but deprivation, corruption and poison. Similarly, just as the soul so possesses and fills the body it animates that the body has no being, substance or life, no strength or action, save in its soul and through its soul, so also does St. Paul, considering us according to what we are in ourselves, call us 'the body of sin,'[8] because sin is like our soul, our spirit and our life. Of ourselves we have no existence, life or strength except in sin; and we can perform no action except through the spirit and movement of sin."[9]

In these views, the Saint believed himself wholly unworthy of living. He often said that he did not merit that the earth should support him, that God should think of him or trouble to exercise His justice in his behalf. He was amazed, like holy Job, that God should deign to turn His eyes upon him or to stretch forth His hand to condemn and punish him.[10] St. John Eudes used to thank almighty God for the grace of being tolerated in His presence, and for the favor of preventing, by a perpetual miracle, his downfall and destruction. He would acknowledge that he had deserved the wrath of God and of all creatures; that he had merited hell, and that he ought never to glorify himself in anything; that he was infinitely unworthy to receive assistance or good from the Creator or any creature.

It seemed to St. John Eudes that, since he had no right to the privileges of the state of innocence, he was no longer entitled to sunlight, air, fruits of plants or service of animals. He judged, rather, that the whole universe ought to use its forces against him to avenge the injury he had committed against the Creator by offending Him, as will indeed be the fate of sinners at the end of time. He considered that his being and life, his body and soul with all their powers, no longer belonged to him; that he deserved to be stripped of them by divine justice and deprived of all the graces he had ever received.

The Saint never wanted anyone to pay the slightest attention to him personally nor even to think of him, since he believed that he was not worth it. Sometimes he did not even dare, feeling as he did, to ask prayers of others. He used to say that there was no mind capable of understanding his unworthiness except the mind of God, and that no evil could come to him from any source whatever that he did not deserve in greater measure.

He considered that his own will was potentially diabolical, because all the malice of the demons and the antichrist spring from pride of mind and unruliness of will. He realized that he could become capable of committing every crime; that at any moment he might fall into the abyss of sin if God did not preserve him by continual grace. For that reason, sharing the sentiments of St. Philip Neri, he frequently exclaimed: "Lord, take care of me, for I shall infallibly betray Thee today and commit all the sins in the world if Thou dost not help me with Thy grace."[11]

St. John Eudes did not set himself above anyone, not even a notorious sinner. He had, on the contrary, deep compassion for the spiritual lapses of his neighbor, and far from being amazed about them, he would thank God whose all-powerful arm sustained him. He believed himself to be more culpable than those who fell, declaring that if they had enjoyed the same graces as he, they would have been incomparably better. He was convinced that if God had left him to himself, he would have suffered the same tyranny of sin as the demons, and that he would have been wholly transformed into sin, as the saints in heaven are transformed into holiness. He feared that his sins would bring down vengeance on the places where he lived or visited. Like St. Dominic, whenever he entered a city he would beg our Lord not to engulf it because of his sins.[12]

These sentiments were so deeply impressed on his mind and heart that humility enabled him to resist attacks by temptations of pride so common to learned men and saints. He was amazed how some men, great though they seem to worldlings, bear the marks of their ignominy, that is, the characteristics of sinners, and yet are still so prone to vanity and self-esteem. Like St. Paul, he regarded them as seducing themselves into false notions of their own grandeur.[13] With the same Apostle he looked upon them as liars who boast of good in themselves which they do not really possess;[14] as thieves who rob God of the glory that belongs to Him alone; as demons who have no desire to accept their infamy, although they are the most wretched of creatures.

The Saint was willing to forego his own judgment to yield to others in matters secondary to his apostolate. He respected his equals and inferiors because he considered them all to be above him. Rather than censure the actions of others, he would praise them for whatever good he could find. He never said anything detrimental about anyone. He used to rejoice whenever his labors were frowned upon. If he began to feel pleasure in his holy undertakings, he would immediately humble himself profoundly before God, remembering that all justice comes from on high, and that nothingness and sin are the lot of every creature. He believed that he had more to fear from the faults and imperfections of his own actions than he had reason to exalt himself. He protested countless times at the foot of the crucifix that in all things he was seeking only the glory of God alone, confessing that he deserved to be banished from God's presence and swallowed up by the earth. He never considered, when receiving any grace, that it was being granted to him because of himself or by virtue of his prayers, but because of Jesus Christ, the Son of God, to whom the eternal Father has given all power and to whose merit He refuses nothing.[15] The humility that revealed his nothingness did not hide from him what he was in our Lord, to whom he was always most grateful for the favors received from divine bounty.

Whenever St. John Eudes happened to commit a fault, he would humble himself without becoming discouraged. Trying always to preserve peace in his heart without allowing himself to be troubled, he would confess at the feet of the Sovereign Judge that it was through his unfaithfulness that he had fallen; that if God treated him according to his merit, not only would He deprive him of graces in the future, but would even strip him of those He had granted him in the past and would abandon him entirely. These very humble sentiments enkindled in his soul fresh fires of love and renewed confidence. He persevered in giving himself to our Lord in order to use His graces more faithfully and to live with greater devotion to the service of Him who still tolerated him so mercifully after his failures. He lamented his shortcomings because they were displeasing to God, but consoled himself because they gave him occasion to love God more strongly and to unite himself more intimately with Him. He longed to be delivered from faults because they were contrary to the love of Jesus, but he humbled himself when he committed them, turning them into fresh reasons for having recourse to our Lord.

The Saint gave similar advice to the persons under his guidance. "No, my dear Sister, no," he wrote to a Benedictine nun, "as long as we remain on earth we shall never be entirely free from the shortcomings and imperfections of the world. O earth, how unbearable thou art! O abode of sin and misfortune, wilt thou hold us here yet a long time? O Jesus, wilt Thou not call us soon to join Thee? Tell us, most lovable Jesus, when will there no longer remain anything in us that is contrary to Thy love? When shall we love Thee perfectly? Let us hasten, my dear Sister, to labor for the accomplishment of God's work in ourselves, so that we may soon leave this place of darkness and horror to enter into the kingdom of eternal love.

"Furthermore, let us always humble ourselves profoundly in view of our shortcomings; but at the same time, let us cast off ourselves, flee from ourselves, as from a place filled with all sorts of evils and miseries, that we may enter into Jesus who is our house of refuge, our treasure in which we possess every kind of wealth and shall find all types of virtues and perfections to offer His eternal Father in satisfaction for our sins and imperfections. If we dwell within ourselves, we shall find nothing therein save only cause for grief and sadness; but if we emerge from ourselves in order to ascend to Jesus, we shall behold in Him so many delights, perfections and wonders that, if we truly love Him, we shall rejoice exceedingly in the sight of these things, exclaiming with the most Blessed Virgin: 'My spirit hath rejoiced in God my Saviour.'[16] That is one of the uses we should make of our defects. O blessed shortcomings, if I may so express it, when they give us cause to cast ourselves aside in order to ascend to Jesus and unite ourselves with Him, who alone is free from shortcomings and imperfections! Belong to Him alone; remain wholly and forever in Him. In this Jesus I am devotedly yours and ever more and more. Live Jesus and Mary!"[17]

One can see that the Saint found strength in his weakness, reason for his elevation in his lapses. Instead of yielding to discouragement as cowardly souls usually do after committing sin, he would find in such occasions a new incentive to throw himself with humility and confidence into the arms of our Lord who was always so merciful despite his unfaithfulness.

St. John Eudes abhorred praise and considered it as a poison very pernicious to the virtue of souls. He would shudder when anyone spoke well of him, recalling the words of our Lord in the Gospel: "Woe to you when men shall bless you."[18] At such times he used to raise his heart to God who alone is worthy of praise. He kept on his lips, and still more in his thoughts, the words of Sacred Scripture: "To me be confusion and shame, but to Thee, O God, be honor and glory."[19] He wanted himself to be out of the minds of creatures, not wishing men to see anything in him but God. Such was his humble prayer frequently offered to God with an ardor and earnestness beyond the power of a biographer to express. In the following chapter we shall see in greater detail how deeply he loved humility which he had chosen as his spouse and which he always sought with the affection of a true lover.

NOTES

[1] Phil. 2:5–9.
[2] Mt. 11:25; Lk. 10:21.
[3] Eudes, *The Kingdom of Jesus*, p. 39.
[4] Lam. 3:1.
[5] Ps. 69:1.
[6] 2 Cor. 13:9.
[7] Ps. 21:7.
[8] Rom. 6:6.
[9] This excerpt may be from a sermon or conference by St. John Eudes. The exact source is unknown. It is quoted by A. Pioger, *Un Orateur de l'Ecole Française* (Paris, Bloud et Gay, 1940), pp. 128–129. Compare this extract with passages in *The Kingdom of Jesus*, pp. 40–42. See also E. Georges in *La Spiritualité de l'Ecole Française et Saint Jean Eudes* (Paris, Notre Vie, 1949), Lecture IV, "La Philosophie de l'Homme dans la Spiritualité de l'Ecole Française," p. 25.

[10] Job. 9:14.

[11] Father Herambourg gives this quotation in Latin: *A me tibi caveas, Domine, te enim hodie traditurus sum et omnia perpetratus mundi peccata, nisi me tua gratia benigne protexeris.* See Pietro Bacci, *The Life of St. Philip Neri* (St. Louis, B. Herder, 1903), Vol. 1, p. 227.

[12] See A. T. Drane, *The History of St. Dominic* (London, Longmans, Green, 1891), p. 194.

[13] Gal. 6:3.

[14] 1 Cor. 4:7.

[15] Mt. 28:18.

[16] Lk. 1:47.

[17] Eudes, *Letters and Shorter Works,* p. 271.

[18] Lk. 6:26.

[19] In this ejaculation St. John Eudes combines the thoughts of two biblical texts: Prov. 13:18; 1 Tim. 1:17. See "Profession of humility," in Eudes, *Meditations on Various Subjects,* p. 55.

Chapter 29. Love of Humiliations

I AM BEGINNING THIS chapter with the thoughts of St. John Eudes himself, who used to say that humility of mind without humility of heart is diabolical. The devils possess humility of mind because they know only too well their disgrace and accursedness. They lack, however, the loving acceptance of their wretchedness and abject state, which is the essence of humility of heart.[1] As a faithful disciple of Jesus Christ, the Saint had learned to know himself. Moreover, he sought constantly to practice this knowledge, essential to sanctity. He often cast himself in adoration at the feet of his divine Master, pronouncing these words: "If any man will come after me, let him deny himself, and take up his cross and follow me."[2] He passionately strove to love humiliations and induced a number of saintly souls to request that grace for him. We have every reason to believe that God granted it in full measure.

Our Blessed Lord gave us the perfect example of humility in His avoidance of honors and His acceptance of scorn. The Gospel narrates how He fled from the crowd that wanted to make Him king[3] and how He delivered Himself up to the troops and mob coming to take Him prisoner and completed

His humiliation even to death on the cross. St. John Eudes chose our divine Redeemer as his model. Few can be found who were so far removed from everything that savored of prestige and position. He abhorred honor and compliments. Although he had founded a religious Congregation that became distinguished, even in his lifetime, both for the immense good it accomplished and for the brilliance of its founder, he never assumed the title of Superior General. He would not let himself be called by that name, and he always prevented its insertion in the contracts and public enactments of the Congregation. He believed it too great an honor for him even to be the servant of servants of God. His love for humility prompted him to refuse important benefices in the Church; he wanted none because too much pomp and magnificence were attached to them. One of the most distinguished bishops of France,[4] desiring to vacate his see in favor of the Saint, received this reply to the urgent recommendation of acceptance made through a mutual friend:

"I do not even presume to write to his Lordship, for I am so filled with astonishment, confusion and fear, in view of the frightful danger confronting me, that I do not know where I stand. I feel like one who has lost his mind and power of speech, except that, if I dared, I should cry out that I desire no benefice save the one my Saviour chose for Himself, which is the Cross. My only consolation is that I have confidence in the incomparable goodness of my most lovable Jesus, and of His most bountiful Mother and mine, that they will direct all things in the manner most pleasing to them. That is my only prayer to them, save that they grant me the grace to do their most holy will everywhere and in all things. I see all that our dear M. de . . . fears for me, and it causes my nature to shudder and tremble. But my spirit embraces all for the love of our adorable crucified Saviour and in reparation for my sins, the least of which merits infinitely worse, for I have the greatest confidence that my good Mother will not abandon me."[5]

This letter reveals the attitude of St. John Eudes. He deemed himself unworthy to be elevated to a high position in the Church, but knew that God could give him the dispositions necessary to carry out such a great task as it should be done. His humility brought him low, while his submission to the divine will sustained him in that humility. Self-distrust made him reluctant, but his trust in God inspired him not to resist. His fear of human respect and his genuine humility impelled him to write a second time to the same person in these terms, putting an end to all efforts to oblige him to accept the bishopric:

"The fear I have had up to now of resisting the will of God in that matter of which you are aware, sir, obliged me to endure what was being said and done to further it; but at last the crystal-clear view that I have of my great, my very great, my almost infinite unworthiness, and the fear of seeing myself compelled to answer to God for the salvation of so many souls, oblige me to tell you, sir, that I declare openly and from the bottom of my heart that I want no benefice other than the one my Saviour chose for Himself, that is, the Cross. This is the benefice I desire, that I embrace and love with all my heart for the love of my most amiable crucified Saviour, who loved and preferred it to all that the world loves and esteems more highly. I want no other, unless God absolutely wills it. I implore you to read this letter to His Lordship and to the vicar-generals, as well as to His Lordship of. . . ."[6]

It is obvious from this letter that his lack of eminence in the Church came from his personal humility. He preferred to live in a low position, more suitable to his spouse, the beautiful virtue of humility, which finds nourishment in the midst of scorn, abasement and opposition.

Recognizing that humiliation was his heritage, as a son of Adam, St. John Eudes remained at peace. He had pondered at length the inspired words of Ecclesiasticus: "Humble thyself in all things, and thou shalt find grace before God."[7] He profited by this counsel and made it one of his most common practices, knowing it to be the true means of rendering to the divine majesty of God the honor which is due to Him. He always began his actions with a confession of his own wretchedness, declaring he was unworthy to exist, to live or to act, and that he was incapable of doing anything pleasing in the sight of God without the help of divine grace. Several times daily, but particularly in the morning he would approach the feet of our Lord and His holy Mother, saying to them with an affection truly indicative of his strong determination:

"O Jesus, O Mother of Jesus, keep this miserable demon well under foot, crush this snake, exterminate this antichrist with a single breath of your mouths; bind this Lucifer, that he may do nothing today against your glory. I call down upon myself the power of your spirit of humility in order to annihilate my pride and bind me close to you in humility. I offer up to you all the opportunities to practice humility that present themselves in my life and particularly today. Deign, I humbly beseech you, to bless them. I renounce myself and all things which may prevent me from sharing in the grace of your humility."[8] This exercise was so fruitful for him that he also used it to ask for the other virtues which he needed most.

This love of humiliation caused the Saint to hide, as much as he could in a life of public service to God, the great talents he had received from divine bounty. His intellect was remarkably keen, his judgment profound, his knowledge sublime, yet he rarely gave evidence of his qualifications, cultivating the utmost simplicity of manner. In an age noted for elegant diction and richness of oratory he preached simply, not seeking either subtlety of thought or beauty of language. He never spoke like a learned person or a saint, not even in private consultation; rather, he would make the most humble replies. He expected no acknowledgment of the good he did; he believed himself obliged to do it, judging, like St. Paul, that he was indebted to everyone but that no one owed anything to him.[9] He wanted only the most ordinary things, whether spiritual or material. He accepted graciously everything presented to him, no matter if badly prepared, saying that it was too good for him and that he did not deserve it. If given a choice, he always took the least attractive of everything and sought in all things to contradict and stifle natural impulses. He even feared extraordinary graces, which sometimes appear before human eyes, such as visions and ecstasies, ever mindful of the dangers to which they expose the soul unless it is extremely well grounded in humility.[10] Far from desiring such favors, he used to withdraw into the depths of his nothingness, satisfied simply to receive from divine bounty graces to render him more conformable to the hidden life of our Blessed Lord on earth.

In order to destroy natural pride, the Saint sought earnestly and devoted himself humbly to lowly activities despised by the world. Whenever possible he used to go to the kitchen to wash the dishes with the lay brothers of his house, from whom he would take orders. Sometimes he publicly humbled himself in the presence of the community,[11] accusing himself of the sins he had committed, in such humble terms and with a heart so pierced by sorrow that all his spiritual sons were deeply touched to witness it. His intention was to honor, by these practices of abasement, the humiliations suffered by our divine Saviour at the hands of men, particularly at the time of His passion. The Saint also used these practices of humility to make amends to God for the sins that he had committed, and for the bad example he had given his Community; to obtain from our Lord the spirit of humility for his Congregation and to gain new strength to overcome his shortcomings, which he regarded from the viewpoint of God rather than from that of men, who are so easily mistaken.[12]

St. John Eudes considered himself to be responsible for the sins of all who were under his guidance. He looked upon the sins of the world as his own, too, and he deemed himself obliged to do penance for them in his role as priest. He would have been ready, in his humility, to accuse himself publicly and before the whole universe of all the sins of his life, if God had asked it of him. Not being satisfied with humbling himself privately and secretly in the house where he lived, he would frequently do so in writing, too, at the feet of his scattered spiritual children, asking pardon of them for his bad example and beseeching them to implore our Lord to grant him the grace to correct his faults, in keeping with his constant desire to do so.

Eudes was accustomed to anticipate the reaction of those whom he offended, taking the blame upon himself and asking pardon for the opportunity he might have afforded them to become angry with him. He did the same with respect to those whose feelings he had hurt, however slightly. He once did everything in his power to retain a priest who wanted to leave his Congregation, kneeling before him three times while the other remained standing. He always wrote respectfully to his subordinates; being extremely distrustful of himself, he would ask their advice with humility.

For a long time St. John Eudes sought to have someone else assume the responsibility of superior general, believing himself unworthy of the post. After the election was over, he knelt at the feet of his successor[13] to receive his blessing. He was never more lighthearted than when he could be relieved of the obligation of issuing orders, which to him seemed a heavy yoke, so that he might embrace obedience, which he found a lighter burden and more in conformity with the weakness of shoulders already burdened with age.[14]

He welcomed every sort of humiliation, not as a trial, sent by God, but as a chastisement of divine justice. He never complained about anyone except to our Lord and our Lady. Mindful that he had in himself the source of all evil, he believed that he was deserving of every scorn. He used to say that everyone had a right to persecute him, except that he was not worth the trouble. The example of our Saviour who had glorified the eternal Father by His ignominy was the powerful incentive that induced the Saint to find all his joy in humiliations. He expressed his feelings on this subject in a letter to one of his missionary priests: "While you are contending with the seven-headed, ten-horned monster where you are, it is striving to wage war on us here. But, thanks be to God, it does not deprive us of peace. For those to whom God grants the grace to be, to have and to do what they wish, because they desire only what He wills, those, I repeat, always possess perfect peace. And then, too, I agree with our benefactors,[15] for I have resolved to take their part with them against myself and my sins because I find that they are right in wanting to annihilate a sinner who deserves the wrath of God and of all His creatures, provided they do what they are doing with the zeal of divine justice and in the spirit of Christian charity. That is what I should and wish to believe."[16]

Such was the attitude of the Saint, who considered all evil to be in his own person; who, having become his own witness and judge, accused and condemned himself, censuring and criticizing his actions which he saw filled with imperfections. He hated his life as the Saviour orders us to do.[17] He was amazed that creatures tolerated him and did not strive to crush him. He was convinced that he could never penetrate the depths of his own unworthiness; that, although he did everything possible to humble himself, it would always be far removed from the scorn that his lowliness really deserved; that, whenever man worked or plotted to cover him with confusion, he received only a very small part of what he actually deserved, and that God alone could punish him in just proportion. He was ready to be annihilated in imitation of the abnegation of the life, passion and death of Jesus Christ, seeking with our Saviour to be made the opprobrium of men, to bear the wrath of the eternal Father as much as he was capable of doing, to be subjected to the powers of darkness and to suffer all the infamy which is the consequence and lot of sin. He was sometimes heard to say: "O man, how canst thou still be vain, beholding thy God downtrodden for love of thee? O my Saviour, let me be humbled and annihilated with Thee, that I may share thy sentiments of most profound humility and be ready to bear all the confusion and lowliness due to sinners and to sin itself."[18]

It was this deep spirit of humility that made St. John Eudes such a worthy instrument in God's hands and made him perform wonders in his apostolic work. He could truly say with the Blessed Virgin Mary that the Almighty wrought great things in him and through him[19] because God regarded the humility of His servant, who debased himself more and more each day in his own sight that he might be more pleasing in the eyes of the divine majesty.

NOTES

[1] Eudes, *The Kingdom of Jesus,* p. 44.

[2] Mt. 16:24.

[3] Jn. 6:15.

[4] His Lordship Henry de Maupas du Tour (1608–1680), Bishop of Evreux, Normandy. See Sargent, *op. cit.,* p. 251.

[5] *Letters and Shorter Works,* p. 230. For a recently edited letter from St. John Eudes to Bishop de Maupas, see *Saint Jean Eudes, Lettres choisies et inédites,* présentées par Charles Berthelot du Chesnay (Namur, Editions du Soleil Levant, 1958), p. 176.

[6] *Letters and Shorter Works, loc. cit.*

[7] Ecclus. 3:20.

[8] Eudes, *The Kingdom of Jesus,* p. 49.

[9] Rom. 13:7–8.

[10] Eudes, *ibid.,* p. 45.

[11] The Saint prescribed the regular accusation of faults in the Congregation of Jesus and Mary. This community exercise, which is performed every Friday, is called "Humiliation." See *Manual of Piety,* p. 119.

[12] See *ibid.,* p. 120 for the proper dispositions with which "Humiliation" should be made.

[13] Father John James Blouet de Camilly (1632–1711), eldest son of James Blouet and Anne Le Haguais. He entered the Congregation of Jesus and Mary on February 8, 1655, at the age of 23. In June, 1680 he was elected superior general of the Congregation of Jesus and Mary to succeed the founder, St. John Eudes.

[14] The Saint was in his eightieth year.

[15] St. John Eudes frequently referred to his enemies as his "benefactors."

[16] Eudes, *Letters and Shorter Works,* p. 281.

[17] Jn. 12:25.

[18] *The Kingdom of Jesus,* p. 47.

[19] Lk. 1:49.

Chapter 30. His Teaching on Humility

OUR BLESSED LORD came on earth to reveal to mankind lessons in the virtue of humility, so contrary to human values. Our divine Saviour not only practiced humility but gave specific instructions about it. His example was the most convincing argument for its necessity, as the Master told His disciples plainly: "Learn of me, because I am meek and humble of heart."[1] To be under the guidance of St. John Eudes inspired love for humility. One became versed in it simply by talking with him. There was an indefinable quality in his person which inspired humility; even the sight of him was an education in humility. Not satisfied with a humble outward demeanor, he also strove, in imitation of our Saviour, to teach humility by word of mouth both in public and private, and particularly to his own spiritual sons and daughters. He made humility the foundation of the structure of his Congregations, and of the formation of their members.

St. John Eudes believed that the grace of the priesthood, which surpasses all others, obliged priests to be the most humble of all creatures. He commanded his spiritual children to esteem other religious congregations and orders more highly than their own, while they were obliged to love theirs best because God had called them to it. He gave them an example of humility on every occasion that arose, leaving them the beautiful prayer of humility beginning with these words: "Lord Jesus Christ, we are nothing,"[2] like a mirror in which to see themselves as they really were. Persons in the world, even if they are not especially curious about their physical charms, need to look at themselves in a mirror each morning, and even several times a day, in order to keep neat and clean. Similarly the Saint believed it necessary for servants of God, in solicitude for the spiritual beauty of their souls, to pause frequently before the mirror of Christ's lowliness to see if secret pride or self-esteem had diminished their humility in any way.

On Monday of each week, his spiritual children were to take the virtue of humility as the subject of meditation. Working to eliminate the feelings of jealousy that usually spring up in communities because some members have preference on account of their talents or qualifications, the Saint advised the members of his Congregation who were important in the eyes of the world for high rank or learning not to seek to be more highly esteemed in the community, but to believe that the only true merit in the sight of God is that which is acquired through virtue. His praise for preachers was moderate and was chiefly for the encouragement of beginners. He constantly admonished his spiritual sons about their shortcomings or else directed some other prudent person to do so. Whenever a superior was removed from office, he was to take the last place among the priests of the house for a year, and was to live in the midst of his brethren as if he had never been put in command.

Pride was the vice that the Saint feared most in his spiritual children. He taught them to humble themselves at every suitable opportunity and ordered them to defer to the opinions of others when the issue was not contrary to the morality of the Gospel. This point he stressed very strongly in one of his letters. "Over and above all, let us avoid disputes and quarrels that arise from adhering stubbornly to our interpretation of things, and have their source in pride. Pride cannot humble itself, and it never wants anyone to believe that it is ignorant of anything; rather, it always desires to triumph and have the advantage in all things, and to appear what it is not."[3] During the course of each year, the Saint also outlined a number of practices to be followed in order to preserve within the hearts of his spiritual children the all-important spirit of humility.

St. John Eudes also endeavored to implant this virtue deeply in the souls under his guidance. When his niece, Sister Mary of the Nativity Herson, was preparing to take the holy habit in the Order of Our Lady of Charity, the order for women that he founded, he gave her this advice: "The principal thing you must do is to humble yourself profoundly at the sight of your own unworthiness, wretchedness and lowliness, and earnestly to beseech the most Blessed Virgin Mary to obtain for you from her divine Son the grace to regard and treat yourself always as the least of anyone in the house. That, my dear daughter, is what I particularly recommend to you; implant it deeply in your heart that it may never escape, and in that way you will truly be one of the daughters of the Mother of love and humility."[4]

To a Superior of the same Order[5] who had told the Founder of her spiritual state and of the insight God was affording her into her nothingness and unworthiness, he wrote: "It is true, my dear Mother, that the miseries of the children of Adam are infinitely great beyond the power of speech or thought to describe them, for we bear within ourselves two unfathomable pits of wretchedness: the first is the abyss of our nothingness, and the second is that of sin. God permits you, or rather, He gives you the special grace to see in yourself some portion of these two vast sources of miseries, and for two reasons: first, He desires you to use this means to close all the approaches of your heart to that accursed vanity which so singularly ravages many souls who profess to be virtuous and pious—who even aspire to perfection—and which, alas, precipitates many into the fires of hell! Then, too, it is to preserve, strengthen and increase within you the most essential of all virtues, that of humility, which fashions the souls it possesses according to the Heart of our Lord and of His most holy Mother. Secondly, it is to render you conformable to our most adorable Master who is Jesus. According to the testimony of the Prophet Jeremias our Lord says of Himself: 'I am the man that sees my poverty.'[6] The humanity of Jesus recognized perfectly that of itself it was nothing, and stemmed from nothingness. The God made man also penetrated even to the depths of the abyss of nothingness and sin, a sight that caused Him the most profound and inconceivable humiliation, as well as inexpressible pain. Adore the Word Incarnate, my dearest Mother, in this state. Thank Him for having deigned to assume human nature for love of you. Give yourself to Him so that you may accompany Him on whatever road it may please Him to take you. Offer your little troubles in thanksgiving for His immense trials. Ask Him to make good use of them in your name. Finally, abandon yourself with your whole heart to the divine providence of God, that He may lead you wherever He will and in His own way.

"For your part, remain always humble and submissive to the guidance of God, but take care never to become discouraged; rejoice, rather, and give thanks to our Lord for the graces He grants you. For I repeat, my dearest Mother, what I perceive quite clearly to be true: that your present state, as you describe it to me, is a great gift of God. 'Blessed is he,' says St. Paul, 'that condemneth not himself in that which he alloweth.'[7] When anyone feels and believes himself very good, he is not good; and when anyone thinks himself quite wicked, he is most worthy in the eyes of God. But let us abandon ourselves entirely to the judgment, will and guidance of Him who knows and loves us infinitely more than we ourselves do. Let us dwell in the house of our nothingness and await with patience, humility, simplicity and submission Him who desires only nothingness as the material and substance with which to do whatever is pleasing to Him. With my whole heart do I deliver you, my dearest Mother, to His omnipotent bounty, beseeching Him to annihilate you so completely that He may be all things to you. Please offer the same prayer for me."[8]

This letter shows how perfectly the Saint possessed the knowledge of humility. His plainness of speech reveals how noble were his sentiments on this subject, but it is also evident how humble he himself was, since he practiced everything he preached. "When God," he once said, "gives us but a single good thought after we have worked hard for Him, we should consider ourselves handsomely rewarded for our trouble, and acknowledge, furthermore, that we do not deserve even one."[9]

Humility was the greatest good that he desired for souls. He judged that other blessings without humility were valueless; and that, in possessing it alone, one possessed them all. That is how he explained it to his daughters, the Religious of Our Lady of Charity, in whose perfection he took such great interest. "Be very humble, my dear daughters, be very humble. Oh, how greatly I do desire you to be humble, for when you achieve humility, our Lord will abundantly infuse

His graces into your hearts. A soul which is truly humble is indeed wealthy, for it possesses all; but a soul lacking in humility has nothing. It is like a sieve through which everything passes, and thus God takes no care to bestow and shed His graces on that soul, since they would be lost."[10]

Because St. John Eudes was well versed in the knowledge of his captivity under the law of sin,[11] his unworthiness in the service of God, his inadequacy in anything pertaining to good, his infinite need of Jesus Christ and divine grace, which caused him to cry out unceasingly to the divine Liberator, he tried also to inspire others with the same realization, saying to them: "God sometimes permits us to work a long time in order to conquer our predominant passion or to become firm in a special virtue, and yet to make little progress in what we are striving for, so that from experience we may recognize what we are and what we are capable of doing by ourselves, and thus be obliged to seek outside ourselves, in our Lord Jesus Christ, the power of serving God. God did not choose to give His divine Son to the world until it had yearned thousands of years for Him, and had learned from experience that it was unable to observe His law or deliver itself from sin, and that it needed a new spirit and strength in order to resist evil and do good, which proves to us that He wants us to be well aware of our own unworthiness so that He may give us His grace."

The Saint considered humility so necessary for salvation, as our Lord teaches in the Gospel,[12] that he often made humility the subject of his sermons, zealously denouncing from the pulpit the vices opposed to it. He gave to the public meditations on humility full of divine unction.[13] In them he so penetrated the depths of the nothingness and wretchedness of mankind that it seemed as if humility had wholly revealed itself to him. This was the testimony given by a number of learned and spiritual souls, who heard him and contended that it was impossible to reflect even a little on his message without feeling impelled to practice humility more faithfully. Humility is the sacred field in which the just can unearth the precious treasure of self-knowledge,[14] the fruits of which are apparent today in a countless number of souls who have been seeking it for a long time.

NOTES

[1] Mt. 11:29.

[2] See Eudes, *Meditations on Various Subjects,* p. 95.

[3] This is a fragment of a letter that is not found in the editions of the correspondence of St. John Eudes.

[4] See Eudes, *Letters and Shorter Works,* p. 78.

[5] Mother Margaret Patin, a Visitation nun, became superior of the Monastery of Our Lady of Charity at Caen on August 10, 1644. For twenty years she guided the nascent community and trained the first sisters of the Order. Mother Patin died on October 31, 1668. See Eudes, *ibid.,* p. 80; Rev. J. Ory, *The Origin of the Order of Our Lady of Charity* (Buffalo, Leader Press, 1918), p. 32.

[6] Lam. 3:1.

[7] Rom. 14:22.

[8] Eudes, *Letters and Shorter Works,* p. 81.

[9] This extract is from a letter that was lost. It is not found in the *Oeuvres Complètes.*

[10] Eudes, *Letters and Shorter Works,* p. 253.

[11] Rom. 7:23.

[12] Mt. 23:13; Lk. 14:11.

[13] Eudes, *Meditations on Various Subjects,* "Meditations on Humility," pp. 96 ff.

[14] Mt. 13:44.

Chapter 31. Chastity and Mortification

PURITY, WHICH ST. PAUL calls the sanctification of the flesh,[1] resembles the guardian angel of a person consecrated to God. If our bodies are living temples of the Blessed Trinity,[2] purity is their sacristan and high priest, says Tertullian.[3] Since the office of priests or guardians of temples is to remove anything that may desecrate the holiness of such places, as well as to adorn them suitably, purity makes a Christian remote from the vices which profane his body, and are most opposed to the spirituality and holiness of God; it endows the soul with a beauty capable of winning and attracting the Sacred Heart of our Lord. If purity is necessary for Christians, how much more is it for priests, who are the visible angels of this world, who accompany the spotless Lamb everywhere in His Church, and who continually engage in functions which call for imitation of divine purity? The High Priest of the Old Law used to wear small bells[4] stitched on the hem of his garment in order to teach all priests of the New as well as of the Old Testament, that their steps, words and actions should everywhere proclaim their holiness.

St. John Eudes possessed a very special love for chastity. He led the life of an angel in the body of a man, and his flesh became all spiritual, as Tertullian says of virgin bodies, *angelisata caro.*[5] Purity was a hidden treasure, one that he always guarded with reserve and modesty. The Saint feared the very shadow of impurity more than any other sin. He shunned whatever might possibly give rise to it, closing all the doors of his heart by a complete mortification of his senses, especially the sense of sight.

The downfall of some ecclesiastics whom he had known personally caused the Saint to shudder because he realized that they had fallen into the abyss by carelessness about small things. He was circumspect about the most trivial matters, particularly in his conversation with women. He spoke to women only when necessity and charity obliged him to do so, and then always in a place which precluded any suspicion, and as briefly as possible. He did not allow them the liberty of coming to see him except for special and necessary reasons. If he spoke to them in the church, he did so only in passing, while standing, and then for a very short time. In the confessional he spoke only on the duties of their state in life and how to discharge them. In any place whatever, he conversed with his eyes lowered. His own modesty threw a veil over his face which prevented him from seeing them. Being the minister of a jealous God, he never wanted a single look to cause divine displeasure.

To inspire these same sentiments in his Congregation, Eudes ordered the entrances of the houses to be strictly closed to women, with the exception of princesses, outstanding benefactresses and persons of high authority, and even these were not admitted unaccompanied. In each house he ordered a place set aside near the door, open to view, where it would be possible to hold a conversation with women whenever necessary. On his generous visits to the sick, he always took a companion, and whenever he heard their confessions, he had the door kept open so that both he and the sick woman could always be plainly seen. He was ever mindful of the modesty of our Lord and His Blessed Mother and was a perfect image of them.

It was to preserve the precious treasure of chastity, which we carry in fragile vessels, that St. John Eudes cultivated a great devotion to the most Blessed Virgin Mary. He established the practice of having the *Inviolata*[6] sung every Saturday, in each of his houses, in honor of the most immaculate purity of our holy Mother, physical as well as spiritual, and to implore her to obtain from God for the members of his Congregation a great love for this virtue, together with deep horror for the vice opposed to it. For this same intention he particularly honored the holy virgins in the great company of saints.

To these precautions St. John Eudes added penance and mortification. At meals he ate only the most commonplace food. Whenever the presence of guests obliged him to do otherwise, he felt great aversion. He would do so, nevertheless, in condescendence to his neighbor, and for fear of giving some persons reason to murmur against him and so to offend God. He deprived himself of everything that went beyond the limits of pure necessity. He was a true Nazarene who never violated the rules of sobriety. He would have imitated the austerity of John the Baptist if he had been able to do so. Never was he happier than when he lacked even the necessities of life, considering himself fortunate to be able to imitate, on such occasions, the poverty of our Lord and His holy Mother. Indeed, he conceived such a high esteem for mortification that he nearly always bore outward signs of it. He wished to practice it not only with regard to food but even in his manner of dressing. He glorified in wearing the livery of the heavenly princess, Poverty, the adornment of Jesus and Mary and most of the saints during their mortal life. He considered poverty to be one of the virtues contributing most to the preservation of chastity.

The Saint did not believe that it was enough to eliminate the superfluous and deprive himself sometimes of necessities; he also chastened his body to an extraordinary degree, practicing every kind of penance. From the time he was fifteen years old, vigils, fasts, hair shirts and iron chains were his usual means of doing penance. He used them until he passed the age of forty, with such severity that he completely undermined his strength. He bore, as St. Paul recommends, the mortification of the Saviour in his body.[7] He made himself, by his own hand and without the help of anyone, a man of sorrow. He immolated himself daily in bloody sacrifices that Christ, whom he offered on the holy altar, might be better received by the divine majesty. He went to such extremes that his spiritual adviser obliged him to moderate his rigors in order to spare himself for missionary work, to which he had dedicated himself at the age of twenty-four, and with which he continued for the rest of his life. His director ordered him to take strict care of his health because God willed to use him as an instrument to further divine glory. He believed himself obliged to obey and to relax the terrible severity he had inflicted on himself. He knew that God had not been pleased with the sacrifices of the Jews because their own will had entered into them, and that the victims offered to God are always less important in His eyes than obedience.

The Saint also strove for interior mortification, annihilating and renouncing his own will and senses on all occasions. Knowing that almighty God sometimes permits us to fall into humiliating sins in order to punish and cure intellectual pride and a puffed-up heart, he spared no effort in their destruction. He was constantly on guard against himself. He looked upon the practices of interior mortification as the principal activity of the Christian life, and the most powerful means of forming and establishing Jesus Christ in ourselves. He believed that interior penance was the only road to salvation, and that our private practice should be to renounce Adam and all that remains of him in us.

St. John Eudes cultivated special devotion to our Blessed Lord as the Victim who bore in Himself all the sins of mankind. For him Christ was the divine Victim in all the states of His life, but particularly in His agony in the Garden of Olives. He would implore our Saviour to let him share in His victim spirit. As soon as he felt an inclination toward a special object, he would sacrifice it at the feet of Christ, declaring that he wanted nothing except the desires of our Lord. He used to do the same thing whenever he became aware of any manifest affection. Turning his heart at once toward Jesus, who must be the sole object of his love, he would return what he was receiving to the God of all consolation. All his happiness was in doing God's will; all his joy was in knowing that God exists and that He is the God of our hearts. In short, he could truly say with St. Paul: "I live, now not I: but Christ liveth in me."[8]

The Saint renounced voluntarily even permissible pleasure of mind, but deprived himself more drastically of bodily satisfactions since they are more opposed to the virtue of chastity and to the life of a man obliged by his vocation to imitate the angels. He therefore joyfully seized every opportunity to mortify himself and blessed God for the occasions granted him to practice austerity. Such should be the conduct, in imitation of St. John Eudes, of all who are called to the religious life or to the holy priesthood. For them the death of human nature must be a gain and an advantage, since it renders them more capable of representing in their person the dying life of our Lord and of preserving the precious treasure of purity, which renders them so great in the sight of men and angels.

NOTES

[1] 1 Thess. 4:7.
[2] 1 Cor. 6:19.
[3] Tertullian: *De cultu foeminarum,* l. 2, chap. 1; P.L. 1:1316.
[4] Exod. 39:23.
[5] This phrase sums up a sentence in Tertullian, *Ad uxorem.* l. 1, chap. 1; P.L. 1:1281. *Iam in terris non nubando de familia angelica deputantur.*
[6] *Manual of Piety,* p. 132.
[7] 2 Cor. 4:10.
[8] Gal. 2:20.

Chapter 32. Love of the Cross and Patience

TO SUFFER PERSECUTION for the sake of justice means to be happy indeed.[1] The maledictions of men, borne as they should be, are invariably followed by the blessings of heaven.[2] This is the teaching of our Lord in the Beatitudes, from which we learn that the cross is the most efficacious means of advancing along the path of grace and progressing toward a very high degree of glory. Such has always been the dispensation of God toward chosen souls, subjecting them to tribulation in order to render them more worthy of carrying out His plans. He refines them as gold in a crucible, tempers them as steel in a furnace, and often makes them victims of His justice before turning them into instruments of His power.

There is nothing on earth more useful to man than to learn how to profit by his trials. It is rightly the knowledge of the saints, for it makes a contribution essential to our sanctification. The Way of the Cross was the straight and narrow road along which divine wisdom guided John Eudes, and he never departed from it. He looked upon the cross in the same light as his Master had done; he felt the same inclination toward it, made use of it and bore it for the same end. It was his treasure and his glory; he declared like St. Paul: "God forbid that I should glory, save in the cross of our Lord Jesus Christ."[3]

St. John Eudes disclosed his love of the Cross to his spiritual children on various occasions. Writing to a priest of his Congregation who was suffering from high fever, he said: "May Jesus be eternally blessed, dearest brother, for the share He deigns to grant us in His Cross. Oh! when shall we be able to say with truth: '. . . God forbid that I should glory, save in the cross of our Lord Jesus Christ; by whom the world is crucified to me, and I to the world.' How very true it is that there is nothing to be desired in this world, save to be nailed to the cross with Jesus Christ. Then let us joyfully embrace our crosses, dearest brother, and try to bear them in the spirit of our most adorable Crucified."[4]

The ordination ceremony by the Lord Bishop of Bayeux at Caen in 1658 gave him visible consolation when three hundred and fifty ordinands entered and left the Church of St. John in procession. They marched and sang with modest dignity that moved even the most bitter Calvinists to bless the missionaries countless times. Afterwards the Saint wrote to the Superior of one of the houses: "Among all these successes, I clearly perceived that periods of humiliation, suffering and crosses are much more desirable, pleasing, advantageous, useful and precious than those of eulogy, exaltation and comfort. However, we must accept the one with the other from the hand of God, and endeavor to accomplish His most holy will."[5]

To Mother St. Gabriel, a religious of Montmartre, who had made remarkable spiritual progress, and had great confidence in St. John Eudes and sympathy for his tribulations, he penned this letter: "Thank you, my dearest daughter, for your participation in my crosses; blessed be our Lord and His most Holy Mother for them. I hope that in their incomparable goodness, they will grant you a share in all the fruits and blessings derived from my trials through their great mercy. Oh, what an enormous treasure is the cross which our Lord so loved, and which His holy Mother and all the saints embraced and bore so lovingly! Surely, if there were a more excellent way in this world to glorify and please Him, our Lord would have chosen it for Himself and given it to His dearest Mother and all His saints."[6]

Because of his supernatural attitude to crosses, St. John Eudes always deemed himself most fortunate whenever God sent him trials and difficulties. He looked upon them as manifestations of His divine mercy towards us, and as the most obvious testimony of His love. "The grace of graces, the favor of favors," he said frequently, "is the multitude of crosses which my crucified Lord has granted me; may He be eternally praised and glorified for them."[7] The Saint believed that our Lord was pleased with his services whenever He gave a cross as a reward, thus honoring us with the chalice that the Son of Man drained to the dregs. "I bless God with all my heart," he wrote to Mother Frances Patin, Superior of our Lady of Charity at Caen, "for the favor that He has granted you in having controlled the wind and tempest, filling your soul instead with calm and tranquility. But I thank Him even more for the grace He has given you in allowing you the sufferings that I realize from your letter you have endured. O my dearest Mother, how precious is the state of suffering! What a rich gift from divine bounty it is! Ah, how much more should we render thanks to God for such desolation than for all the consolation on earth! For crosses are the greatest gifts that God can bestow in this world upon souls who are very dear to Him. If we were to remain on our knees for a century in thanksgiving for the most trifling affliction possible, we still could not thank Him worthily, as He Himself revealed to Blessed Henry Suso[8] of the Order of St. Dominic."[9]

St. John Eudes found joy in the cross. He was never happier than when he had to suffer a great deal. We can apply to his days of tribulation the very term applied by the Holy Ghost in Scripture to the passion of the Saviour—the day of the joy of His Heart.[10] This was the customary explanation of his sufferings that he confided to his spiritual daughters in a letter written to them: "Truly, my dearest daughters, there is no real cause for joy on earth other than this: to perform the will of God and to be despised and crucified with Jesus Christ. Oh, would that we shared the sentiments of St. John of the Cross![11] When our Lord asked him what he desired for the services he had rendered Him, he made this reply: 'Lord, I ask only to suffer and to be despised for Thy sake.' It was indeed the Holy Spirit who inspired him to ask the greatest blessing of this life."[12]

Writing to two Benedictine nuns of Montmartre Abbey, who were grieved and troubled, he said this: "I am writing you, my dearest daughters, to assure you that I feel your crosses very keenly, that is, humanly speaking. For, speaking as a Christian, I shall tell you that the greatest cause for joy on earth that we can have is to be crucified with our lovable Saviour. Human nature does not understand such language, but it is an article of faith that therein is the sovereign good of Christian souls. So true is this that the saints in heaven who suffered the greatest torments here on earth would very gladly exchange the glory and joy they possess for the sufferings they endured in the world, if God allowed them to do so. That is why I give infinite thanks to divine bounty for the holy dispositions that fill your heart in this circumstance. Courage, my dearest daughters, rejoice; rejoice because our all-lovable Jesus is granting you a share in the one thing in this world which He most dearly loved, and of which His holy Mother had the greatest share. You must not doubt that I am doing my very best for you in the presence of God."[13]

"I beseech my dearest daughter," he wrote again to another nun, "to help me love God. She has much, indeed, for which to show Him great love. For, just as the greatest love that He manifested for us was in His sufferings, so also the greatest love we can show for Him is to suffer for His love. . . . I give infinite thanks to our most adorable crucified Saviour for allowing this dear sister to participate in His most sacred crown of thorns, and for the grace He is giving her to make such a good use of her sufferings. I urge her always to continue to bear them with all possible humility, resignation and love."[14]

The cross was so deeply rooted in the heart of St. John Eudes, and he strove so much to instill it in the hearts of others, that his greatest comfort was to lack all consolation and his highest happiness was to be overwhelmed with sorrow. Cowardly and timid souls, who tremble at the least approach of misfortune, who draw near to Calvary only with a shudder, cannot bear to hear the cross mentioned without accusing of hardheartedness those who make the slightest reference to it. How far from these was the Saint, who always asked God for tribulations and sufferings with an earnestness beyond the power of expression. In addition to attacks against his labors in spreading the Gospel and in all his undertakings for the salvation of souls, he suffered many personal attacks. His enemies made every effort to blacken his honor and ruin his reputation. Many lies were told about him, including the blackest calumnies. Actually, a campaign of hate was organized against his name.[15] A good example is the exclamation of the aristocrat[16] who was informed that John Eudes was at the door, seeking an audience. The nobleman gave an immediate order for the missionary to be forcibly driven away, adding indignantly: "Tell that priest that I never want to hear his name mentioned, and that I should be happier to see him hanging from a scaffold than calling at my door." On another occasion the Saint had to visit an official[17] to request a favor for his Congregation. This man, taking the Saint by the arm, introduced him with mockery and exposed him to the scorn of all who were present. In such circumstances St. John Eudes could well have repeated the words of St. Paul: ". . . we are made as the refuse of this world, the offscouring of all. . . ."[18] Insults like those, which would have discouraged a lesser soul, made John Eudes happier and never caused him to swerve in the least from his duty.

At one stage in the Saint's life the weight and number of his crosses became so burdensome that several kind, devout persons felt pity for him, even to the extent of complaining to God on his behalf. "Crosses," he wrote to one of his colleagues, "are coming to me from all sides. If almighty God did not sustain me, I should be overwhelmed with them, for lately I have received several of the heaviest and most painful that I have ever had to bear."[19] Divine wisdom made the apostle of the devotion to the Sacred Heart embark upon a rocky and thorny road because He wished him to make great progress along the path of perfection, laying the foundations so deep that his advancement in grace would not occasion his downfall.

St. John Eudes made use of his crosses to prevent, not to cause spiritual pride. At their incidence, he would prostrate himself to adore divine providence and to ask, despite all the repugnance of human nature, for the fulfillment of God's intentions for him, the satisfaction of divine justice and an increase of love. Never did he return a curse for a curse; his silence was the only reply to the accusations levelled against him. He never sought justification other than the integrity of his life. His patience was eventually to convince his bitterest enemies of his innocence; it was proof against all their attacks. His virtue was an imitation of Jesus who, as a reward for His singular merits, received from men only shame, scorn, torture, the cross and death.

Despairing of conquering John Eudes through temptation, the devil tried him with calumnies, which St. John Chrysostom calls "the last arrow of the devil."[20] Slander is the last arrow that the devil aims at the steadfastness of the just, hoping that, if their care and fidelity have weathered his first attacks, at least they may be surprised into sins of impatience or worry upon finding themselves persecuted by unjustifiable slanders.

Everyone warned St. John Eudes about the attacks being made against him, so that he might plan a method of coping with the libels. His reaction was so far from the natural instinct of self-justification that he made no reply except: ". . . Jesus held His peace."[21] The attitude of silence is to be noted in many of his letters. The one quoted here was written to the superior of the Rouen Seminary, who had taken the liberty of expressing how he and other prominent persons thought the Saint should react to a particularly vicious libel. "A thousand thanks, my most dearly beloved brother, for the charitable and cordial letter you wrote me; I am most grateful to you and to those gentlemen who are noted therein. I beg you to assure them of my gratitude and thank them profusely for me. Their zeal and goodness are most praiseworthy, but because I can find no evidence in the holy

Gospel that our divine and adorable Master ever used the ways and means indicated in your letter to defend Himself against the injustice and cruelty that He suffered at the hands of the Jews, I cannot bring myself to do otherwise than to imitate Him in His patience and silence: 'Jesus held his peace.' Perhaps God will raise up someone who can answer this libel. Be that as it may, I gladly embrace all the crosses it may please God to send me, and I earnestly entreat Him to grant pardon to me and those who are persecuting me. My numerous sins are deserving of a thousand times worse."[22]

To those especially in his confidence the Saint revealed even more intimately the feelings in his heart. "It is true," he wrote to his niece, "that our most lovable Saviour is loading me down with crosses, but at the same time He is granting me such a great abundance of graces that all my afflictions are turned into consolations. Many lies and calumnies about me have been widely circulated, but God will use them for His greater glory, while the father of lies, who is their author, will be put to confusion."[23]

Writing to a Benedictine nun at Montmartre, he said: "Pray for me, my dearest daughter, for I have great need of it, being more laden with crosses than ever before. But the least of my sins is deserving of a thousand times worse. My consolation is that God is ever God, that He always derives the greatest glory from all things, and that all the powers of earth and hell cannot prevent me from performing my sole duty, which is to love and serve my most benevolent Saviour and my most loving Mother."[24] "I should be crushed beneath the weight of my sufferings," he wrote to another nun of the same monastery, "if our Lord and His holy Mother were not sustaining me, but they are giving me an altogether singular strength, for which I entreat you to help me to thank them.

Help me, too, I beg of you, to pray a great deal for my benefactors, to whom I am most indebted for giving me such precious opportunities to practice the most beautiful virtues, particularly humility, obedience to the divine will, a love of Jesus crucified, and a love for His most holy Mother, also crucified with Him."[25]

Such were the admirable dispositions of the patient heart of St. John Eudes. Like the stars which continue to follow their regular course in the firmament and assist men to find their way on earth, even though the world is ungrateful and harbors wicked men who abuse heaven, the Saint ignored the outrages perpetrated against him, except to thank God for having sent him these great humiliations to destroy his pride and afford him additional opportunities to practice Christian humility. He pardoned his calumniators, whom he called his good friends, and looked upon them as his greatest benefactors.

St. John Eudes never ceased to pray and to enjoin others to pray for his enemies. He offered the Holy Sacrifice of the Mass and had it offered for their intentions. He implored divine mercy to make great saints of them in eternity. He was deeply grieved by their misfortunes. When one of his slanderers died suddenly, he was manifestly sorry, declaring that there was nothing he would not be willing to do to redeem him, if possible, in case he had not found favor with God. He offered himself to divine justice to bear in this world the pains his enemies were to suffer in the next, and to obtain pardon for their sins. Such were the virtue and character of our dying Saviour, whose meekness and patience St. John Eudes imitated so perfectly. The holy missionary seemed to have a heart made of diamond, as Origen says of John,[26] a heart which resisted all the blows of the envy of men and malice of the demons. He could be compared to the moon, which during an eclipse appears dark and shadowy from the earth, but is at the same time brilliant with light on the side facing the sun.

NOTES

[1] Mt. 5:10.

[2] Mt. 5:11–12.

[3] Gal. 6:14.

[4] Eudes, *Letters and Shorter Works,* p. 283.

[5] *Ibid.,* p. 119.

[6] *Ibid.,* p. 258.

[7] This may be a quotation that Herambourg received directly from one of the Eudists who had lived with St. John Eudes or who knew him intimately.

[8] Blessed Henry Suso, a Dominican mystic, was born at Constance, Germany, in 1295 and died at Ulm in 1366. St. John Eudes in the letter quoted by Herambourg refers to a conversation of Blessed Henry Suso with our Lord who said: "Suffering is a hidden good that no one can purchase; and if a man knelt before Me for a hundred years in return for the gift of suffering, he would not have deserved it." See *Little Book of Eternal Wisdom and Little Book of Truth* by Blessed Henry Suso, translated by James M. Clark (New York, Harper, 1953), p. 97.

[9] Eudes, *Letters and Shorter Works,* p. 150.

[10] Can. 3:11.

[11] In this letter St. John Eudes refers to "Blessed John of the Cross," because John of the Cross was not yet canonized. His beatification took place on January 25, 1675, and his canonization on December 26, 1726. For the words quoted by St. John Eudes see Crisogono de Jesus, O.C.D., *The Life of St. John of the Cross* (New York, Harper, 1958), p. 268.

[12] Eudes, *Letters and Shorter Works,* p. 64.

[13] *Ibid.,* p. 272.

[14] *Ibid.,* p. 273.

[15] See Sargent, *op. cit.,* pp. 262 ff.

[16] This nobleman has not been identified by the biographers of the Saint.

[17] Nothing in the source books on the Saint reveals who this official was. This incident and the one mentioned before it may have been related to Herambourg by one of the Eudists who lived with St. John Eudes.

[18] 1 Cor. 4:13.

[19] An excerpt from a letter that is not found in the *Oeuvres Complètes.*

[20] We have not been able to find this expression, "the last arrow of the devil" in the works of St. John Chrysostom. The expression recalls the words of St. Paul in Ephesians 6:16 where the Apostle refers to "all the fiery darts of the most wicked one." See St. John Chrysostom's homily 24 on this epistle of St. Paul and another passage in P.G. 49:31.

[21] Mt. 26:63.

[22] Eudes, *Letters and Shorter Works,* p. 249.

[23] *Ibid.*, p. 240.

[24] *Ibid.*, p. 252.

[25] *Ibid., loc. cit.*

[26] This reference is not to Origen but to St. Basil and St. John Chrysostom. See St. Basil, *Homilia de gratiarum actione,* P.G. 31:232 and St. John Chrysostom, *De diaboli tentatione,* "Homilia 3," no. 6; P.G. 49:272.

Chapter 33. His Use of Spiritual Suffering and His Advice about Crosses

SINCE CHRISTIANS are on earth to pattern their lives after the life of the Word Incarnate, and to fulfill in themselves what is lacking in His mysteries,[1] they must all carry their crosses in order to conform to the Saviour who was crucified for love of them. Two kinds of pain divided, or to put it better, consumed the life of our Blessed Lord: pain of body and pain of spirit. The latter, which is not usually apparent, is nevertheless harder to bear. The interior sorrows that our Lord suffered in His passion were very much greater than the physical torture. He bore uncomplainingly the scourging, the crowning with thorns and the cross, but He could not suffer the spiritual abandonment of His Father without voicing its bitterness.[2] God alone is the witness of this kind of martyrdom. Men and angels, who are ordinarily the witnesses of bodily torments, see nothing of the others. That is why authors of the lives of the saints tell us little of the spiritual pain that they suffered, and that made of them the noblest and most perfect images of our Lord.

We know beyond a doubt that St. John Eudes suffered

interior pain. His spirit was frequently overwhelmed by it. The number and weight of his crosses reduced him to profound agony, but we have no particulars as to their nature. He put to wonderful use, however, all the painful states in which he found himself. At such times he would adore Jesus Christ in the privations, humiliations, troubles and griefs that our Saviour had borne in His soul. He would unite himself with the dispositions of the Sacred Heart, imploring Him to bless and sanctify his own pains, which he would offer in thanksgiving for those Jesus had suffered for love of him. He would beseech the Son of God to atone for all his deficiencies toward the majesty of the eternal Father.

During such periods of interior suffering, St. John Eudes used to serve God with extraordinary diligence. He showed then that he loved our Lord truly for Himself, not for the comfort our Saviour grants to faithful souls. He did not neglect any of his devotional exercises, but performed them all as perfectly as possible. The more he felt interior coldness and weakness, the more did he have recourse to Jesus Christ, his strength and his all. He would abandon himself into the hands of God with greater firmness; his elevation of mind was more frequent and he would make many acts of love. "What does it matter," he would say, "if we are happy or not, provided Jesus is!" Whenever he found himself afflicted with spiritual darkness and aridity, he never neglected to present himself, like David before the Ark, there to behold and adore the power and glory of the Lord, to sing the praises of His mercy which is worth more than all lives, to affirm to Him that he would bless Him as long as he lived and that he would always have his hands outstretched to invoke the name of the Most High.

St. John Eudes felt that what we do in the state of spiritual dryness and desolation, provided we have the intention of honoring Him, is more pleasing to God than what we do with feelings of joy and love, which are usually accompanied by self-love. He never faltered in his firm resolution to serve and love God perfectly, no matter what happened, and to be faithful to Him to the last breath of his life. He steadfastly hoped for this grace from divine mercy. Can we doubt, then, that he found in the Cross what the Saviour of the world had put therein, sanctification and a certain means of advancing along the paths of perfection? He looked upon this state of interior suffering as an effect of the immense mercy of God upon his soul. For that reason he urged everyone to make holy use of crosses, no matter what their nature. His principal concern about the souls under his guidance was to teach them to realize the importance of crosses and how to profit from them. This is evident from the following advice that he offered to various persons.

When Madame de Budos,[3] Abbess of the Royal Monastery of the Blessed Trinity at Caen, was stricken with a violent illness, he wrote several letters to comfort her. From them we have chosen this one in which he emphasizes the way to sanctify her sufferings.

Jesus, Maria

Madame, may the grace and peace of Jesus Christ our Lord be with you for ever!

I am filled with compassion for you at the sight of your incessant pain and weakness and I should be filled with sorrow too, if I did not perceive Jesus in your weakness and pains. In them I see only Jesus, only His goodness and love.

He is there, Madame; He abides within you. He is present in your anguish and sufferings. He is there, all love and completely transformed into love for your sake. He is there, preparing and ordaining these sufferings through love of you.

He is there, guiding and leading you along the paths of His love, and drawing you toward the perfection of love by means of those trials and severities.

He is there, bearing with you through His love all the anguish of mind and body that is yours to bear. Even though you may often be unaware of it, He is nevertheless infallibly present, for if He were absent, you would find it impossible to support even the least of the infirmities you are suffering.

He is still there, purifying and sanctifying you and preparing great things for you, provided you, on your part, give the cooperation He asks.

He is there for the purpose of filling you completely with love for Him, and much more so than you are filled with suffering. I will say even more: not only does He wish to imbue you with His love, but also to transform you entirely into love for Him through crosses and sufferings, as His Cross and sufferings transformed Him into love for us.

He is there, finally, with a most ardent desire to draw you to Himself, to perfect and consummate you in Himself, along the path of these same sufferings. St. Paul says that it was fitting that Jesus Christ should be consummated by suffering: "For it became him . . . to perfect the author of their salvation by his passion."[4]

O dignity, O holiness, O admirable excellence of suffering to be used for the honor and consummation of a God, for the perfection of Jesus, God and Man, for the consummation of Him who is the consummation and perfection of all things! Great was the humiliation of Jesus, who humbled Himself to a state in which He was capable of being perfected and consummated! But immense was the dignity of suffering, chosen and used by Him and His Eternal Father to achieve this perfection and consummation!

Is it not a great honor for you, Madame, is it not a great favor and should it not be a great comfort to you to be consumed and perfected through suffering, as Jesus was consumed by suffering? Does not Jesus show a rare and singular love for you by using the same means for your fulfillment and consummation as He employed for His own? May Christ Crucified be forever blessed, for so giving you a share in the blessings of His Cross! I implore Him to crucify you completely with Him, and to do so through the same love which nailed Him to the Cross for your sake.

I see a countless number of crucified persons in the world, but few who are crucified by the love of Jesus. Some are crucified by their self-love and inordinate love of the world, but happy are they who are crucified for the love of Jesus; blessed are they who live and die on the Cross with Jesus. You will be numbered among these, Madame, if you bear your cross lovingly, like Jesus, accepting, embracing and cherishing it with all your heart in honor of and in union with the same love with which He accepted and bore it for you.

To achieve that end, cast your eyes frequently upon Jesus who is always with you, who penetrates and pervades you much more than do the pains and sufferings which seem to take complete possession of you. See only Jesus in your pains and sufferings; see only His goodness and love, which are responsible for all that happens to you. Adhere only to Him; be attentive only to Him. Forsake your weariness and displeasure; disregard them utterly; ignore them entirely. Turn your mind gently and firmly from all thoughts and objects which may cause you worry. Turn to Jesus, who is turned toward you, and always has His eyes fixed lovingly upon you. Cling closely to Him and His divine love, as to One who is your all and outside of whom you wish nothing. Let there no longer be anyone but yourself and Him in the world, and let yourself be entirely unaffected and unclaimed by anything at all that is not He. Lose every thought and consideration of your own interests, of yourself and everything else. Yes, lose yourself holily and happily in the abyss of this goodness and love of Jesus which encompasses, penetrates and possesses you, and is always considering you, always watching over you and all that concerns you; which is more zealous, more attentive, more preoccupied to an infinite degree in procuring your welfare and advantage in all things than you yourself are.

O love! O bounty! O Jesus, God of love and bounty! Adore, love, bless this Jesus so full of love and kindness toward you. Adore, cherish, glorify all His attentions, all His plans and all His desires in your regard. Surrender yourself frequently to Him and offer Him your whole state of spiritual and bodily sufferings, in homage to the sufferings of His body and divine soul. Adore, too, the peace and tranquility of that holy soul in the midst of its pains and torments, and pray Jesus to let you participate in that same peace and tranquility, as well as in all the other dispositions with which He suffered.

These, Madame, are the practices and duties which Jesus asks of you now. They are the allegiance and the honor you must render Him in your present condition. I pray that He Himself may impress these thoughts and sentiments on your heart. I entreat Him to honor and glorify Himself in you. I implore Him, finally, to carry out all His plans and desires for you, allowing not even the slightest hindrance on your part.

And as for you, Madame, I beg only one thing of you, which is that you remember and put into practice something you said to me the last time I had the pleasure of seeing you. You told me that you no longer wanted anything except what God willed, and that you were submitting yourself unreservedly to all that it pleased Him to ordain for you. You spoke these words with a certain strength and energy which consoled me a great deal. I beseech you, therefore, not to contradict this statement, but to prove, whenever God may afford you occasion to do so, that you spoke those words not with your tongue alone but also with your heart and will.

You see, Madame, how freely I speak to you? But it is prompted by my zeal for your soul and my trust in your goodness. Let me say just one more thing, and that is to beg you to continue—for I believe that you are doing so now—to have something devotional read to you from time to time. I think that the acts of love for Jesus which were recently sent to you will serve the purpose. Have them read to you now and then, and dwell tenderly on them, without strain or exertion.[5]

This letter, so full of the spirit of God, reveals how the Saint esteemed suffering, and how wisely he utilized it.

Writing to a lady of rank[6] who was very distressed over the prospect of being separated from her daughter,[7] who wished to enter the religious life, he said: "May God forgive you for your over-anxiety on the subject of the greatest happiness that can befall the fair 'Lily Bud'[8] and her mother. You have a very great reason for rejoicing, inasmuch as the noblest, richest and most powerful Lord in the world loves you so much that He wants you to give Him your daughter as His spouse. . . . The Way of the Cross is most pleasing to God, since our Lord Jesus Christ chose it for Himself and for you. Be at peace, then, dearest daughter, always humbling yourself, however, and trying to do whatever you can on your own part. Do not be discouraged, though, when that fails you. Pray our Lord and His most holy Mother to supply for your deficiency, and they will surely do so."[9]

"It is a special favor," he wrote to a Benedictine nun, "that our adorable crucified Lord is granting you in still allowing you your headaches so that by this means you may pay some small measure of honor to His divine head crowned with thorns. Exercise the utmost care, my dearest daughter, to use this illness to the best possible advantage by supporting it with humility, submission to the divine will and love for Jesus wearing His crown of thorns."[10]

A prominent man[11] who considered himself wholly indebted for his conversion to the Saint, next to God, was stricken with a painful illness. Whereupon his charitable spiritual director wrote for his consolation: "When I look upon you through human eyes in your present condition, I am indeed deeply moved to the point of great compassion. But when I consider you through the eyes of faith, I am prompted to bless and praise our divine Saviour for the singular effects of His infinite goodness toward you, for I see quite clearly that everything which is taking place is a command and inclination of His mercy in your regard. He wishes you to do penance for your sins in this world in order to pardon you in the next.

"We are indebted to His divine justice for a hundred thousand bushels of wheat, but He lets us off for a portion of it. O great favor! We have merited eternal torments, and He is satisfied to let us suffer a few small temporal afflictions. I call them small, very small, in comparison with those our offenses deserve. Ah, what goodness! What an obligation we have toward such goodness! What care should we take to make good use of our afflictions! That is what I exhort you with all my heart to do, my dearest brother, that you may not thwart His plans for you at this time. He intends for us to be cleansed and purified of the filth of our sins by that lye-bath of suffering which may seem very strong to us; but the stronger it is, the more will it whiten us and make us pure and pleasing in the sight of His divine majesty, provided we, on our part, cultivate the necessary dispositions which are chiefly these four:

"The first is to accept our sufferings from the most adorable Trinity and the most lovable Heart of our heavenly Father who chastises us, not as a harsh judge, according to our merits, but as a very kind Father, and infinitely less than we deserve. If we accept them as coming from the latter, we shall not attribute them in any way to our fellow creatures, who are but the rods used by this good Father to punish us.

"The second disposition is to humble ourselves under the mighty hand of God, considering ourselves not as just and innocent, but as guilty criminals who time and time again have deserved the wrath of God and all His creatures. But let us be convinced that the humbler we become in our nothingness and lowliness, the more will God be exalted therein, and the more, too, will He take care to protect us and convert all things to our welfare.

"The third disposition is to regard sin as the sole author of all our ills, and consequently to turn all our hatred, indignation and vengeance against this monster which is our only enemy; to employ all our strength to persecute and destroy sin by true penance, and to banish it henceforth beyond the doors and avenues of our souls. Let us remove the cause and the effect will cease.

"The fourth is to guard well against allowing ourselves to subscribe to pagan sentiments, which are to hate those who hate us. Rather should we follow those of our gentle Leader, who gives us this commandment: 'Love one another as I have loved you, and by that shall they know that you are my disciples.' "[12]

In reply to a religious who had unburdened her heart to him about her painful condition, he wrote: "If I were to speak according to the senses, I should indeed pity you for your sufferings, but speaking according to the spirit, I find you more worthy of envy than pity. The greatest happiness that can befall you is to be in conformity with Jesus Christ our Lord, who is our most adorable Master. Now, your present state of privation, death and annihilation is highly conformable to that endured by our most lovable Saviour here on earth. Therefore give yourself to Him, my dearest Mother, that you may suffer with Him in that condition and in His spirit as He desires. Try to do these three things:

1. Strive not to become disheartened, guarding well against discouragement. Surrender yourself to virtue and to divine strength, that they may sustain you.

2. Accept this state of death and annihilation with the Son of God, saying: 'Father, into thy hands I commend my spirit.'[13]

3. Abandon yourself completely to the most holy will of God, repeating with our Lord: '. . . not my will, but thine be done.' "[14]

Such was the use which St. John Eudes, so learned in the wisdom of the Cross, would have us make of the crosses that divine providence is pleased to send us. When we view them in that light, they lose all their bitterness; they become like fruit delicious to the taste of those who possess enough love of God and zeal for their own salvation. He was convinced that to suffer in this way was, of all ways, the most satisfying and the most useful to a soul. He sometimes said that the more crosses one encountered in the affairs of God, the more advantageous were such affairs.

Since he realized the merits of crosses, the Saint always sought that none be allowed to escape without becoming an occasion of merit. Judging that the rigors of the seasons were crosses from divine providence, he would exhort his spiritual children to endure intense heat and cold in union with and in thanksgiving for the endurance of our Lord on earth. He even wished us, in time of blessings, to recall our misfortunes, and to remember, in the midst of the joys and consolations of this life, that true happiness consists in being outstretched on the Cross with Jesus Christ and bearing pain in His spirit.

These were the sentiments and practices of this faithful disciple of our Saviour, from whom he had learned them. Like St. Paul, he gloried in being ignorant of all things and knowing only Jesus crucified.[15] He tried at every opportunity to absorb knowledge of the Cross and to clarify the mystery, which was a source of scandal for the Jews and mockery for the Gentiles.[16] Many persons have profited from his enlightenment and example. They have learned to regard with esteem and bear with respect the crosses that are theirs, believing them to be the most indisputable indication of God's intention to grant them the reward of His glory.

NOTES

[1] Col. 1:24. See *The Kingdom of Jesus,* p. 3.

[2] Mt. 27:46; Mk. 15:34.

[3] Madame Laurence de Budos, Abbess of the Holy Trinity Abbey in Caen. St. John Eudes met her when he was still an Oratorian. Recognizing the profound wisdom and great prudence of the Saint, she placed herself and her community under his spiritual guidance. She died in the odor of sanctity on June 23, 1650. *Letters and Shorter Works,* p. 2, footnote 2.

[4] Hebr. 2:10.

[5] Eudes, *Letters and Shorter Works,* p. 20.

[6] Madame Blouet de Camilly. *Ibid.,* p. 29, footnote 2.

[7] *Ibid.,* p. 39, footnote 4.

[8] *Ibid.,* p. 38, footnote 2.

[9] *Ibid.,* p. 43.

[10] *Ibid.,* p. 274.

[11] Augustine Le Haguais, brother of Madame de Camilly, Councillor of State. He resided in Paris, where he died in 1666 at the age of 63. Intelligent and devout like his sister, Le Haguais was deeply grieved by the desertion of his wife who took with her one of their sons. St. John Eudes, his "closest friend," did much to console and guide M. le Haguais in this bitter trial. See *Letters and Shorter Works,* p. 109.

[12] *Ibid.,* p. 109.

[13] Lk. 23:46.

[14] Lk. 22:42. This letter was written to Mother Margaret Frances Patin. See Eudes, *ibid.,* p. 152.

[15] 1 Cor. 2:2.

[16] 1 Cor. 1:23.

Chapter 34. Spirit of Martyrdom

MARTYRDOM IS THE perfection and consummation of Christian holiness, the greatest miracle of God for His servants; it is the most signal favor with which our Lord honors them, and the most certain indication of love that they give Him. St. John Eudes considered himself obliged to live in the dispositions and spirit of martyrdom because of his ties to Jesus Christ. The Saint acknowledged that he had received being from the divine majesty of God only to procure glory for Him, and that there was no better way to do so than by offering his life to God in sacrifice. He knew that creatures are obliged to love their Maker with their whole soul and their whole strength, and that this commandment is never more perfectly carried out than when we risk our lives or shed our blood for Him. The intentions of the Saint were the same as those of the Saviour who, desiring nothing so much as to suffer and die continually for the honor of His Father and love of mankind, wishes to fulfill in His members what He himself can no longer do in His present state of glory.

St. John Eudes realized the obligations of baptism which compelled him, through his union with Jesus Christ, to be host and victim perpetually sacrificed to divine love through homage to the terrible martyrdom which Jesus underwent in His passion. This thought he stressed repeatedly. "What truth can there be in the claim that we are Christians and adore a crucified God, a God agonizing and dying upon a Cross, a God who for love of us gave up so noble and excellent a life, a God who sacrifices Himself every day before our very eyes upon our altars for our salvation if we are not ready to sacrifice to Him all that we hold dearest in the world, and even life itself, which in any case belongs to Him by all rights? Surely we are not Christians if we are not in these dispositions."[1]

The responsibilities of the priesthood obliged St. John Eudes to live even more strictly in the spirit of sacrifice, since he knew that our Lord had united in His person those two noble qualities of priest and victim, and since he experienced daily at the holy altar an admirable example of that abasement and sacrifice of self which should be a subject for the consideration and imitation of every priest.

All these reasons made John Eudes long most ardently for martyrdom. For many years he asked it of God, seeking with unbelievable fervor to shed his blood in defense of the truths of faith and in testimony to His divine Saviour of the love he bore Him. Since there was no tyrant at hand to put him to death, he was ready to seek martyrdom in foreign lands, and he would have done so if his spiritual directors had not prevented it. Being unable to satisfy his ardor, he longed for the death of all those who die by the executioner's hand. With all his heart would he have liked to be in their place in order to die a death more in conformity with that of his Master. Perceiving, however, that all these desires were fruitless, he prayed to God to overwhelm him with all sorts of afflictions and this God granted. He was heard frequently to exclaim: "Come, crosses! Come, sorrows! Come, that I may suffer in imitation of my Saviour and for love of this divine Jesus who suffered so much for my sake."

"It is not enough," he used to say, "no, not enough to have but one body to immolate, but one life to lose, to die but once. Surely, dear Jesus, if we had all the human bodies that ever were, are now and ever shall be, we would most willingly, with the help of Thy grace, deliver them up and abandon them to every kind of torture for Thy sake. And if we had all the lives of men and angels, with how glad a heart would we not offer them to Thee to be sacrificed to Thy glory? Were it possible to die as often for Thy love as there are moments in time in all the past, present and future centuries! How happy would we then esteem ourselves! Thou one and only Love of our hearts, who will grant us to behold ourselves covered with our own blood and filled with wounds and suffering for love of Thee, as Thou wast once for love of us?

"If only we might one day see ourselves in this enviable state, how we would then praise and bless Thee! Oh, blessed be that day, yes, a thousand times blessed, in which we shall accomplish the extreme desire to be sacrificed for Thy pure love! Come fires, flames, swords, guns, gibbets, come all things that confound us, come all contempt and shame! Come all you torments, all rage and cruelty of men and devils, earth and hell, come upon us! We defy you, if only we may ever love our most lovable Jesus; if only we may love Him by our death, and die for His love, in order to love and bless Him forever in eternity."[2]

St. John Eudes made a vow to Jesus Christ, offering himself as a victim to be sacrificed purely to the glory and love of our Saviour. Here is the text, as it was found in his handwriting.[3]

Jesus, Mary

O my most loving Jesus, I adore Thee and glorify Thee endlessly in the most bloody martyrdom that Thou didst suffer through Thy passion and death.

I adore Thee and bless Thee with all my might in Thy state of offering and victim in which Thou art continually sacrificed for the glory of Thy Father and for love of us.

I honor Thee and venerate Thee in the most sorrowful martyrdom suffered at the foot of the Cross by Thy most holy Mother.

I praise and glorify Thee in the various martyrdoms of Thy saints who endured so many atrocious torments for love of Thee.

I adore and bless all the thoughts, intentions and infinite love Thou hast had from all eternity with regard to the blessed martyrs who have been in Thy holy Church since the beginning and will continue to be there until the end of the world.

I adore and venerate in every way I can Thy extreme desire and most ardent thirst to suffer and die in Thy members until the end of the world in order to fulfill the mystery of Thy holy passion and glorify Thy Father through the way of suffering and death until the end of time.

In honor of and in homage to all these things, and in union with the boundless love with which Thou didst offer Thyself to the Father from the first moment of Thy Incarnation as a sacrifice and victim, in order to be immolated for His glory and for love of us through the most sorrowful martyrdom of the Cross; and also in union with love of Thy holy Mother and all Thy holy martyrs, I offer and abandon myself, I vow and consecrate myself to Thee, O Jesus, my Lord, in the capacity of sacrifice and victim, that I may suffer in body and soul, according to Thy pleasure and with the help of Thy holy grace, all manner of pains and torments, and even shed my blood and sacrifice my life for Thee through any death pleasing to Thee; and this for Thy sole glory and for pure love of Thee.

I vow to Thee, O my Lord Jesus, never to revoke, that is, never to make a formal act of disavowal of this my oblation, consecration and sacrifice of myself to the glory of Thy divine majesty. And should there arise an occasion on which I should have either to die or renounce Thy holy faith, or else do something of consequence against Thy divine will, I make a vow and promise to Thee, as firm and constant as possible, while trusting in Thine infinite goodness and the help of Thy grace, to confess, acknowledge, adore and glorify Thee in the presence of everyone, at the price of my blood, my life and all the martyrdoms and torments imaginable, and to suffer a thousand deaths, with all the tortures of earth and hell, rather than deny Thee or do anything serious that is contrary to Thy holy will.

O good Jesus, receive and accept this vow of mine and this sacrifice which I make to Thee of my life and my being in homage to and by the merits of the most divine sacrifice Thou didst make of Thyself to Thy Father on the Cross. Look upon me henceforth as an offering and victim dedicated to be wholly immolated to the glory of Thy holy name. Grant, through Thy great mercy, that my whole life may be a perpetual sacrifice of love and praise for Thee. Grant that I may live a life that may perpetually imitate and honor Thine own holy life and that of Thy Blessed Mother and holy martyrs; that I may never pass a day without suffering something for love of Thee; and that I may die a death conformable to Thy holy death.

That is what I beg of Thee very humbly and earnestly, O most kind Jesus, by that ardent love which brought Thee to the death on the Cross for us, by that precious blood Thou didst shed, by that most sorrowful death Thou didst suffer, by Thy overwhelming love for Thy most holy Mother, the Queen of martyrs, by Thy love for all the holy martyrs and their love for Thee; in short, by all whom Thou dost love and all who love Thee, in heaven and on earth.

O Mother of Jesus, Queen of all martyrs, O ye holy martyrs of Jesus, implore this same Jesus, I beseech you, to effect these things in me, through His infinite goodness, solely for His glory and most pure love. Offer Him this vow of mine, and pray Him to confirm and fulfill it by virtue of His precious blood, just as

I am about to sign it with my own blood in testimony of my desire to shed it even to the last drop for love of Him.

Done at Caen in the Oratory of Jesus, this 25th day of March, 1637. John Eudes.
Live Jesus and Mary,
Whom I love more than my life.[4]

To this vow the Saint added the *Credo* together with acts of love, an invitation to martyrdom and an invocation of Jesus and Mary as King and Queen of martyrs, as well as of all the saints known to have suffered torments for the glory of God.

Such was the longing of the noble heart of St. John Eudes, who frequently adored our Blessed Lord as the sovereign Martyr of the eternal Father. He urged special devotion to the blessed martyrs because they command the greatest admiration in the presence of God and belong to Jesus in an entirely unique and special manner as the Church sings on their feasts.[5] He read the martyrology daily in order to ask the martyrs commemorated each day to obtain for him the grace and the opportunity to shed his blood for love of the divine majesty. He even constrained one of his best friends, with whom he was very closely united by the ties of grace, to accept a copy of the martyrology and to read it each day so that this friend might offer the same prayer for his intention. He composed in honor of the martyrs an anthem and a prayer in which he asked our Blessed Lord, through their intercession, for the grace and spirit of martyrdom.[6] He desired it not only for himself but also for those who were destined to suffer, and among the latter, for all living at the time of the persecution of the antichrist, which will be the most terrible of all.[7]

No one could please the Saint more than by speaking to

him of martyrdom, nor could anyone wish him a greater blessing. Thus did his closest friends give proof of their sincere friendship for him. Among others, there was Father Ignatius of Jesus and Mary,[8] a Discalced Carmelite who, knowing the feeling and longings of the Saint's generous heart, would use this signature in his letters: "Your most humble and obedient servant in our Lord, who desires for you the crown of martyrdom."

Throughout the entire course of his priestly life St. John Eudes continually championed the interests of God. He was certainly a martyr in spirit. Neither severity, promises nor threats were in the least capable of undermining his courage. Always faithful to his sacred obligations, he vigorously opposed the enemies of His divine Master's glory. He feared sin alone and would rather have shed his blood to the last drop than commit the least deliberate venial sin. He mortified his flesh and passions; he patiently endured the miseries of life; he joyfully suffered insults and persecutions. He blessed those who uttered curses against him. He tenderly loved persons who hated him. The help that he extended to his neighbor for love of our Lord during the ravages of the plague exposed him to death a thousand times over.

At every moment St. John Eudes offered his life in sacrifice to God because his greatest desire was to suffer and shed his blood in testimony to the divine majesty of his love and zeal for the establishment and expansion of the kingdom of Christ. We pray that all Christians, and particularly all priests and religious, may work to share the holy desires of John Eudes, since Christians are obliged by the contract of their baptism to bear within themselves the likeness of Jesus Christ, while priests and religious, by the dignity of Holy Orders and the profession of their sacred vocation, must work for the salvation of souls even though it should endanger their lives, in imitation of the example set by our Blessed Lord on Calvary. "Look and make it according to the pattern, that was shown thee in the mount."[9]

NOTES

[1] Eudes, *The Kingdom of Jesus,* p. 96.

[2] *Ibid.,* p. 99.

[3] The original copy of this vow in the Saint's own handwriting is now in the Monastery of Our Lady of Charity at Chevilly-Larue, near Paris.

[4] Eudes, *Letters and Shorter Works,* p. 315.

[5] Our Blessed Lord, speaking through the Church, calls the martyrs "my saints": *Roman Breviary,* "Common of Many Martyrs," Matins, resp. 8. See also *The Kingdom of Jesus,* p. 89.

[6] Eudes, *The Kingdom of Jesus,* p. 101.

[7] *Ibid., loc. cit.*

[8] Father Ignatius Joseph of Jesus and Mary (1596–1665), a learned and saintly Discalced Carmelite, who filled the important position of Master of Novices of his Order in France. His many works are evaluated by Father Cosme de Villiers in *Bibliotheca carmelitana,* edited by Father Gabriel Wessels, Rome, 1927, col. 707–709.

[9] Exod. 25:40.

Index

A NOTE ON THE TYPE

IN WHICH THIS BOOK WAS SET

This book is set in Caledonia, a Linotype face created in 1939 by W. A. Dwiggins, which is by far one of the best book types created in the last 50 years. It has a simple, hard-working, feet-on-the-ground quality and can be classed as a modern type face with excellent color and good readability. The designer claims Caledonia was created by putting a little of each of Scotch Roman, Bulmer, Baskerville and Bodoni together and producing a lively crisp book type. This book was composed and printed by the York Composition Company, Inc., of York, Pa., and bound by Moore and Company of Baltimore. The typography and design of this book are by Howard N. King.